ETHICALIMPLICATIONS OF ENVIRONMENTAL CRISISONPRESENT-DAY SOCIETY

A Challenge to Future Humanity

Part I: Fundamentals of Ethics & Environment

Dr. Rupali Devi Barua

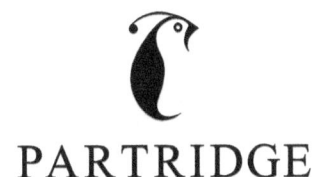

PARTRIDGE

ISBN: Softcover   978-1-4828-4410-8
            eBook   978-1-4828-4409-2

Print information available on the last page.

To order additional copies of this book, contact
Partridge India
000 800 10062 62
orders.india@partridgepublishing.com

www.partridgepublishing.com/india

This Book is Dedicated To.......
My Father who inspired me to 'Love Nature'
And also My Mother Who Taught Me How to
Take Care of Different Species of Birds and Animals
Which I Came Across in My Life.

CONTENTS

THE PURPOSE
OF THE DISCUSSION _____

At the threshold of twenty first century, we, the present generation of mankind is at a dilemma over whether to allow ourselves be restrained from the path of development by stalling the process of utilization of natural resources and to act as the good Samaritan to safeguard the living world from the brink of extinction or to allow the developmental activities to be carried out unabated for us the human beings' benefit; The resultant outcome is that man, (as we are represented by the species of man or Homo-sapiens on the earth in general_) is trying to find a middle path that would allow him both the benefit of the natural world for his society to make progress and have his conscience at its clearest point by not destroying the natural world's paraphernalia further and rather safeguard them for the future, because he wants to safeguard it both for the reasons of newer, coming generations on the Earth and also as for his kind being part of the embodiment of the universe, called as Nature,_ human beings as the protégé of the nurturer only. The nurturer, that is Nature and in scientific term,- the Environment is the provider of succour for the organic world to sustain life on earth. So, man suffers from a sense of conscionable impropriety committed against Nature when he discovers the extent of destruction of its resources for the benefit of human, that is, his society.

However, in the process of committing to his conscience, man is in a dilemma and conflicting over various issues and prejudices to whether his agenda of prosperity, that is the progress of his society should attain precedence over his agenda of safeguarding the natural resources, as many of his society believe themselves to be superior to other animals on the earth and therefore owning the downright prerogative on the resources of it. However, again the question comes over that no one, not even God has, in any written or un-written law attributed the right of natural resources on man; and therefore man having the dilemma of continuing over undue use and misuse of them remains.

As we are aware and can notice already, now-a-days, along with the tremendous technological progress we have made, there is wide spread devastation of our surroundings caused by wanton destruction of nature. This devastation has been allowed to occur to attain technological achievements only at the cost of our surroundings. It is caused by destruction of forests, as well as due to desertification and desalination processes caused by over-usage of fertilizers and other reasons. The monumental creation of human civilization, _ the urban and industrial conglomerations have contributed to the devastation by causing pollution from factories and other industrial establishments which has highly un-purified and therefore contaminated the air, water and ground around us.

However, as has been mentioned before, since the beginning of twentieth century when technological inventions such as cars, aero-planes etc. have started becoming part of day to day life for human society, there has been wide spread concern for our surroundings and its various components_ air, water and ground and for their conservation and future protection and preservation from the degradation caused to the components of nature, the nurturer of the living world. The relentless destructive process against the environment has caused grave concern among a few who believe nature to be part and parcel of human life. In fact it is to the knowledge of every human being that mankind grew up in the cradle of nature. However, in spite of such knowledge being ingrained in each human being, the temptation to destruct nature seems to be far greater in him than his restrains from doing so. Only proper rationalization of his own actions can make a man refrain himself from committing such damages to natural properties and it seems not all human beings are capable of such rationalization. Besides, "Nature'∞1,(study of which in scientific terminology is called as 'ecology'), forms a part of the greater objective identity called 'Environment'. It comprises the air and the atmosphere, and the overall soil on ground, the ocean etc. _ that is, all the biotic and non-biotic components and therefore all the organic and non-organic substances on earth. As we can notice, the degradation of environment has not only created resentment among its well wishers, witnessing the rapidity with which it is all occurring, a tussle has been going on between them and the propounders of prosperity over the conscionable propriety of such wide spread exploitation. When we find the former questions the moral authority of any one committing such an act, the latter believes it is their 'utilitarian right' to commit and carry on such acts. This conflict of views however reflects the dilemma mankind is facing as the destruction is gradually becoming beyond any redemption or remedy. The biggest question however, which is intriguing us mankind is that – since most of the components of nature are degrading day by day, and many of its inhabitants, i.e. species are getting extinct from the earth, then, in retrospect of what we have to be concerned about is – 'will the world be able to survive without the existence of nature?'

Again, we find that there were many great scholars who could presage the future crises,

---

1. ∞ **'Nature' and 'Environment'**:- 'Nature' describes by us to denote our larger surrounding comprising trees, birds and animals, hills, rivers, landscape on earth etc. is a term more descriptive in nature and has a subjective perspective to our imagination. Environment, on the other hand is more of a scientific term indicating atmosphere, ground, natural resources expressing materialistic approach of definition. Here, both the terms are being used according to each one's the application.

dilemmas and the dichotomy regarding the views and values relating to our surroundings and which would put into turmoil the contemporary convictions that had allowed the world to face degradation and destruction of the Environment -or to be precise- the 'Nature'. Author William Cullen Bryant expresses in the following manner on 'man-nature' relationship, while representing feelings of the nature's eulogizers by referring from Thanopsiss,_ "To him, who in love of nature, holds communion with her visible forms, she speaks a variant language."(Thanopsis)[*1]. However, their voice was never allowed to be highlighted in the advent of the 'neo- intellectualism' that preceded the ideology of progress and development, inundating with 'narratives' that influenced the minds of laymen with consumerism and market-values. The other alternative left is to technologically solve the mammoth crisis of environment waiting to cause and by now being known as 'global Warming'_ a condition of climate disorder which is already being apparent with the conspicuous reduction of icebergs in Arctic regions and the ensuing results of climate changing in a very distinct way, ascribed by scientists as outcome of it. However, the human society as a whole is much too conflict ridden to act in overall manner against the precarious and vulnerable conditions as has been evident with the disconcerted effort at the podium of the united nation organization, the conglomeration of the world- nations' interest on the earth. Therefore it is time for all concerned individuals to pick up the onus of reinventing methods and rejuvenating our conventional conceptions, so as to find some and definitely a perennial one, to bring in the solution for all the self-created hazards in the moral life and material world for humankind, so that our proceeding generations pass their lives blissfully in the lap of nature on the Earth, once again.

As the world is coming to the brink of introspection of what blunder has been committed in the process of materialization and enhancement of human welfare, it gives scope for studying what role ethics of modern society may have in the whole, although at the first instant, the development of technologies and its applications and achievements including those of radio messages, television, sending man to moon by the rocket or even computer storing knowledge and information etc. seems to have no relationship with the abstract connotation of ethical views and values.

Ironically, however, while the present generation of the society has experiences and also aware of the fall out of such technology-oriented development because of the repercussion of it becoming evident on both individual and society at local and global levels (such as Greenhouse effect or Climate Change), there are fewer persons relating ethics or role of ethics to such events or even mishaps in overall manner. But there were some of the ethicists back in eighteenth century who could foresee the increasingly deviated ethical values endorsing utilitarianism(that is, exploiting resources of nature for human welfare) and its possible fall out on the natural surroundings of the society. It is the increasing influence of utilitarian values, born at the beginning of modern era and resulting out of possibly contemporary concept of new found views of domination and exploitation espoused by certain western nations on different other nations and societies of the world by colonizing them, which, the ethicists believe, lead to the concept of mass production in form of industrialization and urbanization in large extent. It also lead to the mass destruction of natural resources in particular and forest areas in general in the process, further resulting in reduced number of particular species and sometimes extinction of some of them. Therefore, there are many scholars and environmentalists in twenty first century who believe that it is the degenerated ethical values, or rather the new-found values generated from human mind and motivating the society to adept to the utilitarianism, but such degenerated illusion needs to be rectified and put and applied in proper perspective for the betterment of the society and bring the 'man and nature' relationship to the earlier mode of reverence and sustenance amidst human society.

The most important feature of the observation to such a situation is that what role human 'conscience', a part of or rather the conceived 'high order' ethical value of human society had played in his conscious effort in safeguarding the nature from overall degradation and retrieving the values to reestablish the age old reverence for nature in society. Scholar D.H. Green speaks in the following way,_ "The(is) delight in nature and longing for a time when man lived in harmony with nature has always been an undercurrent flowing counter to prevailing exploitive Utilitarian attitude."[2] It is also important to note that while degenerated ethical values are believed to be responsible for degradation of qualities of nature's various aspects, the degraded natural conditions again leads to ethical demoralization, causing a vicious circle of overall degradation of the society.

However, what remains questionable is that, would barely finding an ethical solution of the damages caused to the environment in epic proportion halt the process of degradation of it presently leading to a possible catastrophe to happen at an unforeseen moment in the future, permanently damaging the bond of man-nature relationship; Therefore, it is required to establish a new set of thinking of ethical importance that would solicit the future generation with guidance to respect our surrounding nature in a manner that every act of thinking and action would be propitiated with the notion of well-being for the nature and its future. Therefore, the great ethicist of modern period of twentieth century Nigel Dower has expressed in the following way, _"There is here a kind of ambiguity about the relationship of human beings to nature. If human beings are morally bound to respect nature and life in it, we seem at the same time to be both part of nature and apart from nature. On the one hand, we are just part of 'biotic community', with no privileged status: our role is to fit in and be part of the wholeness or integrity of nature/creation. On the other hand, the very fact that we have moral obligations makes us different from the rest of nature so far as we can tell, since the morality or ethos of a higher animal is seen as quite different, not barely by virtue of our rationality and our freedom which means we are not wholly determined by our environment. However hard we try to be literally a part of nature or to abrogate our special status, we undermine the attempt, for the trying is a part of what makes us different."[3] For that matter, a 'Think Tank' should be introduced not only as a part of the curricular activities in school, but also among the intellectuals and concerned individuals, so that it can become a permanent part of the psyche in the common man exercising his day to day activities in life. It should be remembered in the words of the great scholar of Ethics, John McKenzie pronouncing_ back in nineteenth century about what may happen at the end of the millennium_ that the elite generations of twentieth century would worry more about the environment and pollution than industrial development and material benefits for posterity. The very prediction of McKenzie shows that mankind is aware of the possible repercussion of all their activities. Therefore it seems to be necessary way ahead of time for preventing all the possible fallout of the environmental apocalypse with all possible human output and if required, even with the help of technology itself. Therefore I would like to bring into focus what influence there would be of man on his mental and physical worlds by scores of environmental problems he is going to face soon as the implications of environmental crises(Σ) is bound to affect a man

---

ΣCrisis or Crises? Whether the environmental problems causing havoc on our society is a crisis or crises is a matter of much speculation. When looked at it from overall point of view, as especially viewed by established scholars and environmentalists, it is a 'crisis', all the problems related to nature put together. However, here it is being used as 'crises' to indicate a common man's perception in society, which is albeit fragmented and he/she not always relating them to nature on her own, of the problems and their repercussions, and quite often harangued by them without being aware of them, but not having any inkling to the 'root causes' or their own responsibility and seeing each one from different perspectives, not necessarily from environmental point of view only.

both ethically and physiologically. The world, overcome with problems like global warming, 'Greenhouse effect', ozone layer depletion or hole besides a host of other localized problems of environment is surely going to pose a challenge for its concerned inhabitants who would not like to see people trying to cope with assorted health problems due to pollution, besides the qualms an individual suffers as being the perpetrator of it. Hence there is an increased importance for the study of environmental problems in relation to ethical values in present day society. Asserting such an exigency of implementation of ethical values, scholar R.J. Berry has opinionated in the following way,_ "Thus, environmental ethics are more than self interest. Obligations to protect the environment are incumbent to everyone but responsibility, which is increasing function of power, rest in particular with communities, government and corporations. Furthermore, basic justice demands that any sacrifices ought to be distributed according to capacity."[4] Lynton Caldwell, the author expresses in the following way,_"The essence of an adequate ethics for man's environmental relationships must surely include a sense of wonder and respect for the familiar."[5] Therefore, *the purpose of the study* is to highlight that it is becoming very important for the society and imperative for each individual to think and practice the middle path, which now, under the guidance of UNO is being known as 'Sustainable Development', that is, safeguarding and conserving the natural resources on the Earth while the process of 'development' of the society will remain unhindered; The purpose of it is not only meant as for the future generations to enjoy the natural resources, but also pre-supposedly to help mankind as to remain eternally integral to the whole of the universe only. Only such a practice, underlined with ethical perspective and principles will ensure the stopping of the destructive processes currently going on against nature and further assure of a secure future for the animate world on the Earth. It seems, for the time being it is the best way out to keep at bay the crisis of the environment and also keep us the mankind's conscience at clearest point for our posterity and the future.

To discuss the ethical implications of the impact of environmental crisis on modern society I would like to put forward the following chapters as study of discussion:-

1. Introduction: Man and Society
2. Man and Ethics
3. Man and Nature
4. Relationship between Ethics and Environment
5. Environmental Crises and Its Ethical implications of environment on Society
6. Conclusion : *Challenge to Future Humanity*

References:

1. **William Bryant_ Field Biology and Ecology-p.1(i).**
2. **Green, B.H._ Environmental Dilemmas: Ethics and Decisions; Ch.Perception of Nature-p.111**
3. **Dower, Nigel_ World Ethics, Ch. World Ethics: The New Agenda,-p.163**
4. **Berry, R.J._Environmental Dilemmas:Ethics and Decisions-p.255 Caldwell,**
5. **Lyndon Keith_ 'Environment", Ch. Environmental Management as a System-p.251**

FOREWORD

The book 'Ethical Implications of Environmental Crisis on Present-Day Society' is based on the thesis work submitted by me for Ph.D. and there is minimal change to the original content written as the work of research. It is an inter-disciplinary work in which both the genres Ethics and the environment have figured prominently, in spite of both being two complete different entities,_ the former being abstract in nature whereas the latter is materialistic,_ yet each connected with humanity in intrinsic manner and therefore had conversed in a plateau where their inter-connection and how it does affect human society has been discussed. Looking at problems of present-day society from environmental perspective has become imperative today as major part of its activities are related directly or indirectly to the natural 'environment' around us

The work is definitely an outcome of my love for nature and a result of my eagerness to research in the field of Environmental Philosophy.. I remain grateful to my family,_ first my children and then my husband who had encouraged me to complete my Ph.D. pursuance and achieve the degree, thereby allowing me to further dabble in the field environment and philosophy by attending various seminars or submitting papers in them or even pursue fellowship in linguistics despite the kind of busy household schedule.

Last of all I would also like to thank the dept. of philosophy, Gauhati University, Guwahati and also the staff members at Administrative office and various libraries I visited in connection of my research work, such as the library at Delhi University, New Delhi, the Asiatic Library at Mumbai, the British Council, Mumbai and also Krishna Kanta Handique Gauhati University Library, Guwahati.

Hopefully, my book based on my thesis work will be well- accepted among readers and they will appreciate my perspective regarding the modern day crisis in relation to the environment, which also will mean success and spell significance for me if I find the book achieve a place of honour when it would be found among all other contemporary works of ethics and environment meant for posterity of the present-day society.

With Best Regards,
Rupali Devi Barua
Guwahati

CHAPTER 1

INTRODUCTION

1.1. MAN AND SOCIETY

'Man is a social animal'-goes the age old truth since the beginning of human civilization incepted on earth. Man can survive without fellow human beings in nature, but he will remain without a purpose and goal in life. He does not become separate from the identities of other animal beings in such conditions. Man becomes motivated and inclined to implement his intelligence only in presence of other fellow beings. Man was born as one of the species on earth towards the latter part of the evolutionary process of species on earth. He is endowed with the gift of intelligence unlike most other species and therefore he is borne with the ability to rationalize his decisions or thinking on basis of perception of right or wrong. However, all of these abilities become meaningful and applicable only when he lives in a society. The gift of abstract thinking has helped man and his kind progress and function in life in a relentless manner. It has also helped him to decide upon his future actions and activities. According to the philosophy of some of the modern thinkers like Hobbes and Rousseau, in primitive time, folks of man sat down one day to sign the treaty of society, by which they became bound by its laws. Although the treaty is defined differently by different thinkers, in reality there had never been any, as human society did not develop uniformly in all places in the world or was literate enough at the beginning of it to sign it univocally. It makes only a symbolic representation of the rules of society since in all probability man and his society had existed simultaneously since the beginning of humanity. Therefore, Man and society remain integral to the identity of each other.

Man remains a unitary part of his social identity in spite of his ability to function alone. Man and his unitary family in the society is like the atom in the molecule that expresses its individuality through its togetherness. But then, since human and his society is part of the evolutionary process, it is a part of nature also, which is the receptacle of all the natural embodiments, living or non- living. Therefore in spite of human effort in establishing its identity separate from the rest of the species in the world for various reasons, it cannot ignore its umbilical connection with its surroundings, which is nature. Therefore, for human society, when man is its unit, then nature or its surrounding is its basis or receptacle of functioning. Human society, therefore, is born into and functions within the periphery of nature and its objectivity only. But then, since human being happens to be the most intelligent of the species, who, by gift of God is also attributed with the ability to function and create on his own besides that of rationalizing, he is also being endowed with the ability of judgment as well. Man's periphery of action and function had been far wider than that of any other species. Besides, man's own ability of judgment has asserted him himself to be superior to other species also. The sense of superiority ironically has made man to carry out his own activities, apart from the necessities of natural kind. In the continuing evolutionary process on earth, man has become the most domineering species on it by not only using or over utilizing natural commodities, but also by pushing the other species to the edge of their existence, occupying, chasing or even by destroying the forest and land of their habitats in the process. However, man does not believe only in his intelligence. Prior to executing his act of intelligence, he likes to scrutinize the 'righteousness' of his act, whether from individual point of view or that of society. He also believes in 'conscience', the ethical guide to assert the rectification of his act.

However, often the acts of intelligence by man supersede the dictation of ethically rectified amendment of it, so as to comply with his sense of superiority. In some other cases, over a period of time, he would even change his ethical views to keep intact his sense of propriety that fits into the need of time. Thereby, we can conclude that ethical views and values and 'conscience' are complementary to each other. However, like the supreme truth, which often gets clouded with half truths only to be clarified over a period of time, man's conscience also treads its rightful path by following the truth of nature. Therefore following the path of conscience, man realizes the extravagance of his felony of over- exploitation of nature, the implications of such acts and its fall outs too. Therefore, man's ability of 'ethical' scrutinizing has lead to the realization of not only retrieving the qualities of nature back to its origin, but also to remain ethically bound to do so, that is, to reinstate his ethical values of believing in the equilibrium of man and his society with the nature and its various components for the well being of all men, his ethically guided society and nature.

1.2. MAN -*the Basic Unit of the Society*

According to the theory of evolution, man, one of the species on earth, was born nearly at the end of the evolutionary process. In scientific terms of anthropology he is called Homo-Sapiens because as in the process of it, he is also born as the most intelligent of them all. Reflecting on human existence and its relation with the earth Holmes Rolston, III expresses in the following way, "Really the story is little short of 'miracles', wondrous fortuitous events, unfolding of potential; and when earth's most complex product, Homo Sapiens, becomes intelligent enough to reflect over the cosmic wonderland, everyone is left struttering about the mixtures of accidents and necessity out of which we have evolved."[*1]. The root of human society is none other than but man himself. Man, together with other fellow beings only comprises the entity called human society. Man, on the other hand as an individual identity is a species on earth, born at the end of the long evolutionary process of innumerable kind of species, belonging to different families of flora and fauna.

However, man is also the most intelligent among all the species who is also attributed with the ability of functioning by application of his intelligence. Therefore, he is able to utilize his surroundings that are nature and natural objects for his own benefits and formulate the development of the society and give expression to his intelligence in form of civilization.

The entity of a man, as an individual, however, has gone through numerous definition and elaborate explanation by man himself. About the origin of man, different religions have forwarded different theories. The various philosophical lineages of Hinduism have emphasized on the spiritual entity of human in form of 'Aham' only, which is a part of the cosmic reality called 'Brahman'. Such a definition attributes man with existence of eternity only. He attains, or rather ultimately emerges with the entity of eternity through the performance or fulfillment of duties, which is dictated as law of Karma. He attains his zenith only after repeated births on earth till he achieves his moral goals.

The definition of man by some other oriental religions is equally nature-oriented or related. The nature-defining religion of Confucianism believes that the first man on earth was the child of Ying and Yang, the Gods representing sky and earth respectively.

Taoism, another oriental religion, explains that the earth is a combination of two natural forces called Ying and Yang and the man is their natural child. Christianity on the other hand believes that man was created by God who exists in the personalized form of an entity, along with all other inanimate and animate beings on the earth at the same time. Therefore, it does not believe man to be necessarily a part of nature, but an entity entirely independent of others and on its own. It does not belong or connect to nature anyhow.

Apart from the great religions in the world, different societies believing in different forms of worshipping also express their views on the first man on earth. Many tribal societies believe the first man on earth was by the name Adim or Adam and he started his family on earth to give birth to mankind.

The most revealing and possibly the most authentic description of the origin of man was given by anthropologist of nineteenth century Charles Darwin in his scientifically based knowledge oriented book 'The origin of Man'. In the theory, he had proclaimed man to have originated from the primate species, monkey, on earth, which was preceded by many other species of flora and fauna in their different forms. According to him, life first originated in the sea and eventually gave way to the invertebrates and later the vertebrate animals – the latest being the mammals to dominate on earth. Different species dominated it at different periods of time and one of the dominating species was the dinosaurs, with minimal brain but a huge body, which failed to survive on earth as they failed to adapt to the newer ecology on earth. However, man is believed to be one of the latest species coming to earth as part of evolution, and his late induction ensuring a superior intelligence for him to all other animals.

However, for larger part of human civilization, man is being considered in light of the individual religious or cultural definitions only as superior being to other animals or at least as separate in his identity on earth. Therefore, the discovery of man at the latter part of second millennium A.D. as the protégé of the primate has revolutionized the conventional ideas about himself although no-how it decreased the idea of exploitation of nature thereafter.

Man, on the other hand, also a social animal, who, like many other ones, mostly the mammals is considered comparatively even more intelligent than other species_ such as apes and other primates living together in large congregation or the elephants living in herd. However, with his ability of intelligence and more so that of rationality attributing him with the ability to define his values of morality and other ones also with ethical propensity cause him to differ from all other intelligent beings on earth. Therefore his intelligence becomes significant in presence of his society only in which he can make applications of both his intelligence and values for its development –both in psychological and technical dimensions. Therefore, the identity of man and the concept of society are complementary to each other and their individual identity.

1.3. ETHICS: *the Moral Guide of the Society*

The twentieth century has brought revolutionary ideas and their applications in all spheres of human lives in this world. We have witnessed tremendous success and development in the field of science as it was in the beginning of the last century. The new entrants to the areas of scientific development such as the automobile and the aeroplane have made unprecedented metamorphosis in the living conditions of human life. Since the beginning of human civilization, it was twentieth century that man has only been talking in terms of these scientific accessories, besides the nuclear power and the newest addition being the electronic gadgets that can solve (or it seems to be) all human problems. There are also tremendous developments in some fields that have flourished since the inception of human civilization, _ education, Transportation, architecture etc. which are being facilitated in growing and developing by other scientific inventions.

Man has been practicing 'Ethics'- the act of moral obligation and responsibility in scrutinizing all his works, in judging the righteousness or 'goodness' of them from time to time to arrive at rational conclusions. The present-day crises of the environment as a reflection of overall degeneration of ethical values has been interpreted by Titus/ Keeton, the authors of 'Ethics for Today' in the following manner:-

"The hypothesis is this:- The current doubt, turmoil and despair reflect a loss of consensus among men about what is 'good' or 'right' or what is 'better' or 'worse' in human conduct for present times. This loss of consensus arises from many causes. <u>Among them, paradoxically, are charges that enlarge our opportunities charges that, interacting with other conditions, create unwelcome as well as beneficial effects</u>. One cause of loss of consensus is the conflicts and disagreements about who gains and suffers and about who should gain and suffer as these changes occur-----"[*2]. Again, the authors say:- "During the late nineteenth and early twentieth centuries there was widespread optimism, faith and confidence. A few lonely voices in the nineteenth century warned the West about the dangerous trends and possible disaster ahead, but the 'prophets of gloom' were largely disregarded………. There was great co incidence in sciences and a belief that it would be odd to solve these problems rather quietly."[3]

Therefore, there is an attempt in the context to bring into topics only those aspects of 'Ethics' that may have affected the human psychology pertaining to the environment i.e. human view related to happiness or pleasure since ancient times, as it has perpetuated a major role as a deciding factor not only in the human psyche of twentieth century and later, but also that of the fate of the earth as such - our mother earth, to be decimated and destroyed to the vicinity of oblivion as the cradle and nurturer of the human civilization.

While _defining 'Ethics'_, we come to know, 'Ethics' is derived from the Greek word 'ETHOS', which means 'Study of Good Conduct', it suggests that Ethics is the subject that studies 'Goodness' or 'Righteousness' of the 'Thinking' or action of person or a group of persons. In precise, it means the 'righteous' or the 'good' conduct of an individual or a group of persons in another word the conventional values of the society. The values, which are in a word safeguarded and nurtured by different societies, vary in dimension of applications depending upon the stringency each society dispenses with. Thus, although every society may have varied system of values, it is not difficult to find out a familiar and uniform pattern underlying all norms of ethics in this world. At the core, the different mode of ethics in different societies world over relate to same or similar issues only, which primarily discuss the major social and morals institutions such as marriage, honesty, duty, restrain of conduct etc., the basic values of Stoicism or even on pleasure, sense of utility and sense of reasoning or rationality etc. Therefore, we may arrive at the conclusion that all the civilized societies in the world believe in similar ethical values only.

When we think of 'Ethics' as the 'Study of right or good conduct we also come to know that Ethics studies or discusses in details the _basic values of human kind_, especially the moral values which we assert or mark as 'good' or 'right'. However, then we must define 'values' prior to defining Ethics i.e. when we say, _ "What is 'Value'?, we understand 'value' to be the standard or criteria by which we try to judge a person or persons' actions, define certain postulates (for example, we say to young children "Respect your elders") principles or tenets imposed by an individual in particular or society in general. For example, when we say we should 'respect our elders' or 'we should obey our parents', we mean to express certain postulates of values of an individual society (which, of course may have, from ethical point of view, universal acceptance as postulates of value).

The Summum Bonum' Of Life

We can surmise that there is necessity to find out the 'Standard of Measure' i.e. criteria for deciding 'what is good' or 'what is bad or wrong'. Ethics as a subject studies in details about 'goodness' or 'righteousness' of a person's or a society's acts or collective actions. In precise, it means judgment of righteousness or goodness of human conduct or in another sense the conventional values of the society. The criterion itself can be called as the 'Value' system of human society. The society, in its bid to achieve the 'good' of it, the standard of which has been set by its own 'value' system, often aspires to achieve the 'good' itself. Therefore, rather than using it as a means for achieving the 'goals' of the society, it strives to achieve the 'good' itself.

Prior to discussing about the goal of the 'good' of the society, we must return to the question of the 'value' of the society to be retained, so that the moral order of the society can be maintained. To further the question we may ask to that what are the reasons behind maintaining the 'values' by the societies. The general answer to the question may be that, since the 'progress' of the society is to be maintained, the society should lean on a 'locus standi', that is, to find a reason to carry out an act,- for its progress and the moral values act as the 'Locus Standi' of it. A society based on strong moral values can progress both morally and spiritually and economically, as is believed by the wise men on earth -bringing both peace and stability to it.

Therefore, we may arrive at the conclusion that the 'good' of the society is to 'achieve' the 'good' it aspires for, be it economic development or achievement for some, whereas it may be interpreted by some others as 'achieving the spiritual zenith'. Still there may be some who may consider 'intelligence acumen' as the penultimate 'good' of the society. The ancient Greek society was one such community which highly emphasized on exercising one's 'intelligence' to achieve the 'good' of the society. The great Greek scholar Socrates emphasized on 'Education' as the 'good' of the society, whereas his equally renown disciple, the great philosopher Plato emphasized on 'Virtue' as the ultimate 'good' of all of human kind. In India, during the ancient times, sages believed individuals should make entourage of spiritual quest so as to enhance the level of 'good' of the society. In modern time, we find western societies espousing the causes of 'economic development' and also in orientation of common man's psychology to adapt to the market values so that the individuals can live materialistically unhindered and an effluent life.

Therefore, the question remains as to whether the 'good' of the society is a means for achieving its goal or is it an 'end' in itself? However, many ethicists, specially those believing in the greater 'good' of society believe that not only the 'good' of society is quite often its 'end' itself, the society itself quests for the 'good' that is not only universally 'good', the epitome of 'goodness', but something that must be the essence of life and the ultimate reality of life too. Like in Indian philosophy it is said that "Satyam, Sivam, Sundaram', That is truth is universal Reality and Reality is Beauty' which otherwise suggests that reality itself is 'goodness' which is eternally beautiful and true.

1.4. ENVIRONMENT

Our surrounding, that comprises the trees, animals, birds and other creatures and the rivers, waterfalls, hills and the mountains together is called Nature. Human beings like all other creatures on earth are borne by and grown on the lap of Mother Nature. In scientific terms it is called Environment. Nature also extends to the air and atmosphere and even the space, the soil and the various elements it contains in the deep of the ground and the sea, the deep of the ocean and even the aquatic animals and plants in it. In that case we can call Nature as our Environment and it comprises all the biotic and non-biotic (that is -living and non living) substances on the earth. Scholar Alok Saklani defines environment in the following way- "The term 'environment' includes water, air, land, human beings and other living creatures."[4] Regarding the presence of life on earth author Holmes Rolston III expresses in the following way- "The evolution of rocks into dirt into flora and fauna is one of the great surprises of natural history, one of the rarest events in the astronomical universe. Earth is all dirt, we human too arise up from the humus, we find revealed what dirt can do when it is self organizing under suitable conditions."[5] In the scientific terminology, the study of Nature is called the Ecology- and it contains various study groups_ the study of the various features of nature-such as that of trees and animals are comprised in the category of Flora and Fauna respectively, that of water-bodies comprising that of lake and river as study of Hydrology and comprising studies of sea, ocean etc. are included in the Marine Biology as it focuses on different branches of it. It defines the various and overall characteristics and various natural happenings to give scientific explanation to them. Ecology can be divided into many divisions which includes subject matters Eco-system, Marine Ecology, Tropical forests i.e. the Rain Forests, Estuary, Bio-sere, Flora and Fauna etc. Thus, Ecology helps in learning extensively about Nature.

In the study of Ecology, we can study in details about the inter-relationship or to be precise dependency between two or among a group of species of living beings or the inter-action between living and non-living substances of nature. According to scientist s Allen H. Benton and William E. Warner,-"Ecology, which deals with all of the interrelationship of nature, is thus a modern version of nature's study."[6] Usually when we talk about nature or refer to Ecology, we mean about various living and non- living aspects of our surrounding only,- such as birds, mammals, rivers, mountains etc. and their interdependency and therefore their interrelationship only.

The flowers and the trees, the birds and the animals, the rivers and the mountains -all these are part of the nature around us. Nature provides us with food, shelter and also cover besides the air, water and the earth to live on. Like a mother it helps us being fed and nurtured to carry on our lives and activities together. Since the beginning of human race on earth, man has been as much part and parcel of nature, as all other inhabitants of it. Man has been living in nature, taking shelter in it and has been using it for his own benefits. However, man happens to be more intelligent than all other inhabitants of it. He can use and manipulate things as no one else can do. He not only can move things from one place to another but also to cook food, construct a house or protect himself with weapons that no other inhabitant could do. However, all these activities by mankind have been carried out for his own convenience and his extraordinary ability in comparison to other living beings has made him assert himself as superior to all of them. However, on earth in geo biological term, man is not the only important factor, there are other major characteristics of nature which only help in maintaining natural balance on earth and make it more livable for all living beings.

1.5. THE EQUILIBRIUM

The three primary aspects of human society, *man as its unit, nature as its basis and ethics as its guidance,* are not only complementary to each other, but also integral to each other's entity as part of society. The three entities create interdependency, as a result of which human society makes progress on earth. Ethics, although abstract in form dominates human psychology to drive him to achieve his goal in a righteous way and nature provides him with necessary and other requirements of life. On the other hand, ethics derives inspiration for the values it espouses such as devotion, dedication, honesty, fraternity etc. from nature only.

Although over the change of time human ethics has turned into a complex system, its roots are based on natural values only. However, nature cannot be said to be dependent on either human or his ethics, but man, his ethics or his society is part of the development of nature's relentless process only. Relation of man with nature is like that of a child with his mother only. Therefore, while like a mother, nature is not dependent on human, man himself is an integral part of it only. But then, man, like any other species and with limited utilization of nature can contribute to the process of its continuity only. **Thus, an equilibrium is created amidst man, ethics and nature of their existence, so that the human society can move ahead in harmony with the law of universe and without any interfering with its on-going process.** The equilibrium is created with the contribution of each component nature, man and ethics and each component's proportion of contribution causes a ratio amidst them, creating a balance on earth that helps the equilibrium continue in its process and therefore the human society. However, any of the components acting beyond its measure can not only create disturbances for other components, but also may destroy any of them and therefore so would be the process of equilibrium, destroyed beyond any remand. For example, if nature causes enough fury to destroy most of the human habitation, than mankind will be in jeopardy and therefore the very existence of human society would be threatened.

Man, if growing in number beyond any proportion, is bound to create stress on nature which provides him with necessities and also his ethics which would be bound to tether and its values ignored if man fails to provide himself with his basic necessities. A hungry man cannot be expected to be within the bounds of morality and not steal to appease himself. Likewise if man's ethics becomes either stringent of its values or laxity is shown in implementation of them in society, the society may become disoriented by harming the integrity of human, its basic component or even the existence of nature.

Thus, it becomes a primary requisite, or to be precise, the obligation of the society to maintain the equilibrium on earth, so that ultimately it is not harmed itself in the process of its existence and continuity on earth.

In modern era, the equilibrium of nature is best expressed in the theory of Gaiaism, which believes in such inter-balance amidst the aspects of nature.

Therefore, we can surmise that man, nature and ethics are the three most important aspects of human society, - man as its unit, nature its receptacle and ethics as its guidance have given human society its mobility and dynamism to function as the most important entity on earth. While ethics and environment i.e. the surrounding of a society remain integral part of it, they also help it in its entire formation, whether metaphysically or materialistically. While ethics has been dictating the necessities to be fulfilled for the development of the society, nature has been contributing to it materialistically, helping it in the process of prosperity and development. However, looking at the process of development the need of the society also changes from time to time. There was a time when the society showed precedence in expressing respect for nature for being like a mother in nurturing all its organisms, including human society. It believed not only in the balance of its components and refraining from over using it, it also believed in not evoking the anger of nature by doing so. Ethics has changed over the period of time and the process of development has also taken over it. When at the beginning of human civilization, ethics was primarily meant to relate to the need of fulfilling the moral guidance. But in the process of development, it has become a more complex and structured genre of thinking. While human society at such a stage derived the 'good' values from natural surroundings, for example learning about dedication, loyalty, care, duty, responsibility etc., gradually it has given way to ethical institutions like marriage, religion etc. as parts of a composite society. It has fulfilled not only the spiritual guidance to it, but also has helped human society to become a complex structure itself, setting it apart from rest of the surrounding flora and fauna to assert itself as a complex system.

Regarding the intrinsic relation of man with his surroundings, and the dependency of human existence on the earth, the Chandogya Upanisad narrated in a hymn in the following manner,-

Esham Vutanam Prithvi Rasah Prithvya Aapo Rasah I
OpaamosadhayoRasa Oshadhinam Purushah Rasa II [*7]

It means essence of all the beings on earth is earth. The essence of earth is water, the essence of water is vegetation and from it is born human kind. Thus it has expressed the interrelationship between man and nature.

Some scholars have been trying to explain the equilibrium of nature man and ethics in their individual ways. For example, some scholars viewing it more from objective perspective explain it from ecological or even anthropological point of view, whereas some others try to explain it in subjective manner. Author Stephen J. Kellert believes that the harmony of the aspects of society depends on maintaining the balance among certain values which will assure rightful affinity and of its integrity. The values mentioned by him are as follows,-first it is aesthetic value, which inspires man to enhance his capabilities and be of orderly nature, then the dominionistic value that causes domineering attitude of man over others. It is followed by humanistic value that inspires love and care towards nature. Moral values help man develop in spirituality and moral affinity towards it. Naturalistic view encourages man to come closer to nature. The last of them all, Negativistic value makes man fear and avoid nature or some of its features. Together they are called as 'Biophilia'- which helps in maintaining balance in man- nature relationship.

The most important feature of the relation among the three genres- man and his society, ethics and nature is that not only are they supplementary to each other but also integral to nature. Their relationship has caused equilibrium of existence and survival, not only of human being and his society in the midst of nature, but also of the natural aspects including flora and fauna and human ethics as well. Any kind of metaphysical or physiological change in one genre is bound to influence the others.

References:-

1. Holmes Rolston III - *Philosophy and the natural Environment*,-ch. *Value in Nature and Natural Value*, p.27)

2. Harold Titus and Morris Keeton-*Ethics Today/Ethics tomorrow-* -p.1

3. *Ibid.* -p.2

4. Alok Saklani-*Impact of Environment*-p.3

5. Holmes Rolstone III-*Philosophy and Natural Environment*-p.26

6. Allen H. Benton &William E. Warner- *Field Biology and Ecology*, p.1

7. Chandogya Upanisad-*Environment and Ancient Sanskrit Literature*-p.129

CHAPTER 2

MAN AND ETHICS

2.1. Introductory: *Man's Relation with Ethics*

Looking at the development of ethics as a subject, we must go back to the days of human civilization to find it in its infantile stage too, as development of human society is much owed and influenced by the guidance of it. In fact, we may be accrued to the fact that it is the sense and 'feeling' inculcated in the human mind by the sense and knowledge of 'ethics' itself, that has helped it to achieve a steady ground for attaining maturity on its own for its over-all development of future prosperity and posterity too. However, when civilization was in its infantile stage, ethics too did not develop further and existed in its crudest form only. It is over the centuries and millenniums that it also has achieved its fullest form with all its pitfalls and nuances developing at all directions of human psyche and touching all the peripheries of human mind. Even in modern time it has made its highest bid and has tried to presage all the human activities and lay restriction on intellectual fervor by decreeing on the 'moral standing' of some such issues.

However, not always Ethics has succeeded in decreeing the moral standard over all the issues that have of late hovered over the human society in general. The reason can be attributed to the fact that after all it is creation of the human mind and it is therefore viable to the change of both human psyche and time. Its 'internal viability' that man has been exploiting time and on to adept it according to his own necessity, it is being his prerogative since in spite of being a 'godsend' messages to mankind, it has always been susceptible to indemnity of human eccentricity man likes to exercise over his own creations. Therefore for man, ethics, as a subject has reflected both stringency of views to 'opportunism' he has exercised when he deemed it necessary, and often for his own survival. We can witness the overall development of it, with reaching its pinnacle perhaps during the medieval period. However, the study of 'Ethics' only scrutinizes and chronicles the true and actual 'Applied Ethics' in society only which has got its own crescendo of happenings and a course of evolving for itself.

Therefore, one of the most important features of the relationship between man and ethics is the 'viability' of ethics, as it has changed over the periods of time along with the change of views and values of human being. Invariably, its viability had much to do with the third component of society that is nature. Although western philosophy, predominated by views of Christianity has never believed nature to be greater than human being- man being an independent creation of God along with nature, nature always has dictated its terms in spite of its viability to the diction human eccentricity. However, like in the eras preceding it, even the modern period gave away to the dubiousness of the contemporary ethical thinking; as in the ancient period western philosophy was conditioned to the duality of Cynics and Cyrenaics to be called Epicureans and stoics respectively in the following period. While Cynics and Stoics believed in appreciating nature and natural ways followed in stringent manner, Cyrenaics and epicureans believed more in the theme of happiness or pleasures in life and defined their reckoning of it accordingly. The same parallel views become apparent in modern period when Utilitarian Ethics has been contravened by the view of Environmental Ethics. While some great scholars like G.E. Moore or John Stuart Mill started endorsing the views of utilitarianism from the altruistic perspective of human welfare, scholars like Joseph Butler or Samuel Clark started portraying the environmental ethics as the forte of contemporary thinking, emphasizing the greatness of natural law and the importance of nature in human relationship with ethics. However, it was called Ethical Naturalism or Ethics of Nature only. In modern time it has been taken over by the applied form of it in the name of environmentalism, Cosmocentrism or Deep Ecology or even as the Environmental Activism.

Ethics and Ethical Disagreement

There has been considerable controversy over whether 'Ethical Disagreement' should exist regarding 'different' moral feeling among different persons occurring to them in the 'same' situation of emotion. The modern philosopher G.E. Moore has put considerable importance to the issue by emphasizing on the basic duality of Ethics. According him, _ "This fact, on which I have been insisting, that different men feel differently towards it at different times, is of course, a mere common place." However, the duality of a concept, which is perceived differently by two different persons or groups expressing ambiguity towards the perception of the other one, may not, according to Moore, be different in opinion in spite of being different in attitude. Therefore, to be actually differentiating from one another ethically means one has to be different from the other one both in attitude and in opinion.

2.2. *'Summum Bonum' Of Life:* The Ultimate Goal of 'Goodness'

Each and every one of us, having positive inclination of life, intend to do good things in our life- whether it is for ourselves, or for our families or even for people in general or for our society or country. However, although we believe in doing our deeds with a 'good' motive its periphery remains limited in most accounts. It is believed that the small accounts of 'goodness' in all of us together can create the 'good' of the world too.

'Man is a social animal'_ the age old adage remains an eternal truth for mankind, although human society has witnessed tremendous social changes in the twentieth century. From pluralistic to 'nuclear' set up, society has come a long way in defining individuality in a person. However, in olden time or now, concern always remains embedded in human mind for the society he/she belongs to in particular and humanity in general. The reason to be found is very simple_ like the drop of water creating an ocean, man too has created humanity and however small or big it may seems to be, he contributes to its development knowingly or unknowingly. Therefore, there always exists the seed of 'goodwill' for the society in human mind, which can either be called 'Philanthropy' or 'altruism. According to John Dewey, the famous philosopher and one of the most well known scholar of twentieth century known for his views as a proponent of utilitarianism, that was interpreted as for the welfare of the society - "A union of benevolent impulse and intelligent reflection is the interest most likely to result in conduct that is good. But in this union the role of thoughtful inquiry is quite as important as that of sympathetic affection." [1] Again he says,_ "In other words, there is a natural response to a particular situation, and one lacking in moral quality as far as it is wholly unreflective, not involving the idea of any end, good or bad ……. but it has affected those who hold that benevolence is is the sole motive which is morally justifiable."[2]

However, like almost all other branches of human faculty, whether it is religion or philosophy, ethics too as a subject is mired in the problem of its inherent dualism. When some believe in man's ego-centric ideology, others vouch for ethos that should be based on 'goodwill' of the society in particular and humanity in general, i.e. altruism or 'philanthropy' that bears

the signatory mark of universality. Perhaps similar mark of bilinear pursuit can be witnessed in between Cynics and the Cyrenaics of the pre-Socrates era and the Stoics and the Epicureans of later period. Therefore, the 'good' of life defined by ethics always seems to suffer from the diabolic predicament of the notion of 'what 'good' we have been talking about and for whom is the 'good' and who should attain the ultimate benefit of it. However, quite a number of theories have been initiating since the inception of ethics over who should take precedence in achieving the 'good' of society: there are the ones who emphasize on Egocentrism i.e. love of self against the ones who are basically preachers of 'society' getting precedence over 'self'. The 'Cyrenaicism' vs Cynicism, the 'Epicureanism' vs. 'Stoicism', 'Hedonism' vs. 'Spiritualism' are the representation of the constant conflict of Egocentrism versus Altruism in the world. Ethicist James Seth believes 'there is at once revealed a seemingly chaotic variety of 'good', for which he comments-"what appears good to me is my good, what appears good to you is yours: there is apparently no moral criterion. Here, at any rate, we seem to be reduced to absolute subjectivity. Each man appears to be his own measure of Good, and no common measure seems possible. Yet the scientific thinker cannot, any more than the ordinary man, escape from the faith of absolute good.......
Variety of opinion as to what is what the Good is, is always confined within the limits of a perfect unanimity of conviction that there is an absolute Good.' Even it is found out that the Utilitarianism which give precedence of self over societal good on basis of deriving the most utility out of our surrounding, is not without the view of overall well-being of the society and believe it to be the ultimate attainment of individual Good.'[3]

However, it is a little bit difficult to arrive at the conclusion whether the 'good' an individual or the society strives to achieve is the 'end' in itself or only the 'means' for attaining the highest goal it aims for. However, the great philosopher John McKenzie believes that 'the term 'good' used (perhaps even more frequently) to signify not something that is useful to a person but something which is righteous and useful at the same time and which is universally acceptable too. He also believes that the 'good' itself is a kind of 'end' for human kind which is aimed to be achieved by it, thereby being the ultimate 'good' or 'Summum Bonum'of life, representing height of spirituality, devotion and dedication for the betterment of society. Therefore, we may arrive at the conclusion that ultimately it is the element of 'Universal Well-Being' or "Altruism' which overtakes the element of 'Ego-centrism' of the individual human being in particular and society in general.. Human being will always strive to achieve the 'ultimate' good in spite of his inclination to do 'good' to himself i.e. being self- centred or ego-centric. He says_ "It should be carefully observed, however, that the term 'Good' also used (perhaps even more frequently) to signify not something 'which is a means to an end', but something which 'is itself taken as an end'. Thus the 'Summum Bonum', or supreme good, means the supreme end at which we aim. *4

2.3. *The Nature, Comparative Study and History of Ethics*

Ethics, as a subject is not only part of the establishing of the 'guiding rules' of the society in the ancient time, it also forbears certain characteristics that set it apart from other subjects. We find that unlike some subjects, ethics does not discuss about its subject matter and make a judgment of Ethics, as a subject of study, is attributed with various characteristics that set it apart from other subject matters. For example, we may find that Ethics as a subject, unlike subject like philosophy does not analyze its content, but only dictates rules that are to be applied according to a situation. Nor does it discusses over issues or the subject matter of it, unlike it is done in case of subject matter such as education, political science or other science subjects.

'As regards Ethics, we may note that:
  (a) Ethics is not a subject of discussion but that of 'Guidelines'. It is therefore called a 'normative' science.
  (b) The basis of the study of ethics is 'morality' or "rightful conduct". However, it cannot be called as 'art' of conduct as it does not carry any instruction how to be of good '; conduct', but what is good conduct.
  (c) Ethics primarily connects itself with the world 'within' only, i.e. the world of 'emotion' only which guides the basic human principle. It means its rationalization is based on the basic human feelings only, which sets it apart from most other subject matters.
  (d) Ethics, as we came to know of it, dictates rules and therefore it confines its studies to various dictions that are similar to that of scientific studies where one needs to adhere certain fixed rules or postulates to arrive at conclusion.

Besides it, it also has other characteristics of 'methods, 'laws', 'standards', views etc. However, ethics calls certain subject matters of it as 'problem' as and when it fails to arrive at conclusion regarding them.

Ethics as a subject bears similarity with many other subjects in many respects- that is, in way of its nature of being 'normative, or idealistic in characteristic, or an applied subject matter having 'bearing' upon practical life, but not a practical science. However, in spite of the similarities, Ethics bears in characteristics that are distinct in nature and sets it apart from other subjects in term of integrity and quality. Because of its importance by nature of its objectivity of the study and its influence over man's relationship with society attributes itself to be a superior podium for studying intrinsic values and further pursuing of spirituality.

(A)Ethics vs. Psychology :- Ethics as a normative study of science is a 'state of mind' and relates to various 'mind related issues that connects it to the society. The relation of mind and society is more evident in Ethics than any other subject matter. Psychology, on the other hand is also connected to the mind as its study is intended to explore the various basically crevices and 'pitfalls' of mental activities only. The purpose of Psychology is basically not to establish the relation of mind with society but rather the influence of society on the mental setup of the individuals. Besides, it is entirely the inner world of mind that that psychology explores rather than the outside one although the mind as the receptive sensory organ relates to the outside world only. Therefore, the difference of the two subjects lies not only in the variation of quest but also on the subject matters each relates individually. That is when ethics lays stresses on the relationship of the mind, with that of society, -psychology relates to the nuances and crevices of mind as a result of the outside influence only. Again, being a normative science Ethics decrees directives on the righteousness or legitimacy on the subject matter. Whereas psychology is more descriptive in nature, detailing on the nook and corner of mental activities, although some section of it looks for the solution for mind related issues only. Thus, in spite of dealing with the same plane of mind by both the subject matters, each seems to have moved into different directions to relate to completely different subject matters only.

(B)Ethics vs. Logic, While comparing ethics with logic, we find Ethics as a subject bears in some semblance with logic also. However the difference between the two subjects remains noteworthy. Both Ethics and Logic are normative subjects_ both dictates its followers with certain criteria to be followed with for farther proceed of the study. However, there seems to be distinction in such proceeding between the two. When, the logical proceedings are scientific, based on certain given laws are applied according

to necessity. It is not so in case of Ethics, although it dictates its norms there is no such hard bound rule, in spite of the subject matter is given, Its criteria are loosely bound and applied according to the necessity of situational subject matter. Logic doesn't deal with any human feelings, only facts, whereas Ethics is related to the emotion of the human beings. When the themes of logic are practical situations to be related to, the themes and ideas of Ethics are abstract ones.

While logical rules are inwardly used for various conclusions, there is only superficial imposition of the rules in ethics such as laws and methods and theories which are only fixed conditions without any supposition and contradiction. Thus Ethics remains socio psychological in nature, while Logic remains scientific in approach covering a long range of subject matter.

Thus, we have already come to learn that Ethics is study of 'rightful conduct' the need is to focus on what is rightful conduct and the discussions on it. We have come to know that being a normative science of study, it imposes its moral values on various issues of discussion and bind the rules for them. However, there are many subject matters that ethics seems to be, even since its early days, in ambiguity of assertions and had failed to arrive at a conclusion. Such subject matters are considered problems of ambiguity and therefore remain controversial among the scholars and ethicists in the world.

Besides, there are other subjects related to human mind and emotions and social issues and practices that ethics as a subject relates to. They can be, besides being categorized into the following divisions as its basic qualities_ Postulates, Standards, Methods, Problems, theories and Laws, 'Idea' and 'Authority' also can be measured as standard of assessment of ethical values. Basically, it is the various postulates of Ethics around which other measures of ethical values develop, as complex ideas of ethics grow.

Regarding various issues of Ethics, Dr. Mc. Kenzie opines in the following way,-"... The treatment of this (subject) is necessarily to some extent historical. It is hardly possible, at the present state of development of ethical study, to lay down the various more or less incorrect opinions that have been current in the course of ethical speculation. Having considered these and formed our view as to the general nature of the doctrine that is to be taken as true, we are then able, finally, to consider the application of this doctrine to the treatment of the concrete facts of the moral life.'"[5] Postulates are basic themes that Ethics relate to and Methods are certain systems of moral order confounded by rules of Ethics over certain subject matters whereas the 'Law' of ethics expresses the rules that confound the issues of their limitations. The necessity of the issues to be contained within the limits of Ethics is to perforce the fact that they are within the bound of the moral order of Ethics.

In the study of ethics we find various divisions to denote the various strata of the notions of human contemplation,_ like the 'laws', 'problems' and 'standards etc., there are many 'theories' of ethics too, to purport the idea of the "right' kind of ethics. We may discuss the issues in the following manner:-

2.4. *The Postulates*

The basic themes, related to human mind and emotion that ethics relates to, are Feelings_ volition and desire, will, motive and intention, freedom or liberty and right, duty and responsibility, the origin of conscience etc. Ethics has viewed the importance of each of the subjects separately.

2.4.1. *Feeling, Volition, Desire and Will* :-

Feeling, volition, desire, wish and will all various of human emotions and achieve certain stage of it association with sub conscious to cognitive states of acknowledgement. When we are talking about 'Desire', we must not confound it with a kind of appetite of an animal, as desire is associated with 'consciousness' of a person. Besides, the 'feeling' of ethical consent is also associated with it. We may find out that while volition is reflective action, not having any cognitive effort in it, and which can be compared with that of feeling of appetite only, has in reality nothing to do even with feeling. Feeling, on the other hand, is the basic recognition of emotion and also its reflective expression, it is the intrinsic quality of it by which it identifies and directs other associated feelings also.

Volition, is kind of automatic action on part of individual, which is carried out impulsively, rather than with any feeling. Desire, is a conscious acknowledgement of 'wish'. The most important element of it is the acknowledgement of 'good' in such a 'wish'. It is generally believed that a person consciously 'desire' for an object only if it is "good' for him. It does not seem to be very redeeming to believe a person consciously desire something after thinking it to be 'good' for himself. It should be explained in the following manner that when a person desire for something, it should serve him the purpose of an 'end' for himself. A comparative note on other related 'feelings' may actualize the position of 'desire' in a person's life.

Desire and Will, when to be compared in terms of each one's inclination of achieving the goal, we discover that the former suggests intense feeling for achieving it, in which it acts as means of will, although it may not suggests as the ultimate way to achieving the goal. In case of the latter, it means a kind of feeling, lasting for a longer period of time, rather than being intense, and therefore added with a sense of determination for the same. When the Will suggests the intention of achieving its end, the Desire simply expresses wish for the end and not necessarily expresses either an intention or any determination for the same.

2.4.2. Motive, Inclination and Intention :-

'Motive' is one the basic agenda of human actions. When we talk of or insist on carrying on a particular act, we call it having certain 'motive' for such insistence and believe one having certain 'hidden' agenda, i.e. reason for that. The fact that, one wants to achieve certain goal within a specific or stipulated period of time, one is induced with a force or reason for that. That particular reason is called the motive.

However, it can neither be a moral reason or a qualified one, as it does not seem to be a cognitive action. While motive may indicate an end in view and itself as the means for the same, inclination only suggests a sense of feeling or will to achieve but not necessarily any presence of end or being itself a means. It iconizes a static perception, whereas the former indicates a sense of mobility, which means action with volition, with an 'Intention' i.e. a strong will to perform which acts as the hidden agenda. On the other hand, 'Intention', which has close affinity with the meaning of 'motive' besides being difficult in identifying separately, can be defined in close heel with the former in terms of achieving its end, in spite of their mutual difference. When a person intends to do something, he means to do it again, with his eyes on the end of it. However, while carrying on 'Intention', to do an act, one keeps one's eyes on achieving the end only and not necessarily to follow the particular way to achieve it. It is the means to achieve the goal or end, which count between the two genres. In 'Intention' one is not very 'particular' about the way to achieve the end and may or may not be 'induced' to achieve the end. Therefore, we may arrive at the conclusion that motive can be a part, or to be precise, complimentary to Intention but not be whole of it. Or, we may say that it includes the 'direct' intention, it does not do so with indirect 'Intention'.

2.4.3. *Behaviour, Character, Conduct and Habit*:-

While a person is referred to, he or she is signified by the pattern of behavior by which to relate or to conduct with the people of outside world. 'Behavior' is the expression of the inane qualities of a person which he or she carries inborn. The word 'good' or 'bad' is attached later to the type or pattern of the particular behavior judged on basis of conventional 'standard' of morality. Usually, the particular pattern of behavior or manner signifies a person, which is called his or her character. The outward expression of it or the applied form of character of a person can be called as the person's 'Conduct'. Again, 'Habit' is particular form of conduct a person carries in an inherent manner. Therefore, we may consider the behavior, character, conduct and habit as different facets of different stages of human psyche of an individual.

When the different parameters of 'Conduct' or 'character' are considered from ethical point of view, the question of 'Good' or 'bad' conduct come up to be scrutinized for the standard of morality. While good behavior suggests a person incurring etiquette that suits the moral standard of society, the opposite of it, i.e. bad manners or behavior suggests the performer's inability to fulfill the moral code, defined for conducting such behavior.

We find that different ethicists defining 'character', 'conduct' and 'habit' in their individual manner. According to Dr. McKenzie, - "we have seen that character means the complete universe or system constituted by acts of will of a particular kind. Character is, on the whole the most important element in life from the point of view of ethics, as we shall see more fully in the sequel."[6] According to him, will is the underlying factor that dominates 'character, although it is confined within the parameters of space and time and a 'good' character needs the support of good acts of will to substantiate its qualities, he believed. Conduct, on the other hand, can be called rather an assortment of various activities, both physical ones as expression of individual morality and mental ones too, which in overall manner symbolizes the individualistic characteristics of a being which is directed to achieving certain end. Herbert Spencer not only defined such 'characteristics' of conduct, he even believed that even a mollusk can be defined in term of its conduct. However, his views can be challenged upon by the fact that while creatures such as mollusk or even higher kind of animals carry themselves around with certain amount of individualistic characteristics of their own moving towards an end at the same time, their acts lacks self recognition and are more of expression of their instinctive behavioral pattern than having any purpose, motive, rationalization or therefore as acts of their own will.

Habit, on the other hand is complete different expression of character. While conduct can be called assimilation of various behavioral patterns of character, habit can be called as the expression of the characteristics of person. It is the outward manifestation of the inane qualities of a human being, which shows not only the level of refinement of behavior, but also the moral standard of an individual. Therefore it can be called, as in definition of Socrates and Aristotle that virtue is not only knowledge but also kind of habit. However, if habit is kind of reflection of the character a human being possesses, then it is a fact that such habits can be improvised upon its former ways or patterns and thereby its moral qualities being boosted to achieve the expected podium. Thus, habit, unlike character, itself reflects certain qualities that are conditional to inane qualities of moral values of conduct and therefore is the ultimate expression of moral standard of an individual.

2.5. _Standard of Ethics_
2.5.1. _Happiness Duty, and Perfection_'
Duty, while looked at in relation to Happiness and Perfection, may have completely different perspective than in terms of its relation with such other postulates as responsibility and the right. According to Dr. McKenzie,-"If we describe the two opposing theories of as those of Duty and Happiness, the term perfection may appropriately be used to characterize the middle theory, which to large extent, combines the other two."*7

(A) *Happiness*
Happiness is one of the primary postulates, which also can be called as the axis of western ethical thinking. It is an end, the means of achieving of which remained a matter of contemplation in western thinking. Followers of different standards of value perceived it different ways_ for example hedonists believe happiness can or should be achieved through sensible pleasures only. So was basically the views of the Cyrenaics in ancient Greece, the land or origin of Ethics, although Socrates, the mentor of its thinking believed it can be attained through acquirement of knowledge and virtue only. At later stage, Epicureans believed in a pessimistic approach, that it can be achieved through the experience of pain, so as to understand the joy of pleasure, and therefore happiness. At the beginning of modern era, Utilitarianism believed it could be attained through altruistic motives,

that is, basically for the betterment and welfare of human kind. For them pursuing such happiness even by relegating our surrounding, that is, nature or its paraphernalia, that is the resources is not committing any misdeed or sin, and therefore conceded of moral justice.

(B)*Duty*

Duty is believed to be one of the primary postulates in Ethics. Duty as the standard and the theories evolving around it asserts it to be one of the primary obligations of an individual in society. In fact, in religio-philosophy of Hinduism emphasizes so much on 'Duty' that it seems to be indispensable and therefore inseparable from its ethical views. It is also the primary postulates of Indian Ethics. However, It does not seems to have occupied such an important place in western philosophy, at least not more than as a postulate of the morality of Ethics.

Human kind is entrusted with certain responsibilities, towards his own family members, to each in an individual manner as well as towards society in general and certain members of it in particular form. The concept of duty, the rudimentary form of which can be found even among the other living beings such as animals, birds and even creatures like fish, spider etc.

(C) *Duty and Respect:*_*Duty as postulate and respect as Its Standard*

Often mankind seems to have so much to learn from some of the other living beings regarding the performance of duty that philosopher like Plato considered a small bird as the standard and ideal forbearer of virtues. However, before performing one's own duty, one needs to bring in certain considerations as rational basis for fur more complex set of duties other than those carried out by animals, as man needs to substantiate his values to be based on certain rational criteria. Among such criteria, we find freedom, judgment etc. to be considered for as the basis of duty. However, such criteria or postulates are to be considered as the object of respect (or respected as the primary criteria for consideration) for duty. The postulates to be respected as the basis for duty are rectified for various considerations.

(D) *Duty and Responsibility*

A man comes to the earth, duty bound, and he may bear in many responsibilities entrusted upon him. For example, when we say that it is our duty to take care of our children and educate them, we under stand that we are taking the responsibility for fulfilling them, besides being bound to do it. From the example, we may derive the fact that man, as a social animal is bound with certain duties to other human beings if not all, but with those he is socially or situation wise connected with. On the other hand, man may have responsibility, to which he may be bound or not, although complying responsibility may be part of fulfilling one's own duty only. Responsibility may not always be binding situation wise but by socially only. Therefore, we may believe that carrying out responsibility is the means for fulfilling one's duty. While Duty is a reality, responsibility is a condition only. The former is long lasting, whereas the other is temporal and exists for certain duration only. To perform duty, one must be having responsibly for taking charge of the situation, otherwise it would remain unfulfilled. Likewise, a man is ethically bound by duty towards his family that born him, to the nation that feed him and the society that nurture him and to the children he gave birth to. A man is duty bound to them all due to the situational bond to them. But, being responsible always does not suggest to be duty bound. For example, the eldest boy of a group took responsibility to get them work through out the day. Here, the boy is not duty bound but taken responsibility of the work to be done. Again, the ethical responsibility a person holds towards his society is not duty bound but conditional only.

2.5.2. *Conscience:-*

The conception of Conscience holds important role in ethics. It is believed to be higher kind of psychological exercise that may be lacking in animal habit and tribal self of a person. The state of conscience in the mind of a man transcends his basic feeling and act as a superior conduct in terms of judgment, and rationalization. Regarding the origin of conscience as an ethical instrument, Clifford brings into context the tribal self and its influence on the common beings' selves. According to W.R. Sorley, _"Conscience is supreme in man and represents the divine purpose."*8

2.6. THE THEORIES OF ETHICS

There are many postulates in Ethics, upon which various theories regarding the moral values applied in different concern of Ethics are brought into consideration. In such manner, we get various theories such as that of duty, pleasure and perfection. While most of the theories of ethics, western or oriental revolve around duty and pleasure, emphasized by oriental and western philosophy respectively, the theory of perfection can be called as revolving between the two genres of theory.

However, we may find difference between the various 'Views' in relation to the theories of ethics as views only surmise opinions, whereas theories propound certain ideas which are based on proto typical characteristics derived from various events.

2.6.1. *Right and Obligation:-*

When we talk of the 'Right' of a person, we talk of the person ability to take over or possess of the particular object or matter in whatever manner it is deemed required to do so. Then again, in another context, when we talk of a person having 'obligation' to someone or an institution, whether a materialistic or abstract one, (such as the institutions of family, or marriage etc) we believe him or her to owe the person or institute something or has got certain duty to follow upon towards it, so that in certain way he or she has to make up for the owing or the particular duty. For example, when we say that 'he has obligation towards his uncle' we understand that he must be owing his something for which he has to comply it with. Only, then he will attain freedom or right over the old situation or any object. For example, we may understand from the earlier instance that he has obligation of duty towards his uncle, either because he owes his uncle financially fir which he would have to make up the same way or by fulfilling and carrying out other task, or by fulfilling his obligations the same way, he may inherit his uncle's property i.e. get his right over it in the given way. From here, we may arrive at the finding that right and obligation can be complimentary to each other if not mutually supplementary for the same situation. One way, we can call them (right and obligation) the two sides of a coin, whether in regard to materialistic consideration or moral ones but not necessarily of the same coin, as by fulfilling obligation for owing someone something, a man may retract his freedom or right over it, i.e. moral right only, in which case, he may not gain any materialistic right, unless he did not owe and was 'obligated' to fulfill his duty only to gain the materialistic 'right' only.

However, the same condition is applicable when we are talking about the ethical right and obligation or to be precise, right and obligation of highest order. Besides the self related persons or issues, man has certain obligation towards the society in particular and humanity in general. Therefore, from ethical point of view, each individual should expense with certain amount of time for the society with beneficial works, to fulfill his obligation, whereas, he automatically owns moral right over difference of issues of society for which he can dispense with beneficial ideas.

2.6.2. *Freedom and Liberty*:-

Freedom is one of the conditions that the ethical state of mind craves to achieve. According to Robert Owen, 'freedom of man is depended upon his circumstances only and determined by it as well'. It seems every person is bound by numerous obligations including duties towards others in family and society, therefore is left with little freedom of his mind to allow himself to act upon o his own right. However, freedom does not merely suggest in being free of mind, time and space. It shows the deliberation of one having his 'freedom', that is when it is exercised, and that is when it is applies to one's preferences of something over other things. We find that freedom can be of two notions,_ external and internal and often when external conditions are improved upon to enhance its conditions, necessarily it does not assert the achievement of it internally.

Again, there are other situations to assert that freedom, when unbound of any internal restriction, i.e. obligations or directions, can act in any manner, - right from animal subversion to impulsive actions. Therefore it is believed to be brought into the context of ethical perspective to scrutinize 'freedom.' The act of 'necessity', on the other hand, acts as the detrimental quality going against the interest of it. Regarding both the acts, Dr. McKenzie opines in the following manner, _ ".... But there is no contradiction when we observe precisely what is the nature of freedom and what is the nature of necessity that is demanded. The necessity means simply the uniform activity of a given character. The freedom on the other hand, means simply the absence of determination by anything outside the character itself."[9] Therefore we may find that given freedom, there are various stages of it, to indicate the state of mind by the exercising 'character'. When some exercise lower kind of freedom, a person knowing the 'liberty' of it, may exercise the higher kind which means using it for better benefit and /or for ethical reasons for greater interest of human kind.

2.6.3. *Judgment, Crime and Punishment*:-

Although from analytical point of view, judgment and 'crime and punishment' are two different genres of ethics, they are intrinsically connected as complementary to each other in relation to ethical values. Judgment, to be precise, ethical judgment must take into account various standards of values in ethics_ such as 'righteousness', decisiveness, morality, welfare, duty and above all conscience-related propriety, i.e. Crime, an ethical sin, and theoretically considered as pathological ethics, is considered as desecration of values and therefore antithesis of the good of society.

Since society needs to maintain the values intact to maintain it's goodness, therefore, the onus is with judgment to maintain the parity of it. Therefore crime is followed by punishment of its perpetrator, so as to maintain the ethical balance of the society.

2.7. THE LAWS OF ETHICS

The laws of Ethics can be called a kind of perspective, for the issues it relates to. Over certain issues and perspectives, Dr. McKenzie the famous ethicist has defined and categorized the laws into the following subject matters:-

(A)Law of God:- the Law of God suggests that it is different from the diction of moral Authority, moral or otherwise. Such a diction is believed to be surmised above the land and as words of God. However, on rationalizing its moral authority, the most prominent instance of such a law can be exampled as where it is considered as words of God. But such a claim lacks justification, since if it is a sermon of moral authority by dint of the superior power for God, than it is a 'must' and not an 'aught'. Again, if God is to be considered as self righteous, there will have to be a law which is above the law of God so as to judge his 'actions'. However, such an imagined authority above that of God puts in dilemma with the finality of law of God and therefore it does not hold consistency as calling the Law of God as final law.

*(B) Law of Nature:-*In order to get over the problem of dilemma over the authority of God explained from the point of view of Law of God, it is next in the Law of Nature, which is attempted to be proven as the final authority of morality. The Law of Nature held a considerable importance in ethics of Greek philosophy, as the conception of nature took root as the most fundamental law on earth, therefore the ultimate one. Its importance was so impressive for the stoics that they considered living by the 'standard of nature only (vivre conventer nature). Even it took important role at the beginning of modern time, that is later part of seventeenth century and most of eighteenth, among the elite ethicists such as Samuel Clark or Bishop Butler to base their ethical conception on Law of Nature. Clark justified the inherent difference of logistic existence of ethics and nature as that of any two conceptions with their basic individuality but being rooted of the same law on earth, which is the final and ultimate one. "The differences, relations and proportion of things both natural and moral, in which all unprejudiced minds thus naturally agree, are certain, unalterable, and real in the things

in themselves."*[10] Samuel Clark believed so. Besides, he said, _ "The reason of all men everywhere naturally and necessarily assents, as all men agree in their judgment concerning the whiteness of snow or the brightness of the Sun."*[11] Regarding the difference between the two he explains that the difference and relation of the two subject matters, their applications and non application or fitness and unfitness of conditions are same as that of similarity and difference between two figures of geometry and arithmetic.

However, the inherent difference between the two also counts when we witness two contradictory qualities in Nature. For example, we find that nature's fury may cause the devastation of its own creation whereas on the other hand, the planetary system of it will continue with the eternal rule of its own. Both the qualities stem from the same rule of 'fitness' of things, but stand at the contradictory position of the criteria for the law of destruction to the law of creation at the same time, which is beyond the logical conclusion of any rule on earth, besides being only partially at rhythm with ethics, and not in overall manner, in spite of their relationship and the differentiation.

Therefore, the self contradictory 'logicality of existence of Nature' had put into jeopardy the claim that the law of nature as the final and ultimate Law on the Earth.

(C)*Law of Morality :-* The Law of Nature being proven to be inadequate to explain its superiority to other laws, we may resort to The Law of Morality to scrutinize its supposed ultimate position as the final Law on earth. The Law of Morality suggests that the moral sense which prevails on our mind prior to carrying in out any activity over is 'righteous' ness or wrongfulness of it, is the ultimate law on earth. Ethicist Shaftesbury speaks so in the following passages regarding the conception of being virtuous which means being virtuoso at the same time, _ ... "To philosophize in a just signification is but to carry good breeding a step higher."*[12] That is, we should carry our moral orders, not only for others but also for being of superior order of 'rational' kind, therefore for ourselves too. The theme to be surmised from such a rhetoric is that any rational person would abide by the law of morality i.e. the code of it he had learnt since his childhood, will be applied in all the spheres of his or her life. Dr. McKenzie the great ethicist explains that in the following way, _ "From this point of view it may be quite rightly be maintained that the moral law becomes a second nature, so that the choice of the right and avoidance of the wrong passes almost into a kind of instinct. From this point of view it may be quite rightly be maintained that moral sense is a kind of taste."[13] However, the question that comes over here is that as aesthetical point of view points out, when it comes to the question of taste t may vary from person o person, place to place and society to society. In fact, the criteria for 'ethical standard' vary like wise too. Therefore if according to the law of morality certain act be considered morally 'rightful' in one place or society, it may not be considered so in another place, therefore, the law projected as ultimate diction for man may not be held true elsewhere. Therefore it will lack the criteria of universally being accepted as the ultimate law. Therefore, the duplicity of situation debars it from being called the final and ultimate law.

(D)Law of Reason:-The law of Reason, basically propounded by Immanuel Kant, who established Institutionalism, is based on the idea that there are certain 'universal moral truths which can be deduced from certain rational facts, the same way we may deduct 'thought' from intelligence of our lives. According to Kant, the fact that there are causes for every action or situation created, (for example milk is always the cause of curd or yogurt, or two plus two will always make it four) and which are explainable to one, means that we have a rational insight into it and a kind of moral consciousness lying beneath the realization of the existence of such eternal truths. However, with such a dependence on moral consciousness along with the faith on the irreversibility of nature's way, we may not find too many difference of such a law of reasoning having not much of difference with the law of Nature.

The Law of Reason has, besides, bore striking similarity with the law of Nature, according to the Stoics too. They believe that both are synonymous with each other, as they believed the law of Nature being itself a rational system as it seems to follow certain kind of reasons only.

From, the same point of view, we discover that the sense of reason which encourage a man to carry out his duties and do all the deed he consider to be righteous, so it does give him a sense of refraining himself from all the deeds that seems 'not righteous' too. However, such acts are decided upon by the fact that their 'righteousness is decided upon by its outcome of 'good' or 'evil' only. The great ethicist Immanuel Kant believed that a person would not carry out a wrongful deed because it is inconsistent with his idea of what is good' According to him, the moral law cannot dictate us the righteousness of a task. While "there is nothing good, but the goodwill only." Since again the law of morality cannot tell us more than a way that is comfortable to law only. As according to McKenzie, we find Kant believing in the fact that each act must be 'self consistent', which will assert, as according to his 'categorical imperative' that,-"act only on that maxim(or principal) which thou canst at the same time will to become universal law."*[14] Drawing an example of 'broken promise', he said that it cannot be a universal formula, because people will have to first make promises and only then to be broken. First, 'brokenness' is conditional to making promises, and only then it would be reconsidered to be 'broken'. Therefore, it lacks in universality as it is conditional to another situation, and 'wrong doing' cannot have any universal application and therefore, also be self consistence. By giving the example he asserts his view that moral imperative, which he deems to be categorical, cannot be derived from 'the consideration of any end outside of the will of the individual.' He believed, since every external end id empirical, i.e. based on sense perception, so it will result into hypothetical imperative only. Since again, seeking a particular end means acting in a particular way, which means a kind of 'bound', while performing the absolute Imperative of duty, there cannot be any end attached to it as it is not to look for a good or pleasurable end but goodwill only.

However, Kant's view is not beyond the criticism, not primarily for its 'default' but for the stringent view it carries towards moral perceptions that a 'righteous' person may ask for. For, according to him, not any conduct can be based on 'feelings', but only to be guided by moral reason. Such a postulate i.e. reason is a kind of moral principle which is not based on any feeling or emotion. However, in practical reality, a person's conduct may not be separable from feelings or emotions. Defending such a view, Sir T. Brown, by giving an example expresses that when a person give alms, it is not to appease him but to comply the will of God. However, in stark contrast to it, a philanthropist does carry many more 'beneficial' works out of 'love' rather than by the pure sense of duty to ones that he has any obligation to do so. Secondly, another of his stringent views are expressed through the fact that he 'permits of no exceptions to his moral imperatives' as according to Dr. McKenzie-"Kant is thus led to give us the content of the categorical imperative this formula-'act only on that maxim {or principle} which thou canst at the same time will to become a universal law.*[15] When Kant has put his Imperative in a way of a kind of 'commandment', in reality a person does not follow any such dictum to decide upon the 'morality' of an issue, but rather depend on his own sense of 'righteousness' only. Besides, not every 'righteous' occasion is reflection of 'eternal truth', but may occur as 'exception' to the rule also. For example, the heroic deeds are exceptions only, not common acts carried out in day to day life by everybody. Again, when a person do great activities for his country (for example we may put forward the instance of Mahatma Gandhi who in an act of exceptional courage, put his non-violent battle against the British to liberate his motherland), he or she does it out of the conviction that no one else can carry it out. Therefore, it certainly cannot be a generalized case of Moral imperative of reason.

However, when the Law of Reason propounded by Kant seems to be too 'harsh' to follow in practical life, other laws are considered too 'lax' to be considered as the final and the ultimate necessity as the law on earth. When we cannot hope that every 'exceptional' rule has to be applied by 'everyone' if a similar situation is arrived at, there is no explanation to the fact that the 'act' that is carried out consciously has been done so under the notion of any rational plea for committing it.

(E) Law of Conscience:-When law of Moral sense was strongly opposed by Bishop Butler who believed it to be inadequate as the ultimate law of account because of the fact that morality may have different standard at different places and therefore lack in universal application. According to him, that man has got many instincts to act accordingly in the world and the fact that he has to control and drive them in righteous way to gain his goal, so that the instincts which are subordinate to self love become benevolent to others. However, he further adds that there is certain principle which is superior to such feelings and which presents itself as reflective concern for the law of righteousness. Butler believes it is conscience addiction which is impersonal in attitude and guides us through our deeds in righteous perspective. He said, _"Thus that principle, by which we survey, and either approve or disapprove our own heart, temper, and actions, is not only to be considered as what is in its turn to have some influence; which may be said of every passion, of the lowest appetites."[*16] However, this particular law overshadows our mind with two contradictions the first being_ as it is explained that it is a simplistic and inexplicable law that lays down the guidelines in our lives. The other is that, it is a kind of 'intelligible authority' which guides us by its rational reflections. However, to find a proper definition to his 'Conscience' a close look at his philosophy indicates that the first kind can be called as Intuitionalism, whereas the other can be called as the Law of Reason.

(F) *Law of Tribe*: - The Law of Tribe can be called as one of the earliest ones based on primitive notion of 'moral authority'. The law of Tribe believes in one supreme authority of society, who dictates the acts to be done and make judgment on the result of such acts. However, such a law cannot be considered the final one, not to speak of being the ultimate one, as besides being conditional to the fact that any individual can be fallible in his or her judgment, not to speak of only as the supreme authority, but also because of the fact that what kind of 'criteria' are being applied for judgment of acts. Thus, the Law of Tribe falls short of expectation far more due to its fallibility besides being inconsequential in respect of universality.

2.8. THE HISTORY OF ETHICS: *(Western)*

The developmental stages of Ethics can be divided into three major time periods of namely_

(1) Ancient period, (2) Medieval period and (3) Modern period.

2.8.1. *ETHICS : ANCIENT PERIOD*

Along with development of various civilizations in the world in ancient time, Ethics as a subject also developed along with them to attain its zenith during the period of post medieval era, when European civilization academically achieved its peak. Ethics as a part of philosophy also developed in many other countries such as India, China, Persia etc. However, it is the Greek, i.e. the ancient period of European Ethics when it seems to achieve its fullest development and set the trend of western thinking of its moral values to be followed in the later period. The study of ethics in Greek period started with its appreciation of nature, as many of the scholars believed following the path of nature would restrain them from committing or indulging in excessiveness and would keep them within the bounds of 'morality. But soon they discovered the limitations of learning through 'nature' and started exploring other avenues of philosophy for acquiring knowledge of the world beyond and within the mind. However, it is only Ethics that Greek civilization started its quest for knowledge and Greek philosophy will remain synonymous with ethics as its beginning. Some of the great Greek philosophers, who are considered not only greatest by Greek standard but also the ones of world Philosophy, started their quest of knowledge by experimenting with Ethics only. Their views on Ethics set the rules for its studies for the subsequent periods of history of human civilization. The great 'Trio' of Greek philosophy is namely Socrates, Plato and Aristotle. However, Greek history is replete with the contribution of many other great philosophers such as Democritus, Heraclitus, Aristophanes etc. The former two are considered the harbingers of Stoic and Epicurean Ethics of Greek philosophy. The followers of Socrates were known in Greek philosophy as the Sophist only. Some other well known scholars belonging to Greek philosophers are Aristipus, Hibbius, Aristophanes etc.

(A)The Early Greek Ethics

The early Greek philosophy started, as mentioned earlier, with the study of Ethics only. At the beginning of it, the followers of ethics abode by stringent regulations that encouraged them to respect the ways of nature, which was believed to be the ultimate goal for them. However, over a period of time, such views took change of importance and was replaced in later period by 'quest for knowledge' i.e. Metaphysics. Some of the great Greek scholars preceding the time of Socrates who much emphasized on ethics being knowledge based are as follows:-

1. Heraclitus (circa. 530B.C. -470B.C.) started with his ethical view on stringent moral values an subsequently he was known to be the originator of 'Stoic' Ethics. He was followed by Democritus (circa460B.C.- 370 B.C.) who on the other hand propounded the value of 'pleasure' as the root of all virtues and thereby establishing the 'Epicurean' values of Greek philosophy. Such views on their part signified them as 'weeping' and the 'laughing' philosophers. Their approach to Ethics, which is considered as 'basic' to have influenced the views of many scholars of later period of history of Ethics and has been identified as a major contention of discussion and a 'problem' of Ethics among the scholars of philosophy for all -time to come.

    Heraclitus believed that the great aim of moral life is to secure the victory for the 'bright and the dry' by which he tried to signify his fundamental moral principle to be 'fire' and considered the necessity to 'keep the soul dry', by which perhaps he tried to signify the necessity of keeping one's self in restrain and live in 'pure' form, that is only to live in nature's ways and not indulge in excesses of any material gain. He viewed that such postulates were diabolically opposite to the basic Epicurean postulate of 'pleasure'. However, there was no effort on developing his views on ethics into any system at that time.

2. Democritus (460B.C.-370B.C.) One of the prominent pre-Socrates Era philosophers, Democritus known as the 'laughing' philosopher, moking at people's follies, a contemporary of Aristippus (435B.C. _ 356B.C.), the founder of the conception 'Cyrenaicism, both in views and time and a materialistic in approach towards defining both life and the surrounding. In his scientific approach, he defined that the minimal indivisible matter is 'atoma', which in modern day science is called as 'atom'. He believed knowledge to be of two kinds,_of senses and of intellect. His views relating life was regarded by many scholars as bordering on hedonistic in approach.

(B)THE 'SOPHIST'

The prominent sophists who were believed to precede Socrates and established a certain ethical trend that also speculated upon the political situation were the stalwarts of Greek philosophy_ Parmenides and Pythagoras. By the period of time they professed their kind of ethics, it was the practice of 'live' and 'think' philosophy to quench their thirst for knowledge. However, The Sophists, who were named after the Greek word Sophia, meaning knowledge, had also taken up the cudgel of bringing into the fore of a civilization the 'problem of ethics', which was still in its puerile stage of development. The basic intention of the sophists who were considered the teachers of the society was to educate the young Athenians in proper mould of thinking ability or mental set -up so as to prepare them to be 'able' citizens.

Plato, the great Greek Philosopher, not only chronicled his own philosophical views but also wrote down the philosophical ideas and views of other preceding or contemporary philosophers along with the narrations of their philosophical conversations. In fact, it is from his writings only that the world came to know about the great philosophy of his teacher and mentor Socrates. He wrote in details the views expressed and conversations carried on with his disciples and followers by Socrates which were the treasures for coming generation realizing the in-depth knowledge of great sophist. However, Plato often was so engrossed in details that it had been difficult for readers to comprehend which were Socrates' views and which were his own. There were other authors too, who wrote on Socrates. However, it was more of the satirical version of Socrates' stringent views on life as a sophist, rather than any appreciation of his works and prime progenitor of such works were another rival philosopher Aristiphanes who joked over his works caricaturing his image to be that of a fool.

From Plato's various works only, one comes to know of the views of the sophists. From his book 'Protagoras', we come to know Protagoras' ethical and philosophical views, so as that of Gorgias too.

The Sophists were a term for the 'expert' in any conceivable field of knowledge or skill whether of literature or arts. Their name 'Sophist', derived from the word 'Sophia' meaning expert skill, generally meant 'Wisdom'. In Plato's writing, we come to know of Protagoras' view in the following way- "If (a pupil) comes to me, he will learn... prudence both about his private affairs and affairs of the city."[*17]

As mentioned earlier, the sophists believed in preparing common youth of Athens into able citizens, giving priority to education and knowledge besides being ethically aware of their duties towards family and the nation. In the process, sophist like Protagoras believed they i.e. the students needed to acquire a fair amount of rhetoric, that is, the art of debate and argumentation to counter their opposition as well as assert their own position in society. Such qualities, Protagoras believed, were ways to the success of being good politician and debator.

However, the Sophists were not always met with adulation but rather with consternation from the people of Athens, for the following reasons:- common people believed them to be not only illusionists and tricksters, but also their promises for their youths as hypothetical and hoax, bordering on false and hollow intellectualism. The govt. of Athens believed their ethics to be anti- establishment i.e. against the traditional systems that were running it, and last of all they were despised by the philosophers themselves, believing the Sophists to be scholars for hire, a kind of contempt that was saved by for the common people by the aristocrats. But most of all, what antagonized them of the sophists was their penchant for 'Rhetoric', which was very redundant in context of being pragmatic and finding solution to practical problems. Even more was for the reason that the tenets they put forward to for the 'stronger argument as opposite to the weaker version' of their opponents might have been used by the wrong doers as for their own defense. Therefore, the idea, of ***Dissoi Logoi'*** that is 'counter Argument', has caused counter argument for themselves only, for being too dependable on it.

While Protagoras is considered the most prominent sophist, Gorgias is considered the most 'stylist' of them all. According to him, nothing exists;

If anything exists at all, it is not knowable and thirdly, if it is knowable at all, then it cannot be communicated upon. Considered skeptical in their approach, it personified the 'counter argument' of Protagoras only, besides, parodying the words of Eleatic philosophers like Zeno and Permenides. However, apart from their teutological verbosity and rhetoric, their words were considered not so seriously but rather ambiguously, which is expressed in the words of analyzer of Greek Philosophy Christopher Rowe, _"This is clearly intended as a parody of the arguments of the eleatic philosophers Parmenides and Zeno; but it is at the same time also a quite serious demonstration of the principle enunciated by Protagoras, that for every argument, there exists a counter argument."*18

(C) *The Great Philosophers of Ancient Greece*
1. SOCRATES

The most prominent and earliest Philosopher of Greece, Socrates (469 B.C._ 399 B.C.) was admired for his association with the sophists as much it derived criticism for his support for it. However, unlike the other sophists, he was not a teacher of rhetoric, but considered himself a student of moral science only. It is in fact Socrates only, who established the ethics and introduced 'ethical values' to not only western civilization, but also influenced the proceeding generations till today. It is said that, initially he tried to follow nature and natural ways till he discovered it to be inadequate for finding knowledge the way he wanted and could not quell his thirst for the same. Therefore, he quested for the answers of his philosophical questions in 'Ethics' and ethical values and he thought he established also the basis for his metaphysical pursuit. His very views on ethics has given way to the most prominent division of philosophy, as the Cynics followed his sense of independence and freedom, whereas, the Cyrenaics admired and followed his tact and skill in 'making the most out of his surroundings'. Later they were known as Stoics and Epicureans in Greek philosophy of history.

However, Socrates, throughout his lifetime remained an ethicist of great caliber. It is only ethics in which he found the answers for his queries. As we have mentioned earlier, he tried to follow the rules of nature at the early stage of his philosophical life, but being unable to find his answers, he followed the ethics for finding his answer in moral values.

All his works are being known through the write up of Plato. Right from 'Analogy' and 'Protagoras' to Charmenides and Lyches, Plato has narrated his rendezvous with Socrates. However, even his disciple Aristotle believed that since Socrates put more of 'ethical questions' rather than answers, the conversation put in the mouth of him in the discourses narrated by Plato were answered actually not by Socrates but by Plato himself only.

Even, as another philosopher belonging to the next generation, Xenophanes who also narrated the discourses of Socrates, did so without giving the answers to his queries too. However, whatever were the answers, the questions which were put forward by Socrates were themselves not only revolutionary, but also happened to be the basis of Ethics set forth by himself for the posterity to come in the following time.

Socrates seems to have followed certain tenets of ethical values, which can be named as his 'Doctrines' also. The primary Goal or end for his ethical wisdom was to earn Knowledge and he sought to establish it as the primary 'virtue' for mankind. In 'Protagoras', Plato tells how Socrates emphasized upon all the mortal being in achieving such a 'virtue' which would lead them in life to be not only able beings but also to further their quest for spiritual knowledge. For establishing the ethical truth, he took help of, according to Aristotle, of two philosophical postulates _the first is inductive' logoi' i.e. arguments which were based on examples, whereas the other was 'Universal Definition' (from Metaphysics1078 b 27-9). However, later, soon he mentioned that he never 'separated' the identity of 'universals' and they were instances from Plato's early works only. He mentioned that Socrates called the 'universals' as ideas of things as they are. They also do not figure in some of Plato's other works such as the Charmenides, Laches and Lysis. However, the conversation that was narrated did not arrive at any conclusion regarding the nature of Temperance, or Piety, or Courage, or 'whatever could be the subject of the argument'. By his own admission, Socrates did not know the answers of them either. Even in the works of Xenophanes, as mentioned earlier, the answers to the queries were not found to be expressed by Socrates.

According to him, to achieve 'virtue,' one must not only be 'virtuous' but also make knowledge a condition to achieve it. Christopher Rowe, the ethical critic retorts in the following way, _ only when they (the people) recognized that they did not possess the requisite knowledge of virtue would they be started looking for it".[19] Another quest on part of Socrates was for searching the soul which he called as 'Suche'. One can realize one's soul or 'suche' only by virtue of 'virtue', the eternal ethical quality that purify and make noble of soul.

Plato, in his work 'Apology' has written in details on the paradoxes Socrates used to express his views with. The way 'Virtue is Knowledge' is a paradox, and not a definition, so we come to know of other paradoxes of Socrates as well. For example, -'man can never do any wrongful deed knowingly' is another paradox, which he emphasized on to express that a person who follows the path of righteousness would not commit any wrong doing intentionally. By such a paradox here, Socrates wanted to assert that knowing the illness of 'wrongfulness', a 'rightful person' always prefers the path of 'rightful' act to follow his 'rightful' thinking. The same paradox is put otherwise, that 'no man can do wrong willingly' suggesting, that if a person is to act wrongfully or viciously, then he may commit it out of ignorance, rather than out of knowledge or conscious manner. To emphasize the paradox, he expressed the words 'Hekon' and 'Akon', meaning 'intentionally' and 'unintentionally' respectively. Since according to him, no one can commit 'wrong' intentionally or willfully, and anyone by any such reason may commit it, it must be a 'bad' o 'wrong' condition of the 'soul' or 'suche'. When vice is a wrong or bad condition of it, 'virtue is a healthy or righteous condition of it. However, he treated the definition of soul or suche in rather as a conscious state of mind than as a mute identity. For him, virtue should be a mental condition for a person rather than committing virtuous things.

2. PLATO

Some of the modern scholars of philosophy believe that Plato's Republic and Aristotle's Ethics are the two greatest works of philosophy. In the book Republic, Plato has written in details on the various ethical postulates he believed in, including the manifold application of 'Virtue'. Like Socrates, he too believed in qualities of virtue, but interpreted it somewhat in different manner from Socrates. In 'Gorgias', which can be called a book entirely as of ethical themes, contains no metaphysical or political ideas, which were ample in evidence in either 'Stateman' or 'Law' or in 'Republic'. It is also a book based primarily on the ideas mostly of plato's, unlike in Republic or, Protagoras where Socrates' views play the dominant role than of his own. Besides, in Republic we find that to emphasize certain view point of Socrates such as the Central Ideas, which lacks in the original ones, Plato is driven to the two other important fields_ politics and metaphysics which we find being manifested in the earlier mentioned works Statesman, Law and Republic respectively. However, in Gorgias, which as we have mentioned earlier, we find him entirely dealing not only with ethics, but also expressing his own point of views only.

In Gorgias, Plato starts his dialogue with Callicle, and earlier with one Polus, with whom he discusses about 'whether Injustice, rather than Justice is the root of Happiness'. Through the character Polus, and his conversation we come to know that 'he' believed,- to be committing injustice is worst than suffering it as well and not being punished is worse than actually being punished. From the chapter (474 c-d) we come to know while one can derive pleasure from the notion of 'finesse' of an act or situation, the same way one becomes afraid of being 'shameful' because it can be harmful or painful for the perpetrator, and one who does cause injustice, such a person acts in a shameful manner only. In the following content of the context we find Polus trying to justify committing injustice as it is adventurous. However, ultimately it was arrived at the conclusion that committing an act both shameful and advantageous can be 'ipso facto' disadvantageous for the person. However, what we find a conversational felony is that 'goodness' is being equated with 'fineness' and therefore if it can be compared with 'pleasure' or joy as the latter is the 'cause' of it.

In the book 'Republic', we find Plato trying to define Justice as 'DikoiSuna', which is equivalent to being 'justice oriented'. In the book, it has been discussed in the context of running the state in rightful and proper manner and that of such other aspects as education, jurisprudence etc. Regarding the state it had been said that if it has to be good then it must possess the cardinal virtues of wisdom, courage, self control and justice. While the self succeeds in controlling pleasures and desire, then he or she becomes master of himself or herself. Plato puts in the mouth of Socrates that 'It is education by dint of which a person succeeds in attaining self control of desire and pleasure'. Then only it will lead to the path of Justice. Then again, it is both physical and mental training of education - first physical training and then that of music and poetry that will lead a person in his path of education. When Dikoisuna or justice is attained because of it, Plato maintains,- "If it (Dikoisuna) is the condition of wisdom, courage and self control, then perhaps we should interpret it just as goodness in general, than disposition from which 'all' right behavior flows."[*20]

Regarding The soul, he says that it possesses three parts in all, - Reason (to Logisticon), the Spirited Part (to Thumoeides) and the Appetitive part (to Epithumetikon). According to him, it is clash of the above mentioned parts of the soul, the three that leads to 'injustice'. The three parts are also the indicatives of the states of the soul in order. The role of the higher part is to rule, whereas the second part is to be subjected to the first part i.e. reason. If one is properly educated, then one would roost over the lowest part i.e. Appetitive, Plato believed. In 444 d-e Socrates is made to say by Plato -that, 'virtue will be a kind of health and beauty and well being of the soul, and vice is a kind of disease and ugliness and weakness."*21 At the end of the argument, we can arrive at the assertion that Justice and Virtue 'represent the natural state of the soul.'

In 'stateman' and 'Law', we find primarily the definitions of various political and jurisprudence related postulates; however, we may not miss the traces of ethics in it. In Stateman, we read about the Kronos the divine life which is perfect and flawless, and where individual can pursue knowledge. On the other hand, the world that rotates opposite of it, is the world of fate and innate desire of mankind, that is man controlled and chaotic. Plato also talks about 'weaving together'.

Towards the end of the book 'Law', we find Plato talking about misdeed and punishment, the latter as more of a reforming criterion than as retributionary to one's misdeeds. It is based on the 'paradox' of Socrates, which suggests that 'all vices of man are voluntary.' According to him, the misdeeds cause outcome of 'injustice' kind, and they are primarily the factors of anger, pleasure or ignorance. However, we find believing ignorance to be one reason of committing misdeeds or vices also indirectly justifies the position of the paradox in saying that all vices are committed involuntarily by the committer.

3. ARISTOTLE
Aristotle, being a resident of Plato's academy, by dint of being his disciple or follower, we find that in spite of maintaining his individuality of views in large difference with that of Plato, his ethics is basically an extension of further corroboration of Platonic ideas only. However, his book 'Ethics' is not only considered as one of the greatest work on ethical philosophy, it also distinctly diversified the trends of two of the most important ethical conceptions in the world, i.e. that of knowledge and sensibility. Knowledge in one way of expressing and discussing of virtues, whereas, sensibilities deals with various nuances of the emotions of desires and pleasure and to some extent 'happiness.' Aristotle's writings too bear in distinct characteristics to signify his own method of delivering the theme of his own discourses.

While talking of Aristotle's distinct ways, we find him at very beginning of his writing disagreeing with what we can call as Socratesism :- He refuges to give any vaunt to the 'idea' of 'Forms of the Good', because he believed that 'good' is an ambiguous term and 'is not a common element that can answer to a single form'(1096 b 25-6). In his second point, he mentions that all the sciences or subject matters aim at or seek the particular 'good' to happen and not earn the knowledge of 'good' and then apply it.

Regarding the complexity of ethics, which Plato realized towards the end of his written work, and as mentioned earlier, Aristotle has made it a central theme in his writing, so that the grasp over it becomes easier for those following his ethics. In 1094 b 11ff. he says,-"it will be enough if our discussion has as much clarity as its subject matter allows; for we must not look for the same degree of precision in everything we say, any more than we do in all the products of arts. Fine and just actions, which political science investigates, admit of much variety and fluctuation, so that it seems that they exist only by convention, and not by nature. Good things too give rise to the same kind of fluctuation because they bring harm to many people; for some have died because of wealth, others because of their courage. So, since we are talking about things of these kind, and beginning from these kind of basis, we must be content to indicate the truth roughly and in outline(also in 1098 a 26 ff, 1103b 34 ff)"[22]

Aristotle has detailed on the 'nature' of happiness too. For enhancing the importance of it, he had projected 'Ergon' i.e. work or work ethics suggesting what a person does, and what amount of the element of rationality it carries along with it. Because doing barely some amount of works may not suggest that it bears 'goodness' or 'righteousness' but it needs to be asserted by proper scrutiny. However, the conception of Ergon does not merely means rationalizing the act itself, but act in a proper manner too.

However, like Socrates and Plato, Aristotle also emphasized upon the 'virtue' as a quality of human beings. But Aristotle's virtue is unlike Socrates' 'virtue of Knowledge' or Plato's 'virtue of Justice'. He emphasizes so much on it that it can be separated and distinguished of the 'quality' of virtues into two distinct identities. Since the virtue Aristotle emphasizes upon is 'virtue' that encourages 'goodness' in a person,_ or basically the one who embodies 'Goodness', -or 'Spoudois'. He says,- "the good for man is activity of soul in accordance with 'virtue'; and if there is more virtues than one, in accordance with the best and most perfect".[23] Then again comes the question of 'Happiness'. Can 'goodness' and happiness' go along; or to be precise- can a 'good man' always be happy; or on the other hand, can a 'happy person always be good'.

Aristotle has rationalized his view points in his book X of Ethics in details. He mentions in the book that the happiest man is the man engaged in scientific contemplation; that is, the man who is active 'in accordance with' a different kind of virtue, or excellence, the 'intellectual virtue' of wisdom. He had also explained (in the last chapter of the book I and at the beginning of the book II) the reasons of discussing it,- the first being it will help into the inquiring about 'happiness'. Regarding, the Happiness, we find out that Aristotle expresses it the same way he expresses about 'Form of Good'. The way Platonists believed 'Form' to be the cause of 'goodness', Aristotle too believed 'Happiness' to be the 'first principle and cause of goodness'. As for the distinguishing of virtues, they are being mentioned as the 'virtues' of the 'Appetitive' part of the soul. Which can be seen either as irrational or as rational (irrational because it opposes reason; rational,- because it can obey it.)

The relation of 'Happiness' and 'Virtue', as seen by Aristotle has been divided into two categories, - First, the Nicomachean ethics - whereas the other is called the Eudaemonism.

a. *Nicomachean Ethics* **of Aristotle**:-In the Nichomaecian doctrine of ethics, Aristotle has emphasized upon the role of virtue as the supreme good for mankind. Appropriate and just actions, compounded courageous performances justify the role of such virtues. The argument he purported on behalf of 'Virtue' puts forward the doctrine that 'for ethical virtue is about pleasures and pains; for it is because of pleasure that we perform vicious actions and because of pain that we abstain from fine ones.'

Therefore, since childhood a person should be groomed and taught to derive pleasure and pain in right perspective (1104 b8-13). Again Aristotle defines the objects of choice and objects of avoidance. While 'the fine', 'the beneficial' and the' pleasant' are the object of choice whereas 'the shameful', 'the harmful' and 'the painful' are the objects of avoidance.

The general definition of ethical virtue as given by Aristotle goes in the following manner:-"virtue then, is a disposition concerned with choice, lying in a mean, that is a mean in relation to us, one determined by reason, and in the way the man of practical wisdom determine it."[24]. The 'Phronimos' is the same as the 'Spoudois', the good man found in the writing of Socrates. It is believed to be the practical wisdom for virtue in the full sense, as we discover in book IV, that is which has to be possessed or acquired. Another argument of Aristotle is that the definition of 'vicious' person, as according to Plato-Socrates, who is diabolically opposed to the virtuous one, can not choose his 'end' as he is the committer of 'wrongful 'deeds, "If then the end is wished for, and the means to the end are chose and deliberated about, actions concerned with means will be according to choice and voluntary.

Then comes Aristotle's 'Intellectual Virtues'. According to him, they serve the necessity for superior ideology, as we need to find a 'right reason' for choosing the practical wisdom. The theoretical part, as defined by him is grasping the truth, whereas, the action, believed to be the calculative part, should be cooperated upon by 'desire'. The theoretical part is called Sophia.

In another section of definition of Virtue, Aristotle says that the five states of virtue of the soul are, _ Productive Skill (techne), Deductive Knowledge(episteme), Phronesis (practical Wisdom), Sophia (grasping of Truth) and Nous(Intuition). Nous and Sophia are the states of same mental faculty whereas Phronesis and Techne belong to the same category of states of soul.

In the last chapters of book VI, Aristotle discusses about the relationship of ethical virtue versus phronesis, in which he says about the latter as no person can be virtuous without phronesis or practical wisdom, nor can he be 'practically wise' without ethical Virtues. Regarding relationship of Sophia versus Phronesis he says in here that Sophia (which he perhaps is equalizing with present day version of Conscience) is superior to phronesis, although it has more utility for mankind. Thus Sophia has more 'contemplation' value which precedes the necessity of moral activity as one need to be directed by it to perform such moral activity.

b. Eudemian Ethics or Eudaemonism:-Aristotle defines the conception of pleasure and Akrasia,- meaning 'lack of control' in the book of Eudaemonism. Eudaemonism is what is happiness is all about, - in plain terms of pleasure. He deigned the idea of classifying and considering it as a movement or process. According to him, it is attributed with certain qualities of totality and therefore cannot be considered as a kind of movement only. The conditions of pleasure are, - it will remain an activity as long as things would be perceived as it is; again,- pleasure is desirable; as long as it remain a proper kind of activity. However, according to him, pleasure that is derived from wrong action is not the 'righteous pleasure'. And is like that of animals'. He suggests in book VII (1153 b31-2) as 'people do not pursue pleasure, they think they pursue desire or the once they would say they were pursuing, but the same one; for everything by nature has an element of div. continent' and therefore his reason might clash with desire and than be overcome with it.

Akrasia on the other hand is the conception in which he details the condition of being overcome with desire or pleasure;-An 'Akriti' or weak minded person fails to control the reason by it. According to him, it can be quelled by the presence of knowledge in the being of the person. Thus the 'pleasure' of Aristotle, as defined by him, is pleasure that counts above the pleasure of common human desire, but of superior integrity.

C. Ethics of Hellenistic Period(Greece)
1. Cynics and Cyrenaics

The Cynics and the Cyrenaics of ethical philosophy of Greece belonged to the Hellenistic period and as per the dualism of western ethics beginning with Greek Philosophy both the lineages were divided on the problems of Happiness and pleasure. While the Cynics who believed in transparency of life, that is to live according to the rule of nature (vivantua natura) which for them was 'virtuous' by nature The lineage was steergeared by philosopher Antisthenes, which was not always appreciated by common people for its followers' thinking considered as being antithesis to the common standards of life. Again, according to some scholars their name originated from the Greek word meaning 'dog' and their activities and attitude were attributed with 'dog' like nature. Cynicism of ancient time differed much from the present day's equation of it with 'pessimism' and it was believed to implement the motto 'virtue is happiness' in contradiction to the Cyrenaics' motto of 'Pleasure is Happiness and therefore the End of life'. The Cynics in later time of history became known as the 'Stoics', that is, the one who follows austerity' in contradiction to Epicureans the followers of Epicurus, a reformed version of the Cyrenaics, the believer of the 'pleasure'.

Cyrenaics, contemporary and contradictory to the ethos of the Cynics, were espouser of the theme 'Pleasure is the ultimate happiness' and therefore considered it as the end of life. Aristippus of Cyrene was the originator and mentor of the lineage which was carried further on by his grandson with the same name Aristippus called as Younger. However, the lineage survived only for a century and emerged at a later time as Epicureans, simultaneous to Stoicism that originated from Cynicism, but Epicureanism also took into fold the theme of 'pain', taking into account of 'pain' as the paradox of pleasure and also became a more sophisticated version of Cyrenaicism by admitting the factual reality of pain and pleasure being liketwo sides of the same coin and therefore rather parts of life.

2. *Stoics and Epicureans*

They were the later version of the cynics and cyraenics respectively. However epicureans were believed to be more of pessimistic in view regarding concept of pleasure than their predecessors, as they believed pain takes precedence over pleasure in life.

2.8.2. ETHICS OF MEDIEVAL ERA

Regarding the ethical evolution during the era of medieval time, little can be said as there had been minimal change over conventional beliefs already set during the ancient period of Greek civilization. Whatever developmental change of ethics occurred, it happened so as part of the religious tenets espoused by primarily the apostles of 'church' lineage. Even in India, we come to know little of any newer kind of ethics being introduced to the conventional religion or trends of philosophy during the medieval era.

The Medieval Philosophy, on the other hand can be divided into two sections, - The Patristic Period and The Scholastic Period respectively. Although both the periods indicate their heavy dependency on the Plato and Aristotelian definition of Ethics, still it can not be denied of individualistic interpretations upon it. The medieval period of Ethics, also depended upon its definition defined by contemporary Christianity, did not lack in individuality either in its historical perspective or evolutionary or development point of view. The medieval period was more conservative and orthodox in outlook and influenced by the views of the likes of Thomas Aquinas, but could not do away with the legacy of Plato or Aristotle.

2.8.3. ETHICS OF MODERN ERA

Around the time of industrialization taking root in western world, medieval ethics has given way to modern conceptions being introduced at the behest of primarily those supporting and exemplifying the exigency of pleasure in ethical role in day to day life of common man. However, it was also the time of neo - realization in the philosophical front, and as a repercussion of it, we find many ethicists trying to re establish the classical morality in a rejuvenated way. There were many enthusiasts such as Butler or Samuel Clark trying to bring in the nature's role in ethics, as did the Stoics in ancient Greek days, so that people could not be reprehensive towards it, increasingly being materialistic oriented and oblivious of laxity of ethics in such new found activities. But, like the Epicureans in the same old Greek times, there were whole band of neophytes who were appreciative of not only the new found materialistic adventures, but also tried to vault it by justifying its materialistic morality. A new kind of ethics emerged, which can be called as a refined version of Hedonism that existed since ancient times, making 'pleasure' or 'desire' its primary theme. Such a trend of ethics is being called as Utilitarianism which emphasizes upon exploiting and utilizing best our surroundings for the best benefit of the mankind, trying to base on the idea of altruism. However, it barely succeeds in its ulterior motive of human welfare, as the resources it asks for utilization is not only begotten at the cost of our surrounding but also is exhaustive, for which no such beneficial activities would be carried for long in future.

However, there were considerable number of ethicists born of that period who could foresee the possible deviation of the lineage of ethics during such a trying times of history and therefore tried to put it on a strong foothold of rationality, so that prior to any such deviation, one can introspect the reasonability of such activities, and come back to old value of morality.

Among the new found promoters of 'natural ethics' were known philosophers such as John Lock, Samuel Clarke etc., whereas Descartes, Immanuel Kant etc were promoters of reason as the basis of ethics. There were the even more explorers of the new found moral values, and such neo- ethicists came to be known as 'Utilitarianists'. Towards the middle of the modern period of ethics, covering a period of over two centuries, they dominated the scene of modern philosophy which was personified by likes of G. E. Moore, John Stuart Mill, John Dewey etc.

The modern period of Ethics, which was dominated by newly inducted or defined conceptions, can be divided into the following categories, _ the Rationalism which is followed by the Intuitionism, and then the Utilitarianism. They dominated the ethical scene of modern period till were overshadowed by the consecutively inducted conceptions of Evolutionism and then German Idealism.

1. (a) ***Intuitionalism:-***Intuitionalism tried to reestablish the conventional moralities performed in our day to day life, into some asserted

notions, so that they become part and parcel of our life, rather than being certain optional viability, utilized only in accordance to the necessity of life.

Institutionalism speaks for making such trifle activities of life as duty performing, as it believes 'righteousness' or 'wrongfulness' has its own intrinsic qualities. Dr. McKenzie describes it in the following word:- "(it) is may be described as a theory that actions are right or wrong according to their own intrinsic nature, and not in virtue of any ends outside themselves which they tend to realize."[25] (p.148-manuel of ethics). Thus, we find that there are considerable number of characters that the conception of Intuition(al)ism personifies and that they can be found in the nook and the corners of history. By simpler definition it means to say that there exists the sense of judgment over our sense of conscience, which is beyond the retribution of any other authority or appeal and act as a kind of perception only. However, the perception of conscience is not that of an individual's conscience, but the overall nature of it which epitomizes in every individual. A person not acting in accordance with his conscience, cannot be described as a 'righteous' person and can be compared with any lower being who acts without any conscience-approved motivation. However, the greatest irony of manhood is that he may commit misdeed even when he acts consciously, due to certain intrinsic flaw in human nature. Often man uses his conscience based on wrongful perception too. Therefore, many scholars believe that there must be existing a kind of intrinsic sense of moral value dictating the 'righteousness' and 'wrongfulness' of every act a person performs. However, how latent or emancipated it is, depends upon individual to individual. Again, some scholars find 'common sense' to be accountable for such moral truths. However, again some others bring out the question of 'intellectual truth' which puts into question the viability the common sense and the truth depending upon it. According to Sidgwick, common moral sense needs not be a 'binding faculty,' laying down the principles for our guidance which are not capable of any further analysis or justification' and therefore need not be the tool of justification. However, moral principles can command such rational justification and explanation, so that 'we can distinguish what (I) is permanent and reliable in the decision of conscience from what (II) is varitable and not trustworthy.'

The well known ethicist Dr. McKenzie believed that both the renown Philosophers- Clarke and Kant did not base their conception of rationality on Intuitionalism because of the its basic idea of conscience being based on 'perception' only. According to Kant, there is even more of an authority over conscience to direct it on the 'right' path, and that is 'reason'. He had detailed the principle of reason in his Formalism.

(b) In ***Formalism,*** Kant had tried to establish that there use to be certain pattern of behavior that is being called the 'principle' in the context, whether 'righteous' or 'wrongful' ways. Therefore, human being in general tend to sense or feel similar way in a situation, when he or she in a gathering or alone, without being dictated by any other individual. He also established the conception of Categorical Imperatives to suggest the division of different feelings that ensues the different reflective actions out from them. However, not everyone agrees with Kant, as in certain situation,_ as for 'stealing', we cannot think that everyone feels the same way as the stealer, therefore we can say that there use to be uniformity of situations only and unlike Kant believed, an individual acts in 'unique way' i.e. in an individualistic manner, that suggests that although there use to be universal and uniform patterns of moral conception, he or she is not subjected to behaving in uniform or universal manner or conduct.

2. Utilitarianism

Towards the beginning of nineteenth century and at the middle path of modern era of Ethics, we find a new brand of neophytes of modern philosophy exploring and pursuing newer avenues of thinking, often mixing and reinterpreting the old moral values with those of modern conception. However, as any student of ethical values is aware of, Ethics too as a subject has been suffering from a kind of duality that puts its very conception of morality into a kind of dilemma. Since the beginning of the study of morality i.e. Ethics, we find it suffering from the duality,- in one way, to follow moral value in stringent manner, and on the other hand, accommodate the necessity of pleasure and desire into its fold, and allow it to be a part of moral value system in practice. However, such a 'lax' view creates consternation in the mind of those vouchsafing for following stringent moral values, calling the others as 'hedonists' i.e. one going for pleasure and therefore lacking in admonition of proper moral values. We find the two trends as back as in the days of the followers of Socrates, who were segregated on the two themes as the group of 'Stoic' and the other being 'Epicurean'. Time and on the conflict of the two versions which aimed for 'Happiness' in their individual manner continued over the long period of centuries, till it was time for modern period of philosophy that has become overwhelmed with neo realization of various new conceptions. With the introduction of the conception of industrialization, general population was overcome with materialistic inventions. The primary target of such scientific endeavor was to appease the common masses with materialistic comfort, therefore the commonly defined version of happiness, as well as to continue such effort with financial benefit derived from the consumption by common masses. While the mass consumption allowed them to benefit themselves, it also helped the mass to be benefited immensely and enjoy materialistic happiness. In the west, it also helped the poorer section of people to be relieved of many of their grievances of day to day life, _ such as getting power supply, regular water flow, or even regulated market economy to take part of. Such mass utilization of commodities has inspired a section of intellects, always on the brink of finding a universal theme of 'happiness' of materialistic kind, which to be accommodated into the purview of contemporary ethics, who have found a podium for encouraging and bringing into the fore their forte. Many such ethicists have tried to find a 'system' or principle in the 'mass happiness' and discovered a theory that can incline on the principle of Altruism. On the other hand, we can also explain them as the ones, who wanted to interpret the theory of personal happiness as based on a universal principle, as they felt nothing counted more than the common pleasure of the mass population. According to them, the other necessities, that of intellectual pursuit and other succours of life should follow only later. The followers of the philosophy with an ethical interpretation justifying the universality of materialistic happiness by utilizing the best benefit that has been termed as Utilitarian and the co-related philosophy they established at the beginning of the modern era has been named as Utilitarianism. G. E. Moore has been one of the greatest propounders of the new lineage of ethics. John Dewey, John Stuart Mill, Henry Sidgwick etc are also great followers of such a philosophy, which emphasizes the best of utility that benefit the mankind.

However, utilitarianism is defined differently by different philosophers who identify it with different approaches of life. Therefore, Utilitarianism can be said to be important from environmental point of view, as it is believe to be a concept initiating not only materialism into western philosophy also has vastly responsible for inducing the concept of industrialization in the west. It has professed the need of human welfare in the name of Altruism, meaning love and concern for universal good. Perhaps, the definition of Utilitarianism be best described in the words of W.R. Sorley in the following way, _"The formula of utilitarianism cannot be expressed as the conclusion of a syllogism or of an inductive inference. It seems rather to have been arrived at by the production _ or the recognition _ of a sympathetic or 'altruistic' sentiment, which was made to yield a general principle for the guidance of conduct."[26] According to author Geoffrey Scarre (book-Utilitarianism), utilitarian can be divided into four groups in accordance with their approach and view towards their ideology. They are namely Welfarist, Consequentialist, Aggregative, Maximising and Universalist. Bentham and J.S. Mill, who were followers of Aristotlelian views are considered welfarist by the definition.

3. Hedonism

Hedonism is also a part of western philosophy, which is inducted into its fold since the days of Greek philosophy, much to the consternation of the ethical fraternity. Although, like many of the western lineages of philosophical thinking it's basic theme is 'pleasure', its end being the same, it is the means which puts its ethical content in question. Hedonism does not believe in God and in their atheistic approach in life, its followers have emphasized only on pleasure of life sans spirituality, since they do not believe in adverse outcome of having pleasure and since according to them, unlike believed by ethicists for moral values, pleasure is not a sin and having pleasure during the span of life does nor result into any ill effect or disregard any code of conduct.

In western philosophy, Hedonism has taken shape of its ideology in the early days of Ethics in Greek civilization, when it was founded by Aristippus, elaborating on the views of Socrates, emancipated as Cyrenaics and overall considered pessimistic of views in life. He reciprocated the views of Socrates that the 'true wisdom of life lies in foresight or insight into the significance of our actions, in an accurate calculation of their results, pleasurable or painful, in the distant as well as the immediate future', the pleasure therefore being the sole motif or only good of life. However, unlike Socrates, he did not conjure the idea of 'pleasure of soul' but that of earthly or materialistic ones only. According to James Seth,- "Cyrenaicism' could hardly be the creed of the modern Christian world. For us its counsels would be the counsels of despair rather than of hope."[27]. However, Cyrenaics took the form of Epicureans in the later development of Ethics in Greek philosophy and which was to certain extent influenced by the views of Stoicism, the evolved form of Cynicism, the parallel but agnostic of the views of Cyrenaicism. Epicureaus, who was the founder of it, believed pleasure to the primary 'good' of life. But he also believed that prudence precedes pleasure and conforms to the criteria of good. According to him,-"Of all this, the beginning, and the greatest good, is prudence. Wherefore, prudence is more of a precious thing even than philosophy. From it grow all other virtues,-for it teaches that we cannot lead a life of pleasure which is not also a life of prudence, honor and justice which is not also a life of pleasure; For the virtues have grown with a pleasant life and a pleasant life is inseparable from them. (referred from Letters of Epicurus in Wallace's 'Epicureanianism pp.129-131) ""[28]

However, modern day Hedonism is not ascribed with the notion of pessimism but rather by Optimism, as is evident in the explanatory work of Sidgwick and some other scholars. According to Seth, -"... Ancient Hedonism, whether of cyrainics or of epicurean type, was apt to be pessimistic; modern hedonism is, in the whole, optimistic.""[29]

Utilitarianism vs. Hedonism

The comparison between Utilitarianism of modern period and hedonism, prevalent since ancient time comes into the context of 'pleasure' the primary tenet of both kind of ethics.

However, as we can notice, utilitarianism has a different perspective regarding the application of 'pleasure' in our life as in Hedonism. When 'pleasure' is considered the 'end' by the Hedonists, pleasure is more or less considered a means to achieve the 'good' of life by the utilitarian. Here the pleasure becomes a standard which brings into question from what it would be derived from. While utilitarianism has espoused the view that pleasure can be an instrument, that is, a means in deriving the 'good' of 'Altruism, that is benefit from a universal cause whereas for Hedonist pleasure itself is the 'good' and it has to be derived from any mundane day to day activities. While with Utilitarianism, the moral standard is quest for universal 'good', there is no moral standard so far for which it is considered as a conception with a degraded moral standard which has no value- enhances perception.

4. *Environmental Ethics*:- Parallel to the Utilitarianism, there was usurpation of 'naturalistic values which were defined in terms of ethics. When welfare of human had been the primary tenet of Utilitarianism, environmental ethics first came to be acknowledged as part of naturalism only. Since the middle of seventeenth century, when naturalism came to be acknowledged as a scientific approach, as there was subjective analysis of nature's predominance on man's life, there was a revival of naturalism in western philosophy after the early Greek period only. However, only later it came be known as ethical naturalism as ethics came to be defined by it and even later in twentieth century as environmental ethics. Although environment and ethics are two different genres, here ethics is related to it as man as a species is part and parcel of the environment i.e. 'nature' and more so, man has been related to it in an intent manner, whether as manipulator or a worshipper of it.

The importance of environmental ethics is growing day by day as interference with the environment has put mankind into questioning of the contemporary values in present day ethics. On the other hand, many philosophers believe it to be the panache of the deteriorated values in modern time and also as rescuer from the ethical pitfall. Referring to the need of environmental ethics in our life, Lynton Caldwell expresses in the following way,- "An ethics adequate to man's responsibility for his environment need not inculcate reverence for creation, but at peril of disaster, it must be based upon profound and genuine respect."*30

As in the oriental philosophy, ethics has been part and parcel of Western philosophy since the days of its inception. However, western ethics has always been inductive in characteristics and therefore has perpetually been going through the process of change in an evolutionary manner, although it has been more static in nature during the medieval period. Another Characteristic of western philosophy is it is experimental in nature, as a result of which it has often taken turn which later came to be 'undesirable' by many philosophers. Besides, its experimentation has allowed it to induct too many new conceptions to be added to its context, which has acted hazardous for its ethos. 'Utilitarianism' is one such conception that has been experimented and allowed to deviate from conventional ethical views. Such a conception of ethics has allowed mankind to accommodate the perception of 'pleasure' in form of luxury in the name of well being of mankind. It espouses the idea that every other things on earth can be utilized for man as he is the pivotal character on the earth. However, such a view has come under detailed scrutiny and most of the modern philosophers are highly criticizing and eschewing such a view as basically deviating western values to be economy or market oriented besides being the 'ultimate' responsible for the deterioration of environment for espousing 'egocentric' view and encouraging exploitation of nature.

2.9. ETHICS : INDIAN

Ethics is so much an integral part of not only Indian Philosophy and Hindu religion, it is part of the people's psyche also. In Indian literature, it is mentioned as Naitik Sastra only. Almost all the major religious books and philosophical lineages of Hinduism are basically based on the intrinsic values of Ethics. Only the question is what kind of perspective of views are laid with emphasis by individual scriptures of it and therefore, which of the aspects of life it has touched upon. Almost all the books of Hindu religion lay emphasis upon 'Duty' as the iconic emblem of their rule and thereby have set the precedence of its contents or rules and regulations. We find that while 'Gita', considered the primary religious book of Hinduism is the sermon for ethical values to be practiced upon by individuals to improvise their inane abilities so that the relation with the almighty can be established. Other book such as Manu's Samhita relates to an individual's ethical relation with the society which, with righteous result affected, may lead to one's sublime exit from the ethereal and metaphorical world. Besides the above mentioned scriptures, there are other religious scriptures which too have focused on some other angles of life. Scriptures such as Upanishad, Puranas and Even Sutrakars can be called a bundle of such ethical value- related concern of Hinduism. As is described by author Pratap Chandra,-"With the beginning of Upanisadic Era, a sea of change took place in the values of a section of society reported in these (the religious) texts."*[31] However, the Vedas, which preceded Upanishad or Purana, cannot be called entirely ethical in nature, but more of a bunch of directives of tasks that would ascertain an individual of the sanctimoniousness of his mind and actions. They are more philosophical in nature that would explore the world of its inane realities and rather quest the metaphysical truth than invade the relation of man versus society of its mundane matters, although they are not void of the mention of society or its doable activities. However, they make more effort to direct an individual on how to achieve the eternal state of mind i.e. God, than bring to the book the 'righteusness' or 'wrongfulness' of one's activities in day to day life.

1. The Dictates of Gita: *The Moral Directives*

The approach of Gita in attaining immortality is an ethical one. However, Rather than establishing it through the activities in society a man carries through as part of his obligation to the family or the society, Gita has directed and advised on the purification of mind to such a state of it which would help him in achieving or relating himself with the greatest soul that is God, in where one can achieve the sublimity of one's soul. However, one must be ensconced in some ethical 'feats' to achieve such a stature of one's own personality. With the directives shown in the holy scripture one can attain such a feat.

Believed to have been written by great Poet Vyasa, Gita is consisted of ten thousand verses that originally comprises in the great Epic of 'Mahabharata'. The words of Gita are said through the mouth of Lord Krishna who dictated Arjuna, the warring Prince on the legitimacy or the wrongdoing of actions of life and how ultimately it results in one's 'the here' or 'the other' lives. Therefore, although it speaks of ethical values, it is spoken in terms of 'other reality' or metaphysical terms only, not only as social solution of issues.

In Gita, Lord Krisna has given directives to individuals on how to restrain oneself, of many temptations that come in form of Maya. One has to practice Yoga and be a Karma Yogi, i.e. keep doing one's duty in a relentless manner and, must keep his or her unconditional faith in him, i.e. God and should not look for beneficial results as aftermath of it.

Here, in Gita we discover that Ethics is a plane, or rather be called a means to achieve the ultimate reality, and not an 'end' by itself. Therefore, it is not barely a sermon of dictation of ethical values but a means of achieving the ultimate plane of life too. Therefore, we cannot call it a merely ethical or religious scripture, but as a philosophical notion too.

2. The Upanishads

The Upanisads are another set of scriptures for Hindu Philosophy and religion, which relate to both the world of spirituality and the morality, trying to quest the answers for the metaphysical queries. The search is for 'Eternal Reality' or the personification of God called 'Brahmam' can be attained by jettisoning oneself from the platform of ethical achievements only, and which can be achieved by improving upon one's soul of the ignorance one may suffer from and purified by his or her acquired knowledge. For attaining such knowledge one must again carry out certain actions that must be 'duty' bound to those occasions the scriptures have asked one too. The failure to realize one's duty and perform respectable Godly qualities may not allow him or her soul be one with the Brahmam and achieve eternity or Nirvana, and rather recur in repeated lives on earth due to 'Karma' or non achievement of ethical and moral supremacy such a platform demands for. So the directives of Upanishads suggest that a person must do his duties on earth so as to succeed of eternity after leaving the body on earth by the soul like a cloak, so that they can embrace and be one with eternity. Regarding the spiritualistic views in Upanishad, author N.K. Devaraja had expressed in the following way,-"In the hymns of Rig Veda, we do not find any marked expression of the spirit of detachment towards earthly values. That spirit makes its first conspicuous appearance in our literature in the Upanisads."[*32]

3. The Puranas

There are about eighteen Puranas, ranging over a fairy long period of writing them down, which are rather mythical in nature than spiritual. They are usually compilation of various stories, each of them enacting the saga of various events, portraying right and wrong doings of its progenitors. They also enacts various mythological events to personify the almighty or emphasise certain ethical values, so that common masses can follow them without hesitation or for the reason that being less or without formal education, they could follow their conscience in judging a situation.

4. Manu's Samhita

One of the most enduring books of human civilization and representative of basic Hindu Ethics in form of a scripture for the same religion, Manu's Samhita bears in all the ethical directives a book of religion should bear upon its followers. It connotes in details the rites and rituals besides rules and regulations and the tenets of ethical orders, so that the follower may perform them, again to achieve Nirvana. The primary tenets of Manu's Samhita are:-

Asramadharma, The Four Stages of Family Duties:- The Hindu religion, as we have mentioned earlier, emphasises upon the primary duty of an individual firstly towards his kins and then lays the emphasis upon with the follow up for the society. Fulfillment of one's duty by performing which on the earth one paves his way to attain one's Nirvana or sublimity with the eternity or the God Supreme. The four stages of duty towards the family can be describe in the following way(a) Brahmacharya i.e. till the age of twenty five years, when a person at his youth would remain a celibate and stay at his teacher i.e. Guru's residence and earn knowledge. (b) Garhasthya:-at the second stage of next twenty five years, i. e. till the age of around fifty, a person should get married, do familial duty, along with it performing his other duties towards parents and the society too. By doing so he will not only be discharging his 'debt' towards his ancestors but will be doing so towards God by performing Yagna. (c) Banaprastha:-The next twenty five years till the age of seventy five, one should leave aside the family and duties and must take solace in the forest to do penance for any wrong doing knowingly or unknowingly.(d) Sanyasa:_At the last part of his life, one must completely give away his mundane possessions to the up coming generation and live on meager meal and necessities, thus restraining oneself from temptations and excesses of life till the rest of his or her life.

Cast System or Varna:- The caste system of Hindu religion can be attributed as signatory of a person's duty towards his society. We find that at the beginning of Hindu society, different groups of people, depending upon their authenticity of their identity, i.e. whether one was pure blooded Aryan race or admixed with other races or even belonged completely to other races considered inferior to the others, were put into certain the order, by which they were introduced with certain specific work which were not only deemed fit but suitable for the society as well. Usually, the one with the higher level of intelligence were entrusted with the job of 'priesthood' i.e. a Brahmin, whereas, some others were the warriors i.e. the Khatriyas. Next in the order are the Vasyas i.e. the one doing commerce.

Therefore, we may come to the conclusion that in the Samhita we find that the primary tenet of it is the duty of individual towards it and serve it according to one's own ability. However, the initial divisions which were applicable at the beginning as work division as per one's own ability, had become permanent features of Hindu religion. Consequently, the work ethics has not only become specific to each group, the subsequent generations has started inheriting the individual profession of the father and also had passed on to their coming generations. Thus, the work division also had created the permanent order of 'superiority to inferiority' specification of the groups and the additional privileges some of such groups owned. Thus, the caste system has created as much conveniences to the society as much it has encouraged dubious ethics for the religion.

2.9.1. Karmavada of Indian Philosophy:

One of the oldest religion in the world, Hinduism propagates karmavada and spirituality and after life, Varnasrama etc. Originating from the views of not one person unlike most other religion, but of assorted sages belonging to different eras of time, Hinduism is inherent with stringent ethical values and influence of nature. Except for Manus' Samhita, a treatise on ethical diction of Hindu society, most other scriptures inspired ethical values through the narration of mythological stories.

It has been one of the most enduring features of Indian philosophy in which characteristic of its ethics has emphasized not only on what manner to carry out duty, but also the outcome of performance or as a matter of fact non performance of it. It is called Karmavada and rather than being any ethical diction, it is more of an interpretation or narration of goodness of performed duties. As ethical interpretations can be derived from an assorted number of books such as MadBhagawat Gita, Purana, Upanisad etc. and also Manu's Samhita, one of the common ethical views of the scriptures is the Karmavada, which is significant for the inherited merit of performed duties in next of life.

According to views of Hinduism, it is an un-precipitated principle guided by God who defines and judges the merits and demerits of individuals on basis of his performed duties. According to it, There is an order of several strata of life on earth, and if one fails to perform or is committed to one's duty in a 'callous' manner, then the birth recurs repeatedly on it for one, till one succeeds in fulfilling duties righteously and then attain Nirvana. According to author S. K. Ghosh,_ "The law of Karma is this general moral law which governs not only the life and destiny of all individual beings, but even the order and harmony of physical world."[33] According to the theory, man needs to perform disinterested duty (meaning committing to duty without looking for benefits derived from it) which will liberate him from the cudgel of recurring lives of his on earth. It is also believed not to be spiritual in content.

Both in Jainism and Buddhism and also some other Hindu lineages such as Sankhya and Mimamsa, however, it is believed that the law is autonomous, independent of God and functions on its own.

However, the law of Karma faces criticism in spite of its profound influence on Hinduism and other related religions. According to author S.K. Ghosh,_ "Man is not a mere product of nature; his life is something more than karma. If the law is all in all, than there is no real freedom possible.........The infinite in men helps him to transcend the limitations of finite. The essence of spirit is freedom. By its exercise man can check and control his natural impulses. That is why his life is something more than a machine or mechanical laws."[34] but, when man's freedom is acknowledged and as long as the law does not become a mechanical process, then in accordance with the theory, man can become not only the defining factor of his future but his destiny as well.

2.9.2. *Carvaka*

The Carvaka philosophy of Indian thinking, to certain extent, can be compared with the Cyrainics of Greek period or epicureans of later times. It is known as Hedonism in western philosophy. In both the philosophies, pleasure of life has been emphasized more than other ethical notions such as duty or morality and held ahead of the altruism in western thinking or Karmavada, i.e. theory of 'repercussion' of action in Indian philosophy or oriental philosophies in general. While most of the philosophical lineages of India profess 'spiritualism' on ethical basis, Materialism exists in Hinduism in form of Caravaka and 'Nastik'vada. Carvaka, the philosophy of pleasure and parallel to the Hedonism of west, does not believe in God and can be called atheistic in their supposition of God. However it believes in the 'matter' as the core or origin of the world and perception as the basis of all empirical knowledge and thereby asserts its precedence to western philosophy of modern period when it started emphasizing on knowledge of perception rather than being based on idea of preconceived notions. Since 'Carvaka' does not believe in Karmavada, i.e. the theory of 'merit and effect' of a deed carried out by a human, therefore it does not believe in after life or Nirvana, i.e. freedom from recurring of life on earth. However, not all propounders of Carvaka philosophy believed in indulgence in pleasure only and without restrain and Vatsayana was one of them only. Author R.S. Dasgupta said about Indian Hedonism in the following manner,_ "In conformity with the (above) metaphysical theories that justify the contention that death of the body means death of the so called soul too or that nothing survives bodily death, the only ethical ideal that naturally gets response from human hearts is Hedonism."[*35]

2.9.3. *Buddhism:*

From ethical point of view, Buddhism as a religion commands highest esteem, as it is one of the foremost promoter of peace, amity and non violence in the world. In fact, Buddha is not only synonymous with such tenets, but also symbolizes them as necessity against the tumultuous and disruptive forces on earth. To maintain the peace and amity on the earth, Buddha has emulated certain path, fold and ways to be maintained and which are usually eightfold in terms to conditions and ways of each of its postulates.

Buddhism, as a religious belief has emphasized more on moral values by performing activities in day to day life than attaining it through messages of God. In fact, it can also be included among the handful of religions in the world which can be called either as the most 'Ethics' based one or as also an 'Agnostic' one, that is, not a 'God centric' one since it does not profess about God. Regarding the beliefs of Buddhism, R.S. Dasgupta the author says in following manner,-"Tired of intellectual casuistries and the gymnastics of metaphysicians, who deny one another's ontological standpoints both in respect and processes of results, leaving the unsophisticated mass of general people in the maze of bewilderment, unable to ascertain which way to go and which way to adopt, Buddha the embodiment of love for the living beings, chalk out a line of action, bereft of philosophical speculations, that shall lead to the cessation of all miseries, nay of the life itself, for life is the seed of all miseries."[35] The founder of the religion, Lord Buddha, after much penance in his life has arrived at certain ethical tenants that he believed would give guidance to people to live a life with proper expression of honest, moral and sincere values.

Among the various religions of the world, Buddhism is important from ethical point of view, as it has dictated certain rules called' paths' to follow to achieve the ultimate reality of life. Unlike Hinduism, Buddhism does not believe in the greatest soul to achieve or to emerge with to attain Nirvana, but to attain it through the ethical paths only, i.e. In it, nirvana is not the means but the 'end' itself. There are, however, various paths for various conditions of life to follow.

Buddhism, as a philosophy is more ethically oriented than it is commensurated with the concept of theism, unlike most other major religions in the world. In fact in Buddhism, achieving Nirvana, the highest goal of life, that is freedom from life and rebirth, is but achieving the ethical pinnacle only and its followers should tread the moral paths shown by its founder and saint Lord Buddha only.

2.9.4. *Jainism*

To certain extent being contemporary to Buddhism in its time of origin, it expresses even more stringent set of values when it comes to ethics. Although historically or spatially it is not as extensive as Buddhism, but unlike the later, it is also not known to create war or enjoy the patronage of so many well-known emperors of history who spread the message of it worldwide. It dictates ethical views that may be significant in modern time when a considerable amount of emphasis is laid on 'animal right' and ethics related to it through the processes called Parinamika, Audayika, Aupasmika, Khayika and kshaaiaupasika. Again, it advises seven ways to refrain karma to work upon a being. According to it, with help of Nirjara and Sanvar, one can de3stroy 'Karma' and Attain 'Moksha'.

2.9.5. *Gandhism*

One of the most modern day ethics can be called the philosophy of Mohandas Karam Chand Gandhi of India who retrieved the independence of his own country from the colonial rule of the British regime. To be precise, with the help of his ethical values being applied to great extent in his political views, not only did he recovered the freedom of his country, he set a whole new trend of thinking that has opened up in front of the habitants of the whole world. Gandhi himself did not name his philosophy but its synonymy with his way of life has inspired the common people as well as the intellectuals of the world to believe and call his ideas after him only. The most significant part of his philosophy is the tenet of non-violence for which he was inspired by ancient Hindu scriptures as well as Buddhism and other religions.

Gandhi, belonging to the modern period of twentieth century, did not hesitate in exploring old values in remixing with the contemporary ones for utilizing for modern time, by applying which in an un-definable situation not witnessed in the recourse of history of the country, and skillfully succeeded in bringing into the lives of common man what can be called as spirituality and opportunity to practise it in a 'free' atmosphere attained through his perseverance and neo-emancipated conceptions of morality.

Gandhism, which is a bi-product of modern conceptions born out of the coalesce of ancient ethical themes of most other religions and their applications manifested through Gandhi's own works and thoughts, has not only redeemed the world with the success of its postulates long believed to be irrelevant in modern day context, but also proven the retrieval of our old values as being the saviour of mankind in both the near and distant future. Gandhi believed, like in Buddhism and ancient Hinduism, in the path of 'Non violence' or ahimsa, which encourages both individuals and communities to exercise restrain or prohibition of opting for any destructive means while facing provocation or danger. He believed rather for usage of non-violent means which would neither incur any physical harm to an individual or to any collective groups of people, or to cause any mental difference while looking for justice. However, we find Gandhism to be too intrinsic a value system to be defined and then put into effect in a haphazard manner or in an indiscriminate way, as his 'non- violent' methods might be taken advantage of by the agencies against whom it might be used. It speaks for skillful application against such agencies.

At the end we can surmise that Gandhism, with its non-violent ethical policies, can be the best weapon in the resurrection process of the environment.

References:

1. John Dewey -*The Theory of the Moral life* -p.163
2. *Ibid*. -p.156
3. James seth- '*The study of Ethical principles* -p.11
4. Dr. John Mckenzie- *'A Manuel of ethics'*-p.2
5. *Ibid.*-p.25
6. *Ibid.*- p.67
7. *Ibid.*-p128
8. W.R. Sorley-*The Ethics of Naturalism*-p.123
9. Mc. Kenzie –*Maual of Ethics*. -p.75
10. Samuel Clarke-. *Ibid.*-p.141
11. Samuel Clarke-. *Ibid.*-p.142
12. Shafetbury-. *Ibid.*-p.144
13. *Ibid.*-p.145
14. *Ibid.*-p.154
15. *Ibid.*-p.154
16. *Ibid.*-p.148
17. *Philosophy and the natural Environment*,-ch. *Value in Nature and Natural Value*, p.27
18. Chritopher rowe- *From Introduction to Greek ethics*- by -p. 22
19. *Ibid-*. p. 25
19. *Ibid.*-p.31
20. Plato-. *Ibid*-p.65
21. Plato-*Ibid.*-p.67
22. Plato.-*Ibid.*-p.100
23. Aristotle- *Ibid.*-p.102
24. Aristotle, *Ibid.*,-p.106
25. John Mckenzie- *'Manuel of Ethics'*- p. 148
26. W.R. Sorley-*Ethics of Naturalism, ch. The individualistic Theory* p.65)
27. James Seth-*A Study of Ethical Principles*-p.84
28. *Ibid.-ch. Epicureus.* p.91
29. *Ibid.*- p.94
30. L.K. Caldwell-*Environment*-p.251
31. Pratap Chandra- *The Hindu Mind*-p.60
32. N.K. Devaraja- *Philosophy of Culture*-p.202
33. S.K. Ghose-*Important Philosophical Essays*-p.2
34. *Ibid.*-pp.3-4
35. R.S. Dasgupta –*Some Problems of Philosophy of Religion*-p.34
35. R.S. Dasgupta-*ibid*.54

CHAPTER 3

MAN AND ENVIRONMENT

3.1. MAN AND NATURE

With increasing concern for the environment, that is the natural surrounding around us, we can discover laymen as well as the intellectuals are contemplating on the necessity to stem its further destruction and scrutinizing the possibility of bringing in and re-inducting the ethical interpretation to the relation of man with his surrounding. We may also find out that even with meticulous analysis, it is not possible to disintegrate nature and its influence from man's mental set up and his existence.

From time immemorial, man has been depending upon nature for all the developmental activities for mankind. While human civilization has developed on the lap of mother nature, man has always been trying to strike a balance with her, never outdoing or utilizing beyond his necessities whereas nature has never completely mutilated or destroyed his monumental achievements with her proverbial fury, and man has always looked up at her i.e. his environment with awe and reverence that survived the test of time.

However, this is not the case anymore. The age old bond of mutual understanding and reverence between man and his surroundings seems to have fragmented. Man's outlook has changed and his conception of conventional 'social good' has taken to a beating and being taken over by the utilitarian ones. Man has started using nature for his own benefit so much so that he had forgotten the existence of other animals and creatures on earth. He had explored deep into the air, the ground, the water i. e. the ocean and into the forest also, as a result of which there is wide-spread destruction of forest and animals. The whole of the eco-system being upset to cause inclement weather, erratic rainfall, global warming, greenhouse effects, ozone hole, etc...... It means man's material gain has put into jeopardy the existence of all other animals along with that of human kind.

The man and the environment's equilibrium are in great jeopardy as the former is trying to take over the reign of rule on the earth from the latter.

(a)Intrinsic Value of Nature

Apart from influencing human mind to great extent psychologically, nature has benefited man materialistically too. Therefore it has retained great objective value for mankind in terms of materialistic gain and utility. However, there are many scholars who explain that nature owns qualities, which are not in need to be realized by human being and be utilized for his benefit. The qualities are so intrinsic by nature that they are part of greater realities and designs of the universe and are not necessarily depended on human to be assessed and utilized. They are more inherent in themselves. However, different scholars define intrinsic value in different ways. Again there are those who believe intrinsic value of nature can be defined in both subjective and objective manner.

(b) Ecological Balance of Nature

However, in the ever increasing effort to outdo nature in the latest phase of development of human civilization and experiencing the repercussion of it in form of degradation of our surrounding as a result of it, man is trying to desecrate its own follies and is trying to set right his attitude towards nature and is trying to reestablish the strained relationship with nature. A number of environmental philosophers believe in that amidst the various aspects of environment, an equilibrium exists, which should not be disturbed or destructed so as not to bring imbalance among its aspects and thereby bring in imparity to the intrinsic relation among them. One of the theories that took precedence over others in importance is GayaismΣ which emphasizes in maintaining ecological balance in nature. According to it, the imbalance caused can result into grievous destruction to the ecological relations on earth, which in future may lead to the destruction of the earth.

Nature as an epitome of wonder and therefore being a matter for discussion has eluded all with its treasure troves of wonder in one hand and arousing curiosity and therefore quest for a philosophical or scientific answer to its manifold characteristics and its multitude. Therefore, the study of nature i.e.

our environment has been defined in twofold manners, i.e. both of objective and subjective descriptions:- its physiological characteristic i.e. objective as well as its

Σ Gaiaism was first established by James Lovelock in 1969. However, keeping it at basic core of the conception, different scholars interpret it in their different ways.

its subjective analysis. They are as follows:-

3.1.1. *THE ECO SYSTEM*
Different temperatures, different types of soils and different geographical positions have created different or individual groups of species on earth, although some of them may be available allover the world of these species. Within the group itself or with another group are dependent on one another. They have to interact with each other or one another or among themselves for their existence. For example, a bird makes a nest on a tree to live on it; whereas the bird eats its fruits and helps it in dispersing its seeds elsewhere so that another tree of its kind grows there.

Different types of insects grow on its bark; a woodpecker eats the insects; earthworms living underneath the ground live on the rotten leaves of the tree and help the tree- roots by making tunnels to it in the ground. Thus every single species in this world is dependent on another species or a group of them for its own or their collective existence. Thus, these groups of species functioning together to create an individual system of dependency is called an 'Eco System: Overall, interaction between living beings (that is the biotic community) and the non-living (i.e. a-biotic or non-biotic) substances is considered as the functioning of the eco system. For example, a small rotten piece of wood can be considered as a small Eco-System. Ferns and mushrooms will be growing on it, wood lice roaming under its barks, earthworms and insects like millipeds and centipedes will be nesting under it etc. With close observation we may find most of the insects and the parasitic plants are largely dependent on that piece of wood for their survival, whereas the wood is in the process of decomposition in which substances are turning into minerals on earth with help of variety small micro- organism. A small piece of wood can provide for whole lot of living creatures and its surrounding too. Thus the whole of the world also can be called a big 'Eco System'.

In the world of living beings, all the movable or mobile creatures, that is, the animate objects are called as Fauna, whereas the other ones such as trees, plants etc, that is, the inanimate or immobile but organic by nature are called Flora. Therefore, all the living things of nature, inclusive of mammals, birds, insects, marine creatures, trees, plants etc. fall into the category of Flora and

Fauna. Besides, flora categorizes the species that produce their own food. Usually, they are inherent with chlorophyl, the green substance which allows them to produce their own food called starch from sunshine and which they usually store in the leaves. Therefore the flora species are called as **Autotroph.** On the other hand, there are many fauna species, that is mammals, birds or even aquatic species such as fish, mollusce etc. which depend on plants, or its seed or miniscule aquatic plants called plankton for their existence, which are called as Heterotroph. Besides them, there are other animals which live on the heterotrophs for their survival. Those creatures living on plants, seeds or planktons are called Herbivores. There are those animals which live on other herbivorous animals and they are called as Carnivores. Animals like elephant, cow, deer, rabbit etc. are herbivorous whereas tiger, lion, etc. are the carnivorous animals. There is another category of animals eating both plants and other animals which are called as Omnivores.

If we consider the number of the autotrophs- that is the trees, plants, planktons etc., then we find them covering the land areas most extensively; then comes the number of Heterotrophs which depend on the autotrophs for food; it also include the insect community. Even fewer are the numbers of the carnivores which live on the herbivores. Now, if we imagine all these three categories of living organism into three layers- structured one upon another, we find that from numbers point of view, the autotrophs will form the biggest layer, whereas the Herbivores will form a comparatively smaller layer. The layer of carnivores will be smallest, as their numbers are even fewer. A German scientist named Odum had discovered an imaginary pyramid with these three layers one upon another, with thelayerof carnivores at the top, on that of herbivores which rested on that of autotrophs. This imagined pyramid is known as 'Ecological Pyramid.' The line of 'dependency of food'- that is for example, a rabbit living on grass, a carnivore animal such as or lion or even human living on it as food-or a frog living on the grass eating insects, a snake may eat it as food -is called as 'Food Chain.' Thus we find that in the eco-system it is either self production of food or dependency on others and excepting the plants and trees everyone has to depend on others for food and survive. Thus we find that the whole world is a big Eco- System.

3.1.2. **THE RAIN FOREST**
As we all know, that due to the position of the earth towards the Sun, apart from the Polar regions (arctic and the Antarctic) other regions have different temperature zones. While the Polar regions are the coldest, it is

more and more hotter towards south from the north pole. So it is opposite from the South Pole. Areas falling in the imaginary line going through the middle of earth and called the Equator are the hottest through out the year, The areas adjacent to it called tropical and passed through by the imaginary lines of Tropic of Capricorn and Tropic of Cancer to the north and to the south respectively (lying at 0 degree in each case). The areas falling in these lines are usually quite hot in summer, and cool in winter, but usually poured with incessant rain during the hot season. Unlike the deciduous forest of the temperate zones which lie between tropical and Polar regions, the tropical forests areas are green through out the year thick and almost unpenetrable to common human and light cannot penetrate through the leaves to reach the ground. The top of the trees with thick leaves and branches together form this impenetrable natural shade, which is called as Canopy. Due to lack of sunshine under the canopy, fewer plants grow underneath it, but it itself provide as the abode of innumerous kinds of species, as it is a very hot humid and rainy, which helps in their growth. Besides, usually these forest areas extend over vast areas of land which helps the species in growing their numbers. Due to the fact that these forests are the habitat of maximum number of species on the earth, it is called as the most 'Bio-diverse' region. There are twelve such most bio-diverse regions on earth. The Amazon River Basin in the continent of South America is the biggest rain forest area on earth, which **is** followed by those in the country of Indonesia. The North -East region of India and Sahyadri, i.e. the Paschimghat region in Western coast by the Arabian Sea also are two such bio-diverse regions situated in India. However, the importance of these areas is not barely due to being the habitat of numerous species, _ but due to the role it plays in keeping the balance of atmosphere on earth. This vast forest regions exhale huge amount of oxygen in the nature's way of maintaining ecological balanceon earth. As we know, oxygen is the most vital element on earth for not only the animal kingdom, but whole of living organism on earth. Therefore it is very important that it is available in atmosphere with due amount. The Rain forest helps in maintaining the balance on earth. However, unfortunately for mankind and whole of living kingdom, these rain forest areas are being cut down at a rapid speed where they are found to quelsh the thirst of human greed, who use the wood of it for many utility purposes, thereby putting the whole of living world under threat. We shall discuss about it with other environment related problems.

3.1.3. BIO DIVERSITY

When a species of a particular family order of living organism use to have many more sub- species, then it is caused due to Bio-diversity. It is a complicated biological process which is dependent on various circumstances, but then we can discuss about why it happens, or about its importance and how it can benefit living beings. Authors U.Kumar and Mahendera Jeet Asija have defined bio diversity in the following way, _ "Variation is the law of nature. It occurs everywhere and every moment. The variations take place at micro levels at short space and big time gap. The variations may be linear or cyclic. The variety and variability of organisms and eco systems is referred to as biological diversity or biodiversity. Similarly, the biological variations initiate at the micro level (bio molecular level or genes) and apparent at species and ecological level. The biological variations in nature over time and space form the basis of evolutionary process."[1]

Nowadays, we are all aware of the miniscule molecule existing in the body of a living being which bears in its individual physical and mental characteristics along with that of its own species. These molecules are called DNA (de-oxi Nuclic Acid) or as 'gene' and they help individual species to survive with its own characteristics intact. These genes have the unique capability to adapt and change over a period of time in accordance to its necessity. Often in suitable conditions these genes help individual species to develop into sub- species with newer characteristics added to it. This process of having additional or more diversified species is called as 'Bio_-Diversity'. It is believed that species with more sub species has more chances of survival in face of oddities and of calamities due to its manifold characteristics, than a certain species with uniform characteristics unable to withstand or survive in front of attacking micro-organism(viruses, bacteria etc.) and other calamities. Therefore, scientists believe that bio-diversity will help animal kingdom to survive in face of all oddities on earth. Besides, we find that varieties of flowers, birds, trees and animals bring in not only color to earth, but also make it beautiful. Therefore author Mark Rowland expresses in the following way _ "The preservation of endangered species of flora and fauna is a major practical environmental concern. Similarly, many environmentalists argue that biodiversity is a fundamentally valuable feature of the environment. And one of the constituents here- the concept of diversity is also reducibly relational. Finally, being naturally evolved, as opposed to artificial, is a property which for most environmentalists, confer value on those things that have it."[2]

(A) *Aquatic Kingdom*

Besides the world of birds, animals, trees on and above the ground, we also find another such world down under inside water in a river or a lake or a sea _the animals belonging to water. These animals are generally called as 'aquatic species', although the species living in a river may differ from the ones in a sea and the number of species and their sub-species may be very limted in comparison to those living in a sea. Besides, seas and oceans have species of aquatic animals that are entirely their own. Those living in a river can be called as 'riverine', whereas those living in a sea or a ocean is called a 'marine' animal. Besides, these animals may largely vary in shape and size in comparison to those living on ground. There are some plants too which grow under the water.

Like animals on earth, aquatic creatures range from very minute ones to larger varieties. The small ones consist of invertibrates, i.e. the ones without bones- such as sessile- or larvae of insects, clamps, nymphs, barnacles, arthopodd, etc. whereas even smaller micro -organisms consist of the periphyton, or aufwuchs, which include clumped and filamentous blue and green algae. Phytoplankton includes diatoms, blue and blue-green algae whereas zoo-plankton includes protozoans, microroarpods etc. Plankton in water is like the leaves of plants and trees as they can produce their own food with help of chlorophyll, and thereby to be considered as the autotroph of aquatic world, on which many other bigger animals live. Nekton includes the bigger organisms of the river or sea, which contains fish, larger insects and amphibians and reptiles.

Again, fresh water bodies can be divided into two categories- Lotic and Lentic; Flowing water bodies are called as Lotic and Closed or stagnant ones such as that of lake or a pond is called as Lentic. Periphyton, and sessile invertibrates, cray fish etc are found in these water bodies and when catfish, carp, trout etc are found in the oxygen rich upper reaches, nutrient rich down stream of a river may contain external eco-system such as locthanous and other varieties of fish, amphibians etc.

Lentic water eco-systems may be divided into three zones in terms of light penetration to it, although they may vary in physical, chemical and biological characteristics. The Littoral Zone extends from shoreline to the innermost location of the rooted plants. This zone includes flora species of floating leaves such as water lillies to other submerged rooted-species and nectons such as fish, snakes, snails and other adult larval insects. The limnetic zone, following it, contains Phyto and Zoo-planktons besides the nekton inclusive of fish, amphibian and other larger insects which do not float in water but swim. The profundale zone lies even below the limnetic zone and which contains fishes like pike, pickeral, perch etc. as it is a nutrient poor zone and consists of detritus and decomposed substances.

The Marine eco-System, on the other hand, can be, divided into three zones, called the Neritic, the Aphrotic and the Benthic. In the Neritic zone, which is usually lined with the Bit rocky shore inundated by tides and waves and conditional to extreme of changing temperature, moisture and light, is the habitat of sessile organisms, clamps, crustacean and coral reefs formed by coelenterates besides all other burrowing organisms such as crabs, sand dollars, polychaets etc.

The Neritic zone, which consists of 7% of the total sea areas and continues from sea shore up to around 200 meter into the sea, is usually rich in species and high in productivity due to the presence of planktons in high numbers as result of adequate light penetration. It is full of extensive algae communities of giant kelps as well as of clamps, snails, worms and echiderms. It is full of fishes so much so that it is known as fishing ground. The Pelagic zone, consisting eaphotic and Aphotic zones forms 90 percent of the sea surface. The plankton diatoms and dinoflegellates are the causes of the occurrence of the Photosynthesis. In these zones, besides, shrimps, jellyfish, ctenophoes are its inhabitators. Carnivorous copepodes and crustacae are also abundant here. The Benthic zone, extending from edge of the continental shelf to the deepest ocean trenches nurtures the heterotrophic organisms, which are,_rooted lillies, sea fans, sponges, brachiopodes, snails, nails etc.

The world of the- sea and the ocean, along with its animal world comprises three forth of the areas on the earth, therefore no less important than the world on the ground, although most of it still remains unknown to human kind. However, the necessity to safeguard the sea and its animal kingdom remains a responsibility for humankind before it is destructed by human greed.

(B) The Wild Life, Mangrove and Delta regions, Grasslands : Haven of species

The flora and fauna in the wilderness, where man does not have assess easily or regularly, is usually considered as the Wildlife. Many of the species, especially of the flora have still remained unknown to us.

However, it is mainly the fauna species which get more importance as the wildlife mammals, birds, insects etc., all the heterotrophic organisms that are included in the fauna category of living organism. Now a days, there are many varieties of living organism, big or small whose numbers are decreasing day by day. Many mammals, which used to be very ferocious and strong are getting fewer in number, as man has been destructing them both for the reason to getting rid of his fear from them and also to appease his greed of the skin, teeth, meat etc. for various medical uses and commercial reasons. Thus man has by dint of his superior strength and cunning hood has been killing these animals systematically to reduce the number day by day, or to eliminate them completely from the earth.

1. *The Estuary (Delta) and the Mangrove*

The estuaries are the regions where a river joins- that is- falls into the sea; therefore it can be called as the confluence of a river and a sea. Such a confluence has got ecological importance as these areas are usually replete with triangular shaped islands and they are usually very rich in flora and fauna. Besides, since it is inundated by tidal waves and it is the confluence of pure-water and the salt water of the river and the sea respectively, it easily becomes a breeding ground of various kinds of riverine and marine species. Many types of fishes spawn in here and usually it is a favourable ground for species such as prawns and squids etc. Commercially these areas are considered as valuable by countries endowed with such confluences, although repeated exploitation by such countries have rendered such regions as devoid of many species of important organisms, besides the destruction of the eco-systems or systems existing there. Often the affluences carried by the rivers from the industries flourishing on their shores also contribute in destructing the fragile ecology in these regions. The primary species of organisms, inhabitating in these areas, with the ability to withstand the tide and the constant admixture of river and sea water are- crabs, shellfish, annelid annelids, jellyfish, echiribderms (starfish, sea cucumbers and sea urchins)besides being the breeding ground of marlin, codfish etc.

Redheaded grass, eelgrass, widegreen grass etc. are some of the flora abundantly growing in here. Mangroves are particular variety of plants which grow primarily in estuarine regions. It belongs to Rhizhopora family and it has got long water-resistant branches and twigs that firmly implant in the ground conditioned to the constant exchange of tidal water level. Area covered by these plants is a suitable canopy for the breeding by organisms such as prawn, squid annelid etc. and therefore it is very important from ecological point of view. However as in case of the estuary-born plants which themselves being useful commercially as dye, glue, rayon and tannin are constantly being exploited and destructed by human kind.

2. *Flora and Fauna of Deciduous Forest, Savanna, Tundra, Coniferous Forest, Grasslands, Deserts Etc*

The deciduous forests, are usually found in the temperate zones, that is the region that lives above and below the lines of solstices i.e. the Line of and the line of Capricorn respectively. In these regions, flora and fauna of the forest is not as rich as that of the rain forests as we find number of species of both flora and fauna are limited. Some of the trees in here shed its leaves during winter times as coldness during that time is severe and hence the name 'deciduous' comes into existence. The predominant flora of these forests are maple (Acer) and beech (fagus) growing on moist soil, whereas Oak (quercus) and Hickory (Carya) are found on drier soil. Basswood (tilla), chestnut (castanea), cottonwood (populous), sycamore (platanus), elms (Ulumus) and willow (salix) are some other species of it. The largest harbivore and carnivore respectively are whitetail deer and black bear. Other mammals of importance are red and grey fox, bobcat, weasel, opossum, racoon, voles, mice, squirrels, chipmunks etc. Oven birds T' ruff, titmouse, turkey, woodpecker etc. among the birds and amphibians, insects, reptiles of various kinds are also found in these region of brown forest soil.

The Northern Coniferous forest lying even to further north or south of temperate zones and reaching the arctic zones are much colder than it, (between 50* and 60*latitude) primarily consists of the flora species of spruces, pines, hemlocks etc., whereas the ground cover is of the species of mosses, grasses, sedges and condition-adapted herbs. The fauna consists of snowshoe hare, lynx, squirrel, marten, mink, fisher, wolverine, wolf, woodland caribou, deer etc. These zones are primarily in existence in the Siberian region in Russia and in the northern part of North America and in Canada.

The grassland B community covers vast stretches in middle part of North America, whereas Savannas are grassland growing in such tropical regions as are Australia, South America and Asia. Great varieties of grass, such aslittle bluestem, switch grass and Indian grass(falling into tall grass variety), feather grass, brome grass(medium), and buffalo grass, blue grass, blue grama or mosquito (short grass), are found in the Prairy region of North America, besides variety of legumes, lupine and trefoil etc. The regular rainfall in these regions is about10 to 30 inches per year, unlike that of the savanna, which has average rainfall of more than180 cm. per year. The mostly laterite soil of this region produces variety of fauna indigenous to the type of soil. Regarding the importance of grassland on earth, authors U. Kumar and Mahendera Jeet Asija express in the following way, _ "The significant of grassland has been well realized for the productive capacity. Grassland ecosystems are also expected to play crucial role in the bio-spheric responses to climatic change and in augmenting vegetation in forests facing plunder."[3]

3.2. Subjective Approach to Environment
NATURE'S IMPACT ON HUMAN MIND

Man along with his civilization has grown up in the cradle of nature. Nature with its symmetry, co ordination of its various elements and their alignment has influenced man much aesthetically besides arousing sentiments of reverence for it usually expressed towards motherhood, the sentient of love and care. However, man's feeling for it beside its aesthetical impressions on his mind has been manifested in his day to day activities besides in the expression of his artistic interpretation. In a way it is the primary motivating force in his expression of imitation and portrayal of its various aspects as a mark of his admiration for it. The reason for the same has been explained by W.R. Sorley in the following manner, _ "But man is himself a part of nature, an instrument in the hands of providence."[4]

3.2.1 Old bond of mutual understanding and reverence between man and Nature

We have come to learn about our surroundings as Nature since our childhood days and we have been identifying the trees, animals, birds and all other creatures as part of the same nature. Nature being man' first encounter with outside world, therefore, has deeply influenced man's psyche, and therefore has expressed his own interpretation of it (i.e. Nature) mutely in manifold ways in all his cultural and artistic works. It has been happening since the beginning of human civilization, and it is true of all the tribal and non tribal, small and big racial groups in the world. However, since the beginning of scientific i.e. modern era beginning from around middle of sixteenth century, man has also started studying nature on scientific basis and such scientific study of it has been called as Ecology. Besides, in the modern era its study has become much more extensive and it is called as Environment as a whole. As well, there had come out many philosophers in the modern era, who had brought out many philosophical theories about Environment too. So we shall be discussing about the philosophical theories including the Ethics being related to it. First Nature's impact on human mind is going to be focused as part of analyzing nature's influence on human psychology only. To explain nature's impact on human mind author Stephan Budiansky says,_ 'Over time this (of perfectness) conception of nature has answered a variety of aesthetic, spiritual, ideological and even nationalistic Urges."[5] Also, authors Maarten Hajer and Frank Fischer have expressed their view on bonding between man and nature in the following manner,-"In so far, as mutual help and solidarity have been basic prerequisite of human existence for ten of thousands of years, a rediscovery of respect for and care of the particularities of both nature and cultures can provide us with a way to learn together with nature in particular circumstances."[6]Again they have expressed – "Through archaeological evidence of prehistoric hunter gathering societies that depicts long eras in which human kind lived relatively harmonious with nature..."[7]

3.2.2. *The Manifestation of Nature through Culture, Art and Literature*

The Immensity of Nature's opulence has always been influencing man's mind since the beginning of human civilization. In his finer way, man has been trying to express his adulation of nature in his creative ways- whether through picturization and by painting them or through poetry or literature, or even by song, dance and music.

Literature has always been a very powerful medium of aesthetic expression and eulogy for nature. We find all the great litterateurs of the world were never beyond the bond of nature, although they also wrote the elucidation on the intricate values of the capricious human mind. We find the great poet and dramatist of English language, Shakespeare the great eluding nature in the following way in one of his sonnets_

"Under the green wood tree,
Who loves to lie with me?"

Again, in the great Literature of Sanskrit, written by the great dramatist Kalidas, in one of his renown books 'Abhigyanam Sakuntalam', he had described how painful it was for Sakuntala, who was on her way to meet her beloved Dusmyanta to leave behind the trees, the pea fowls, the little deer and many more things of nature, while they also felt deprived of her love at her departure.

Art too have been a very mutative way of expressing and besides literature, we find nature portrayed in songs, drama, music, dance and in particularly in arts of painting and drawing as well. Most Indian Classical dances describe nature in manifold ways. Many of The Indian classical songs too are named after different stages of daytime, while in the west classical belle dance portrays nature or natural objects and many of the artistes have been drawing and painting pictures of nature in upteem manners. Even the reknown picture of lady Giokonda, called as Monalisa by one of the greatest artists on earth Leonardo da Vinci could not escape the portrayal of nature that it was on its backdrop.

3.2.3. _Emancipation of Nature in Spirituality and Religion_

When these are acts of creative mind, there have been other muter ways to express the hilarious function of nature. Perhaps there is no culture in the world, whether tribal or non tribal, whether known ones or the established and developed ones or simply that of relatively or remotely known groups of them, which do not have their own ways of expressing their adulation and fancy for nature in manifold manners in objects of and actions in day to day activities. In precise, it is the individualistic cultural expressions of portraying and personifying nature by each of the individual groups in its individual ways.

Nature has also highly been focused in religions, especially in ancient ones like Hinduism of India or Taoism of China. Even in ancient times, nature took very important place in the mind of primitive people. Considered now a days as 'fetish' kind of worshipping, in such practice primitive people would revere and start worshipping objects of nature that may look like a human being believing it to be a kind of demi-god or that it brings luck or fortune for some individuals. However, in modern era we still find 'forest festival' being celebrated in many places in the world in different forms since ancient time. While some communities in Europe celebrate 'forest festival', a form of nature worshipping usually observed by consecrating the trees. Similar festivities are also celebrated in almost all the places in the world by different communities in the world - some celebrate as spring festival as in India, so some do for other four seasons in the world.

However, nature's influence is also noteworthy in cases of some of the most ancient and prominent religions in the world. We find nature taking a very important role in the context of Hinduism. We find that nature has been an aspect of Hinduism, which has pervaded almost every context of it. We find that in Veda, the earliest scripture of Hinduism, it has been dictated that the day should be initiated with prayer for Usha, the Goddess of morning.

Thus, we find that Hinduism, in its expression of pluralistic view, has associated all of its Gods and Goddesses with nature or natural objects, each one being accompanied by a particular one or more than one species of flora and fauna, especially animals. Surya, or Sun is represented by eight horses, whereas Saraswati, the goddess of learning is accompanied by a swan, Laksmi the goddess of wealth accompanied by an owl etc. We can even witness the culuralistic expression of religious influence on various activities or work of art. The traditional religious symbols of a pot, adorned with mango leaves considered sacred, atopped with the design of a fruit also considered sacred can be seen as the mandatory pattern in most of the pillars of architecture of temples or at the top of the temples themselves. Banana leaves, kinds of grass, flowers, basil (tulsi) and oregano (drona) leaves, sesame seeds, rice etc. are objects believed to be conduits of objective world on earth and the abstract world of heaven and therefore used for worshipping purposes. Thus we find many other symbolic representations of nature in Hinduism deifying nature and thereby giving it a reverential position. We can also discover similar influence of nature on Chinese religions although in different form. However, both Taoism and Confusianism of China emphasize on nature somewhat differently than Hinduism. Not only they define nature in terms of different forces, they also believe them to be implied with goodness or otherwise. Regarding the close association of oriental religions with nature, author Carolyn Egri reiterates that,-"even so, there are many ways that nature –centered spiritual traditions, Asian religions and philosophies and monotheistic religions have informed and influenced socio religious relationships."[8] Again on overall view and assessment of prominent world religions and their primary motives, she expresses,- "While not totally abandoning their anthropocentric world view, mainstream religions are endeavoring to create a theology which advances the 'integrity of creation' for both environmental and social justice."[9]

3.2.4. *Cultural Adaptation of Man and His Relation with nature* :
1. With the change of time many factors in man's life do change and culture is one of them. Man adapts his cultural views in accordance with the necessity of time. However, nature is another factor which is otherwise an eternal genre for mankind, but susceptible to the peculiar

ethical derivatives from which man draws either inspiration or intimidation. However, influence of nature on the mind of a man is directly related to his culture and it is conspicuous by its absence or presence by the expression of culture itself. Therefore, although culture and nature, two different genres in man's life, they are inter-related and according to some scholars, culture is related to the 'disorder' of nature that occurs time and on to help 'creation'. Believing that 'disorder' is a force to be utilized, the raw material for creativity, "The study of the nature and the role of disorder in biology and in cultural evolution would do much to help interpret the supposed conflict between 'humanism' and 'science'…..",_so says Mr. Van Renaesselar Potter[*10]. However, disorder occurs due to the necessity of creation, as some philosophers believe in and it is the 'fortuitous' occasions that allow such creation to take place, bringing in the possibility of survival. Again, adaptation is another process by which living organism has to survive on earth. The organism has to adapt to the natural surrounding by adjusting to not only the natural condition but also by becoming more morphologically conditioned to such a situation.

However, in the long route of evolution, we can witness the same pattern happening in various other areas related to mankind. It may be found that all activities of man are conditioned to change and his culture is equally conditioned to change and therefore, over a period of time to evolution of it as well. Therefore we can witness change in cultural modes reflecting the social modes or contemporary beliefs and influence of the thinking and psychology.

While discussing cultural evolution in the light of 'adaptation', we have to keep in mind that the present cultural condition also reflects the present day mental set up and influence of our surrounding. From our observation, with regular and the opulent usage of materials like plastic and presence of other chemicals and artificial commodities in our day to day life, we can surmise the increasing influence of technology and less of nature in overall lives of ours. Besides lack of any 'natural' interpretation in the cultural expression in present day society affirms such prevailing conditions only.

The question is -is it also a disorderly condition of cultural evolution as in cases of other areas of human evolution? Even if it is so, it can be hoped that newer cultural creations depicting nature and reflecting 'natural values' will come to prevail in man's life indicating nature's re-induction in man's life.

3.2.5. *Nature in philosophical Definition*

It is not surprising that scholars since the early civilization days were wonder-struck at the diversity_of 'Nature' and the manifold activities of it that use to be going on at the same time. For example, Nature would feed its inhabitants with its aplenty and then again destruct them with her crude hand in time. Abundance of flora and fauna and exuberance of life in forest or dazzling crops may be destroyed with flurry of flood in the next moment. Again small creatures like birds or bates will be fed on by the fruits of trees. Yet again they would be devoured by some bigger animals at the next opportune moment they get to survive in the wilderness. The 'nature's lovers seems to have discovered some pattern in such activities of nature. Many of them believe there must be existing certain invisible forces that are per-forcing its rule to keep nature in particular and the earth in general in moving. Even at ancient time primitive people also believed the invincible forces of nature as Wrath of super-natural forces. However, in relatively modern era, some scholars have tried to put some scientific effort in explaining in the pattern of nature occurring at random and will and letting it continue at the same time. They have discovered many theories in trying to discover and establish explanation that may hold consistent with its 'nature' and its ways.

(A)NATURALISM

When a lot of studies has been carried out on basis of Nature and Nature's ways since time immemorial, it was only at the end of medieval era and prior to the advent of modern time that philosophers started emphasizing on finding a method in what seems to be mayhem order in 'nature'-its mayhem ness resulting into a saggy and distorted picture in which common people fail to find any order. Even in ancient Greece, when Stoic philosophers emphasized on following Nature's ways-that is live a simple life within the bound of Nature rather than by destructing it for one's own comfort, they dictated it more out of reverence for nature than to look for any integrity in its occurrences. However, as scientific inventions started taking roots in medieval Europe, philosophers started looking for certain order in it, more of scientific in nature than being spiritualistic in candor. Some philosophers tried to define it in terms of 'Noumenon' and 'Phenomenon', but it hardly could separate or define it in spiritualistic nature.

However, Naturalism as a subject seems to be void of any subjective approach_ i.e., any metaphysical or spiritualistic approach and is rather based on materialistic desecration for which it is quite often either equated or confused with materialism.

Therefore although it may be studied theoretically of its various characteristics, it primarily relates to various materialistic characteristics rather than with any spiritualistic contents.

(B)Nature's Definition in Ambiguity: G.E. Moore's Naturalism and Natural Fallacy

However, such nature loving scholars were not without competition or counter agencies who tried to deign their 'love of nature' and put it as substances of subsidiary importance to human life. They would not try to find a 'soul' in nature and explain it in terms of human utility only. There are many scholars who vouchafed their opinion opposing the importance of nature or our environment. The great scholar G. E. Moore is one of them. However, the irony lies in the fact that it is G.E. Moore himself is the scholar who brought the 'coined' word of Naturalism into practice and who brought in the discussion of Ethics in its limelight. However, his views and opinions remain a matter of controversial debate among the contemporary and of later period philosophers.

(C)G. E. Moore's definition of Nature and Material Universe

We may learn about his opinion in the following passages:-

"WHAT IS MEANT BY "NATURE"?

What is meant by Nature; & what has philosophy to do with it -what kind of questions about Nature are philosophical, as opposed to scientific, questions.

This term "Nature", with a capital "N", is constantly used in philosophy, as elsewhere, as if we all understood what it meant; but I think it's important for philosophy to attempt to define it.

Again he says in the following ways:-

"What do we mean by "the material universe"?

Let's consider the matter in this way:

There are two prima facie different types of entity, which we certainly consider as forming part of, or included in, the material universe. I mean: physical things & physical events. I mean by "things" what Johnson calls "continuants" & whitehead physical objects. The sun, the earth & planets, the stars nebulae etc. certainly form part of the material universe.

Can we then say that by the material universe we mean the sum of all physical continuants past, present & future, & all physical; events past, present

& future? All these are included in it: can we say it is their sum, or the class of which they're all members?

The first thing I want to say is that though, in a sense, I think we can, yet another sense, & perhaps the most obvious one, I think we certainly cannot.

Both by physical things & by physical events, one thing we mean, is the things and events of a certain character or quality: & the first thing I want to emphasise is that, if we mean this, we can't say that the material universe means the sum of all such things, because there may be parts of such things which don't belong to the physical universe at all.

This is a point which I'm afraid some philosophers might deny, but which seems to me quite clear, & a point that certainly should be considered in philosophy.

Why I say it is this.

When we talk of the material universe, I think it's quite plain we always really mean this material universe: the material universe, for instance, to which the sun & the earth belong. And this material universe does not include necessarily all material things, but only those which have or had or will have a certain positive real relation _ not merely a relation in respect of resemblance - to the sun, or any other object belonging to it which we pick out. You may say the material universe is a unity constituted by the fact that not merely all the things within it are of a certain sort, but that there's a certain real relation which holds between any 2 of them.

Now there may be, so far as I can see, ever so many continuants which resemble physical continuants, & are in that sense physical continuants, & yet haven't got this relation to the sun say. I think we certainly don't know that there are any; but it is logically possible that there should be; & to say this is to say we can't define the material universe simply as the sum of all physical things & events; but only as the sum of all those which have a certain relation to this physical event. This is one reason why Nature certainly isn't identical with the whole Universe.[11]

From the above paragraphs alluded from G.E. Moore's views on nature and his other write up on 'Nature and naturalism give us the notion of the Natural fallacy he propagated against the former. However, as we can already derive upon his antipathy towards the views of Naturalism, which he coined only as a form and looked at as an alternative of Utilitarianism, his views are often looked at critically in the present day context of natural travesties. His contravening attitude towards Nature can be well coined as 'Natural Fallacy' rather than any appreciation of Nature and Natural ways.

In the process it is also very important to take into account the views of Mr. Moore's as it seems to fill up, even in his proverbial critical manner, the gap between ethical values and nature's ways. We may encounter his views in the following manner:-

It is undoubtedly a question of time when the impact of environmental degradation leading to destruction of it will be evident in all spheres of our life. However more than anything else what would be the most revealing facets of our life is the failure of man's ethical values. Man's moral values in particular and ethical outlook have experienced a great beating at the hand of the degraded environmental conditions around us, which had since the time immemorial been consistent with each other in their mutual relationship. Ethics has shown great respects for the rules of Nature, although all the postulates, views and values followed and propounded by Ethics necessarily do not confine to the natural values only. Still the bond between the two had been unique in the history of mankind as man's values i.e. ethics has till the advent of modern days has struck balance with Nature's influence on man, so as never to outdo or outperform the latter's unseen bound on man's values and capabilities. However, reviewing the current trend of values man has been following (as ethics in general reflects the contemporary views and values of common people only and not vise versa, rather than direct and predestine it in most cases, although certain cultures still insist on following the hardbound age old rules of ethics that were set long time back and safeguarded by themselves), it seems the Ethics of modern days man nurtures and espouses has out-stepped its bound of respect for Nature and had shown inclination for its destruction for man's own benefits.

However, as it has been mentioned earlier, man's relationship with Nature had not been as relegating as has been witnessed in the twentieth century and early twenty first. In fact as has been already discussed, man has even derived the basic tenets of its ethics from nature, which had directed him not only to revere it but also to derive inspiration and moral ground to establish the progress of his civilization from the lessons he learns from nature only. However, while walking on the path of civilization, something had gone awry, as man seems to have forgotten his chosen ways and taken to shorter routes to appease his thirst for quicker and faster comforts to achieve the glory of his 'achievement', forgetting in the process the eternal companionship of nature which has uplifted him to reach the podium of success in the path of glorious civilization.

In fact, since time immemorial, Nature has not only helped mankind, but it has been so much of an integral part of life and being indispensable in every sphere of life that it has dominated the human psyche in every possible way of expression. The art and culture of many a human races, the epitome of refinement of a developed and progressive human mind directly or indirectly expresses the influence of Nature of its manifold expressions on human mind only. Literature, the apostle of human knowledge and the earmark for the development of human psychology, has been practically littered with description of Nature. In fact it has been considered also in many developed society as the yardstick of a developed culture and literature. Even many a religions, if not all of them and especially Hinduism has been so much inclusive of Nature that it includes almost every characteristic genre and facets of Nature in its reverential podium. In fact even spirituality, which is believed to beyond the reach of nature or to transcend it, has also been defined in terms of Nature in many a lineages of it only. Therefore Nature's impact on the philosophical ideas of human mind has been carried in the following manner-

We are wonder-struck at the diversity_of 'Nature' and the manifold activities that were going on at the same time. For example, Nature would feed its inhabitants with its aplenty and then again destruct them with her crude hand in time. Abundance of flora and fauna and exuberance of life in forest or dazzling crops may be destroyed with fury of flood in the next moment. Again small animals like birds or bates will be fed by the fruits of trees. Yet again they would be devoured by some bigger animals at the next opportune moment they get to survive in the wilderness. The 'nature' lovers seem to have discovered some pattern in such activities of nature. Many of them believed there must be existing certain invisible force that is per forcing its rule to keep nature in particular and the earth in general in moving. Even at ancient time primitive people also believed the invincible forces of nature as Wrath of super-natural forces_ some even believing them to be God or demigods whom they needed to appease with whatever they could afford. However, in relatively modern era, some scholars have tried to put some scientific effort in explaining in the pattern of nature occurring at random and will and letting it continue at the same time. They have discovered many theories in trying to discover and establish explanation that may hold consistent with its 'nature' and ways.

(D)Nature's Definition in History

However, such nature-loving scholars were not without competition or counter agencies who tried to deign their 'love of nature' and put it as substance of secondary importance to human life. They would not try to find a 'soul' in nature and explain it in terms of human utility only. There are many scholars who vouchafed their opinion opposing the importance of nature or our environment. Time and on, thus the intellectualism of man has been trying to belittle the importance of the nature or its role in our lives, whereas some others, due to their vigil on moral ethics of man have realized the follies of mankind and has tried to reestablish Nature's importance by redefining the Nature around them. Some of such theories are as per below:-

1. Helizoism

Helizoism is believed to be the first attempt on part of Greek philosophers to bring forth the Nature's position in human civilization to the podium of philosophy, so that it can assert its position of roosting the rule of the material world outside our mind. However, it seemed to lack the Abstraction that dominates such implied metaphysicality of any such theories that are believed to be primary cause of the inner or mental forces of the universe. It is unlike the views of Stoics (earlier the Cynics) which spiritualized the presence of Nature in Human life and tried to follow nature's ways rather than utilizing nature for fulfilling one's own necessities.

2. Natural Philosophy:- It is an even more stringently view of
nature if it is considered from subjective point of view; it studies and analyses nature in terms of 'physical' laws and relations and analyses its effect and repercussions on various natural objects. It lacks in any abstract qualifications and therefore is without any idealism. It can be called a form of materialism. Natural Philosophy has been defined by author Peter Simpson in the following way_ "The concern of Natural Philosophy is the world of immediate perception, and the things that directly confront such perception."[*12] That perception is basis of the verificational methods based on scientific enquiries, we can conjecture Natural Philosophy to be more of a scientific approach to the question 'What is Nature' than to be any spiritual explanation. Again we find the author to opinionate in the following way, _ "The study of natural things is consequently a study of things that are marked in their being by a certain more or less distinctive dynamism- it is a study of dynamic things. In a way we can say that its explanation amounts to finding the law of change or motion in matter or natural objects." [*13]

3. Naturology :- Naturology emphasizes on various natural qualities and therefore it also emphasizes on natural laws. It is more of a normative study of philosophy as it professes the 'good' of nature. However, it also fails to metamorphose to any kind philosophical ideas, as it does not relate to any kind of metaphysical explanation.

4. Meliorism: - "Meliorism, stated in most general terms, means that doctrine which believes in the betterment of life and universe in their ethical, social and religious aspects."[*14] Thus has been said about the ideology by the author H. P. Bhattacharya on its views and values on life. It is also believed to be associated with the value factor, which is realized more and more 'progressively', and which actually lies heeded in the mind of an individual. Also normative in nature, Meliorism is a way of life based on certain idealistic conceptions related to nature, rather than being any lineage of philosophy. It is founded by a French person by the namesake i.e. Melior. Mohandas Karamchand Gandhi, reverently called Mahatma Gandhi and considered the father of Indian nation as he guided the country to attain independence and also propounder of non-violence as an application method of politics, was a stout follower of Meliorism.

Meliorism also emphasizes on pragmatic approach to life. Meliorism supports the usage of natural objects or to live in natural ways without using any artificial or chemical materials.

Precisely we can call Meliorism as spiritual enlightenment, which upholds the values of our life in a higher podium, believing its higher application with higher status quo of mind attained through stringent practice of restraint, compounded with simplicity.

3.3.1. *Materialism, Evolutionism and Natural Selection*

A gamut of new conceptions to define nature took root among philosophical ideas of late eighteenth century in western world, as they tried to establish new ideas based on materialistic identities against the overall metaphysical entity of earlier and contemporary philosophy. Attempts were made to base such conceptions on materialistically verified notions, in which natural objects are made representatives of realism in a world void of any metaphysical reality.

(A) *Materialism*: - Materialism is a philosophical trend taking root in the late eighteenth century, as western philosophers had turned to finding realistic explanations to the causes of events on earth, rather than the conventional metaphysical ones. Naturalism, a prelude to materialism, though believes in natural forces, or even unseen order manipulating the forces, it does not profess any metaphysical power at the helm of it. Materialism can be called even more of a stringent view in comparison to the formers in respect of its scientific base for the study of nature, which negates any presence of esoteric force in nature.

(B) Evolutionism and Natural Selection

One of the latest theories relating to natural laws is the Theory of Evolution professed by Charles Darwin in the middle of nineteenth century. However, Darwin was not the first scholar to define 'Evolution', since there were quite a few of them defining it from different perspectives. Besides his theory of evolution projected from the point of origin of species, there are others who look at from other point of views__ Herbert Spencer and Jean Baptiste Lamarck defined it from mechanical and biological point of views respectively, whereas James Martineau defined it in teleological perspective, which advocates 'intelligent' adaptation of organism emphasizing on adaptation to means to the needs of 'ends.' There was also another definition called 'Emergent evolution', which emphasizes that the world constitutes of the constant emergents of newer -on species.

In the perspective of creation or origin of species, the theory of origin of species dates back to the 'Genesis' of testament, where it is defined that species including human beings and each one individually are believed to be created by God himself. It does not believe in the process of evolution. There had been other theories following since then. Hegel in the early modern era, was one of the earliest to do so, although he looked at it from metaphysical point of views. Again, there are others who touch upon the evolution of different genres of philosophies. For example, some of the scholars had defined the evolution of ethics, whereas some others have even talked about cultural evolution they believe to be connected with human development. Lamarck, Spencer etc. are some such scholars relating to it in different ways. Then, there is the theory called 'Abeogenesis' which emphasizes that life was originally born from lifeless matters. However, Darwin's theory defining human evolution in terms of 'Origin of species' is believed to be most authentic, as it is not only based on scientific verifications, but also the most 'conceivable' in its approach to reality. According to Darwin, who wrote two books of immense anthro-philosophical importance, first 'Origin of Species' and then 'Descent of Man', species on earth are the result of the natural process of evolution and it produces varieties of species with the process of Fortuitous (incidental) or Spontaneous variations. In such variations, species 'by chance' due to metabolical reasons of their protoplasmic cells cause changes or variations of themselves, some of which are favorable to their natural surroundings whereas others are not. When the favorable ones succeed in surviving in harsh conditions, the other ones fails to do so. It is the process which is called Natural Selection and thus species survive on earth to further the cause of evolution. Their metabolism again helps them in adapting to the natural surrounding with physical variations.

While explaining the various earmarks of the 'evolution' theory, Darwin emphasized on the fact that the metamorphosis taking place among the species that causes 'fortuious'ly, does occur from 'within' them, i.e. genetically, rather than the 'without' i.e. outside influence of nature. Such a process is called 'mutation' which helps in causing disorder in the orderly process so that newer type of creation may occur for the development of better species to achieve the goal of perfect 'order'.

The process happened per chance per species, which again is an inherited factor and may occur at an opportune moment over a period of time.

However, philosophers like Jean Baptiste Lamark's view differs from Darwin's in such respect and believes that metamorphological change in species happens more due to the 'outside' influence than due to inherited factors.

3.3.2. *Critical Analysis of the Theory of Evolution from naturalistic Point of View.*

Some scholars name it as 'Chaos'. However, why is there a 'disorder' or 'chaos' condition of nature? Scholar Renaesellar Von Potter defines it in the following way,_ "The survival of the fittest was a brutal process for using the raw material or disorder to achieve order, but it served a noble purpose in selecting new and better species, which were widely understood to arise on a continuing basis."[*15]

However 'Chaos' as a form of disorder has been prevalent in Western philosophy since pre Socratic days of the Greek Civilizasation. Philosopher like Heraclitus explained that the universe, an orderly system did originate from 'chaos' i.e. disorder. The philosophy of Christian religion followed the same belief, believing it is the personalized form of God who created the universe and its inhabitants,- including mankind, one by one, created the universe from the state of 'chaos' to an orderly system.

From the various theories it can be surmised that the general belief that the process of 'disorder' or 'chaos' must is part and parcel of the 'evolutionary process' and it is in fact beneficiary to the organic kingdom in spite of the initial confusion or destruction it causes. But to find out the purpose of it or what is it's justification of its occurrence can best be explained in the following words of the Indian scholar Jadunath Sinha from the point of view of 'determination' doctrine, _ "What then is the differentiating mark of evolution as distinguished from dissolution? We must add the further characteristics of determination, which distinguishes evolution from dissolution. Evolution is an advance from confusion to order- from an indefinite and indeterminate arrangement to a definite and determinate arrangement, - from an incoherent to a coherent condition. Evolution is a transition from a chaos to a cosmos, while dissolution is, from cosmos to chaos. Evolution is an onward movement of progress, while dissolution is a downward movement of regress."[*16]

3.4. NATURE AS DEFINED BY INDIAN PHILOSOPHY

The 'Natural context' of Indian Philosophy, with or without the context of Ethical conformity, is very vast and influential besides being an integral part of it. In certain trait of Philosophy even its metaphysical ideas are derived from and depend upon Nature and Nature's intricacy and characteristics too. There are quite a few lineages of Indian Philosophy that purport the Nature's delineation over human life. While equating such trend and comparing them with their parallels in western Philosophy, it may range right from materialism to relativity of physical science to metaphysical origins of Nature in similitude. However, in Indian philosophy, in whatever manner nature is approached, it certainly personifies the quest for the metaphysical truth behind them all. Even in Vedantic philosophy, which is a metaphysical based trait of philosophy only, it has described Nature as the primary illusion on earth, which contributes to the ignorance of human mind from knowing the eternal reality. Even then it fails to escape the bond of nature when it calls the universe to be part of nihilism _an indirect admission to the existence of Nature. In reality, mind or soul transcends natural existence or 'reality' only -it believes. Thus we find that nature is always an integral part of Indian philosophy that propagates subjectivity of reality or the ultimate truth only.

However, what we are emphasizing regarding Indian Philosophy vis a vis nature is the ubiquitous presence of the latter in all the spheres of its reckoning. Even, it seems nature's Flora and Fauna are an integral part of Indian religion and heritage. We find many an animals deified either as God or as the companion of any of Gods and Goddesses of Indian heritage. We find a swan to be the companion of Goddess Saraswati, whereas Lord Ganesh is an incarnated form of an elephant God. An owl is Goddess Lakshmi's 'natural' vehicle, whereas a lion is considered as Goddess Durga's carrier. The animals whether as the incarnated form of God or as the celestial vehicles of the immortal ones, were invariably also prayed.

However, the approach to nature in the philosophical lineages is far more pragmatic, trying to define it in certain qualifying manner. But each lineage had followed its own course of individual version and define it accordingly which we can view from different perspectives.

Among the different lineages of Indian philosophy, the ones which have mostly personified nature into the criteria of its 'standard' and 'judgment', mainly are,_ Sankhya system of Sankhya-Yoga, Vaisesika of Nyaya- vaisesika and to some extent the Vedanta Philosophy. However, Veda the combination of four books of Hindu religiosity of highest order, also portrays nature with optimum amount of reverence for its multitudinousness, has set the trend of making nature into an indispensably integral part of Hindu thinking.

1. The Vedas

The Vedas are the original scriptures of Hinduism and date back to the period of early Aryan time. Although without the complexity of philosophical ideas of later Hinduistic period, it has personified nature in a very reverential position. The religio-ethical script has identified most of its protagonist-Gods with various elements of nature and dictates greater devotion to them to its followers for prosperity and posterity of the society. According to the explanation given in its hymns, man should give away various sacred objects to the various elements in a symbolic manner, so that the sacrifices of the great ancestors of mankind come to be fruitful in manner. In reverence, a devotee should pray all the elements of nature in high esteem right from morning till the end of the day. A person should adulate Usha, or dawn, who breaks the day for the living beings on earth. Then one must pray and worship the Sun, one of the most reverential God in Veda as he gives us sunlight to live on earth. There are certain other smaller objects of nature which are considered sacred, such as certain types of fruits, flower, leaves etc.

2. Sankhya Philosophy

In Sankhya philosophy, all the conceptions and the subjective conclusions have been brought out on basis of Nature only. It believes in two primary characters or fore bearers of nature, which perforce the latter's activities and ensure that the 'system' or the 'process' of it would continue forever in an undeterred manner. However, it has also attributed qualities to certain abstract aspects of Nature, which it believes, dictate nature's ways. In Sankhya Philosophy, we find the emphasis put on both the subjectivity and objectivity of nature -Purusha representing manhood and therefore subjectivity, whereas Prakriti or womanhood represents objectivity or Nature itself. Purusha is born out of Aham or 'Self'. According to it, our mind has three states that are the roots of its equilibrium _ Satta, that is purity of mind and speaks for simplified ways and life consummated with higher ideals of it, Rajah- a thinking mode that perforces the ideas of living opulently, indulging in good food or high living style with less concentration on high ideals or value but within a limit whereas Tamah is the state of mind that encourages all the negative approaches of life, to indulge in or be influenced by wrongful activities.

On the other hand, Prakriti is or Nature is the 'illusion' which time and on allures the mind for the purpose of procreation. After its goal achieved, Prakriti goes back to its day to day activities. Thus the whole of nature keep moving on its eternal process of 'Recreation and Pause.'

3. Vaisesika

Baisesika is also another lineage of Indian philosophy, which explains the various characteristics of nature as its forte to arrive at its metaphysical conclusion. Vaisesika philosophy believes that the different phenomena of nature define our existence and phenomena like earth, water, air, fire and the sky represent various senses of feelings,_ smelling, taste, seeing, hearing and that of sixth sense. Nature is driven by a force which derives strength from the 'Anu'-that is atom of each material on earth. However, Vaisesika's interpretation of nature in overall manner, with its attempt of making of scientific approach, can be attributed as of objective perspective only.

4. Advaita Vedanta

As in Sankhya philosophy, in Advaita Vedanta also we can find nature playing a relative role to arrive at the ultimate truth of metaphysical reality. However, unlike in Sankhya philosophy, nature does not portray a protagonistic role, but a relative one in which it is relegated as a tool to the attainment of the ultimate reality in form of the greater soul (Paramatma). Unlike in Sankhya Philosophy, 'Prakriti' i.e. nature would not entice 'Purusha' to keep the creation on earth in continuation, it is known as 'Maya' and representative of ignorance, in its illusory form and power keeps the mind away from the ultimate reality. Here in Advaita Vedanta, metaphysical entity has taken over the nature's novelty to make it a very conditional existence to greater truth.

According to its definition, Prakriti is Maya, i.e. illusion and it keeps human mind with its mesmerizing power from true knowledge of his own identity, which is in reality a part of a greater reality or truth only.

From the given role of nature in the Advaita philosophy, we may surmise that while pursuing the metaphysical truth of reality, nature seems to have relative role which is rather much insignificant in nature, and held in disdain than in esteem and which is unlike many other lineages or the ethico-religious perceptions of Indian philosophy. The reason can be attributed to the emphasis given on the subjective nature of the 'pursue' and not on the 'natural' characteristics of the 'reality'. However, it may reasonably concluded that Advaita Vedanta remains a philosophy which is void of any definition of nature at all because it has defined universe from subjective point of view nature has got a 'relative' role in it.

5. Gita

MadBhagawat Gita, the Ultimate book of Hinduism on man's morality, attitude and the ideal relationship with God has also related to nature, although somewhat in a 'relative' role same as can be found in Advaita Vedanta, if not in the same negating perspective. However, the words written in hymns conjured in the way of the 'supreme being', has expressed elements of nature as integral to its theme. The supreme God, as in the words of its author, has identified itself with the various elements of nature. However, he had identified them as perceptions of various facets of him only. The God, in the form of ultimate truth transcends in its various forms and ultimately is unified in the abstract reality of the universe.

In most of the religions in the world we can witness nature playing significant roles. However, it varies from religion to religion and one philosophy to another for what importance is attributed to the role of nature. In the Indian philosophy, we find nature and the natural elements being intermingled with religious ethical thinking. We find that almost every element in nature is worshipped in Hindu religion and thus has made it integral to its spiritual thinking. The Karma Vada of Indian thinking is closely connected to various layers of nature with separate ethical implications.

We can also witness nature's influence on Chinese philosophies too, although in different perspectives. Various natural forces are attributed with ethical qualities to purport benevolent atmosphere for the animal kingdom.

However, nature's role in the perspectives of western philosophy is different from the ones portrayed in oriental philosophies, particularly in the Indian philosophy. Here nature is spoken about in a singular perspective, when the creation of universe comes to the fore. In western philosophy, i.e. Byzantine philosophy, with which the various western religions relate to their origin, God is a personalized emancipation and nature and natural objects are his creation only and which are individual entities, not related to one another. The nature or natural objects are not attributed with any spiritual qualities unlike in most of the Indian or other oriental philosophies. Therefore, when it comes for comparison of eastern versus western philosophies on the ground of the nature's importance in each of them, Indian philosophy scores far ahead of its counterpart, as the presence of nature is ubiquitous in every aspect of it, whether in respect of spirituality or in the mere terms of defining it.

Like in other respect, nature and its various objects are attributed with spirituality as they are symbolic of certain level of sacredness. However, when it comes to its comparative study with western philosophy, certain characteristics of Indian philosophy in relation to nature strike similarity with unique keenness. For example, western philosophers of Naturalism believes in the 'relation' of natural objects, which asserts a 'natural law' existing bind them all by such 'relation'. Even in Mad Bagawat Gita of Hinduism, we can find similar definition in the word of Lord Krishna, the believed emancipation of God, who says that the world of different objects is bound to him 'like the pearl in a string' (Sutre Manigana Iba).

Again we find that nature has been given variant emphasis on its role in different Indian philosophies. However, in both Indian and western philosophies we find nature being used to define universe or its aspects. For example, when in Vaisesika philosophy we find definitions of human existence and his intelligence are centering around nature, then also in Sankhya philosophy it is ascribed with certain subjective qualities to define the evolutionary theory on earth. However, its role is more 'relative' in most of the metaphysically oriented philosophies. We find in Advaita Vedanta and also to some extent in the ethically defined Mad Bhagawat Gita the comparatively less important role of nature. More so, in Advaita Vedanta it is found nature to be in the ireful role of both in enticing impersonation in form of Maya i.e. illusion, as well as representing ignorance, which means it is being purportedly given a negative role to emphasise its triviality in man's life. However, it is not true in case all other philosophies, in fact some such as Sankhya or Vaisesika esteem nature highly to make it their pivotal theme philosophy.

We can find similar importance being ascribed to Leibniz's philosophy as in Vaisesika, where he had emphasized in 'atomism' as in the latter. Again, when we can define Patanjali's Sankhya philosophy to some extent with evolutionary theory of Darwin, although it is more with the conformity of metaphysical interpretation than with mechanical one, it also is similar to Hegel's metaphysical theory of evolution although it also draws similarity with Advaita Vedanta where the quest is for greater reality from the confined one by the soul. In Hegel's theory it is the believed to be 'greater truth'.

Thus, we can draw many other similarities between Indian philosophies and western philosophy where the seemingly resembling interpretations of nature are parallel development, although the only difference lies in chronological order, as, usually the branches of Indian philosophies precede those of western philosophies which were formulated mostly in medieval era by approximately thousand years since they were propagated either early in the beginning or in the middle of the first millennium.

3.5 MAN AND HIS RELATIONSHIP WITH NATURE: OBJECTIVE

Man's connection with nature is primarily pragmatic in nature and it precedes its subjective relationship with it. Man is set apart from other species because of his ability to utilize natural paraphernalia, and in spite of the other species being both part of it and live on the providence offered by it, are not endowed with the ability to utilize it beyond the bound demarcated by it due to their limitations they are provided with. Although some species of birds and mammals or even insects can create their own havens and niche' in form of nest, they cannot pervade beyond certain skills and therefore remain limited in their capacities. On the other hand man is not only endowed with variegated forms of skill, he can also adept it in accordance with necessities. However, the most important feature of his skill is that with the progress of time, not only man's ability to apply his intelligence along with his intelligence has increased, it has also developed into multifarious and multipurpose ability to create complex systems that are often equivalent in many respect, if not equal to that of nature. For example, at the height of his civilization, man can construct a dam with variety of materials that can resist even the most fearful river and its energy- accumulated water to turn it into electricity besides the provision of supplying water to previously drought prone areas. At the end of twentieth century, man is in a position to define his necessities and find solutions to it, whereas other species remain confounded by the laws of nature and therefore cannot act on their own beyond their limitations. Regarding the objective value of nature, author Holmes Rolston III expresses in the following way, _"But we will not be valuing Earth objectively until we appreciate this marvelous natural history. This really is a superb planet, the most valuable entity of all, because it is the entity able to produce all earthbound values."*17

Man's ability of utilizing nature's paraphernalia, however, is as old as human civilization and has developed into an 'industry', along with its development in history. It has increased manifold by the end of twentieth century from the nascent ability to create tools out of rocks at the beginning of human civilization. With the increase of his ability, the objects of utilities too increased manifold giving different hues and importance with landmark discoveries and inventions at various stages of time. For example, after discovering how to use iron and make iron tools and other accessories, man discovered copper and gave other interpretations to its utility. With every discovery man, however, reached another zenith of his civilization, culminating into the creation of conception of complex identities such as Urbanization and Industrialization towards the latest developmental stages of human civilization. Although both the stages of civilization have existed at different places wherever there was an early civilization, then it was confined to limited communities for stipulated time periods of history only. But it was never much universalized as at the end of twentieth century. Both the concepts have been initiated and based on the ideas of maximum utilization of natural commodities as never before. The progress of human civilization with the pragmatic utilization of natural objects is given below:-

3.5.1. *The Development of Civilization*
(A) Early Age
The development of civilization is significant from the objective perspective of man's relationship with nature, as the utilization of natural

objects had grown manifold and has taken turn to complexity with the growth of civilization too. Each stage of human civilization is intrinsically associated with particular type of natural object, which again helped it to develop into another stage. With each stage achieved, man's knowledge and skill of utilizing natural objects grew manifold, making the whole process a complex structure and an integral part of development of human society as a whole. The development culminated with the processes of urbanization and the industrialization and which are complementary to each other, in which the level of utilization of natural objects had reached maximum level. The various levels of human society and stages of civilization attained with the help of natural objects are shown below:-

1. *The Old Stone Age (Paleolithic)* :-At the beginning of civilization, man learnt first how to use stone to provide themselves with foray by killing preys of animals and birds with it. Later they learnt how to improve the condition of the stone, with help of another stone to shape and sharpen them and use them for better help and result in their effort to earn their living hood. Simultaneously, they also learnt how to produce fire with help of flint stone, make houses with dead leaves of wood, cover themselves up with them and even try their hand at artistic expression in leisure time. The drawings found on the walls of some caves are the testimony to such effort on their part. The psychological and physiological development of man during different stages of Stone Age is called as Neanderthal, Cro-Magnon etc. as they progressed on the path of development of civilization.

2. ***The Neolithic Age***:- After the stone age man has discovered iron and had learnt how to put them in many fold utilization. The stone tools for hunting and bowls for keeping food got replaced with the ones made of iron. They also started preparing many other objects such as protective shields and weapons for battles and wars with iron and use them extensively. It also helped them in constructing and having spacious niche` and also barrier for their own protection. At such a level of achievement they also learnt how to make boat and carry out riverine trade with other communities living elsewhere.

3. ***Chalcolithic or Copper age***: - After learning how to fabricate iron for tools and other purposes, another age came in which man discovered copper, another element for usage of various utility. It started around seven

thousand years ago i.e. five hundred millennium B.C. and at places lasted till 600 B.C. i.e. about two thousand and five hundred years ago.

4. In ***the Bronze Age***, man became able to use the bronze metal to make utensils and other utility objects. It started around six to five thousand years ago.

5. In ***the Iron Age*** man not only learn how to use iron and fabricate it, but also learnt how to use them for larger purpose of, battle, construction etc., helping in tremendous way in the materialistic achievements of the society. While mining bronze ore saw civilizations like Greek and Egyptian developed, Indian civilization was used with iron at the same time.

(B). Medieval Age

Medieval era of of civilization does not relate to historical divisions of different eras of time and cannot be confined to the conventional 'Medieval Age' belonging to approximately eighth to fifteenth century century A.D. but be considered from since the end of iron age till the end of the same period. The reason behind such consideration can be attributed with the synonimity of development world over and its contrasting mode of thinking with the modern era of history. It has witnessed sporadic development of civilizations but more in frequent manner towards its end world over, as the world became synonymous with various skills practiced by one and all, usurpation of new thinkings in the field of religions and philosophy beside exchange of them with one another. Civilizations such that of Babylon, Egypt etc. along with the ones of India and China in Asia strived time to time, thereby contributing to the source of knowledge in the world with their specific knowhow and skill in particular areas and inspiring the proceeding generations to utilize them in concrete manner in future. But in most cases, due to lack of proper communication methods, most of the knowledge of each individual civilization used to be confined to itself for long or took years or centuries to be conveyed to others. However, at the ending period of it, near around fourteenth and fifteenth century, European travelers, usurped with the notion of development and romance of 'Wonderlust' had ventured world over to gather knowledge, with their 'colonialistic attitude' only, had also succeeded in bringing down the last bastion of barriers of alienation and ignorance among different categories of civilization and thereby have tried to put the world on the track of newer thinking and their applications in the coming era which have come to be known as 'Modern Age' the world over.

(c) Development of Civilization : Modern Age

Although human kind has been experiencing the birth of civilizations and witnessing their development through ages since time immemorial, the rest of the world remained in slumber of ignorance and puerileness of prosperity; However, in the last few centuries, the world has come under the surveillance of scientific discoveries and inventions in western world, which have not only helped in co-ordinating various facets of life, but also had brought different nations into closer proximity through various means such as whether colonialism or inventions like electricity to telegraph and telephoning etc. The most important fact about such development in the last few centuries signifying the era as the 'modern' one is the applications of the concepts that have allowed areas of congregated population to be provided with such applied facilities or mass productions that allow even the common person to live in comparative comfort and luxury of life. Such utilitarian view of commodities had signaled a new phase for humanity with excess utilization of natural resources that has subsequently caused high deprecation of such resources and other impacts on various natural factors and conditions. The concepts of modern civilization which have created profound implications for human society are as follows:-

1. The Concept of Urbanisation

(i)*The Process of Urbanization* :- Process of urbanization has started early in the days of civilization, (specially among the ones that were much developed than their neighboring regions- such as India, China, Egypt) when certain section of the society, specially the privileged or royal acolytes chose to live in congregation for the convenience of functioning their activities.

Unlike in the village enclaves, the residences of the urban areas used to be in rows, the outlet for waste materials being canalled out by drain system and all the utility items necessary for day-to-day life being available in on e place i.e. in the market, unlike in the countryside where it has to be gathered and collected over a period of time. It helped the habitats of the urban areas not only in having easier movement and availability of goods, it also freed them from the cumbersome and tenuous life of its counterpart in country sides, besides helping them in defending themselves in groups against the aggressive invaders.

However, the process of 'Urbanization' has helped mankind on ascending the ladder of progress, at the same time allowing itself to be systematic, organized, acquiring strength for developmental activities. It is primarily the slackness, lack of foresight and non-application of rightful procedure that allows the fallout of the system to really effect environment in particular and mankind in general.

(ii) *The Nature of Urbanization*

There are certain factors or aspects which contain the system of urbanization to its mobility. The aspects are interlinked and supplementary to one another to make the system moving and running in a consistent manner. The aspects are together called 'Infra-Structure' on which the system of urbanization is depended upon. They are as follows:-

1. Habitat, 2. Transportation3. Recreation4. Consumption5. Disposition and
6. Control. Separate areas and inputs are engaged in the process for proper functioning of the system.

The 'Habitat areas within the Urban conclave are connected with the facilities for 'Transportation', and usually on and off separated by recreational i.e. (park, theatre place, stadium etc) facilities. The area for buying day- to-day life's necessities i.e. 'Market place' which is representative of 'Consumption' factor are usually found around the central location of the city. The city area i.e. the urban conclave is controlled by various man-powered administrative facilities which look after the 'running', functioning and maintenance of all the factors by collecting revenues and spending it for the latter.

However, it is only the objective approach to the functioning of the urban process. Environmentalists also consider the process of urbanization from the point of view of 'Energy consumed' and 'energy wasted.' The urban conclave being hub of activities by congregation of people is also the source of energy spent and utilized, as a result of which it produces waste in huge amount which is needed to be managed properly so as not to put the local ecology in disorder and imbalanced therefore degraded and being harmful for the surrounding environment. The relation of energy consumed and energy in waste is being depicted in proper way in the following manner:-

Energy Utilized Energy as Waste

Electricity, petroleum} _____ > Heat
Gas used in household,

Water being **used in}** _____ > Polluted Water
Household, public utility

The energy in used as a result of energy consumed needs to be handled in rightful manner so that with the help of modern technology, not only the used energy can be managed properly, but it also can reproduce energy again for further utility so that no amount of energy resources can go in waste. *After all, Energy in Waste is Energy Unused.*

However, ignorance towards proper utilization and lack of management on the part of administration may result in improper functioning of the infra-structural $ 1 system, thereby resulting in the process of contamination of environmental aspects of air, water and ground, besides the degradation of it.

2. *Industrialization* has taken root in the society specially in western world, way back in early nineteenth century when it has began to experience the joy and benefits of technological inventions, such as that of motor vehicles and electricity and radio signals etc. They have, along with the knowledge of utilizing them for

---

∃ Infra structure in an urban area means the basic facilities of habitation, water supply, transportation and other communication, along with educational, health, religious and other recreation facilities.

mankind's benefit also learned the necessity of using manpower and materials in an extensive manner, being oblivious of its repercussion both on human psyche and the natural surrounding. It also initiated the structural changes occurring into the society in a rapid manner, especially in the west. The society has become nuclear family oriented rather than the conglomerate of families that were encouraged by agricultural back ground. On the other hand, it also brought economic relief to a section of people who had experienced a kind of employment which could be ambiguous with an agriculture related life where economy depended much on the volatile nature of weather to insecurity and uncertainty in the future. The relatively small family life also encourages them to indulge in luxury and become utility oriented. However, the extensive usage of natural materials has made him not only dependable on the products made of natural objects along with being unaware of the destruction of natural flora and fauna, but also to be oblivious of the extra ordinary and fortuitous repercussion of it.

However, on the other hand, it has done tremendous boost to the development of mankind. Besides the luxurious commodities, it has also helped in technological achievement in the field of medicinal sciences and carries on 'mass' product to serve the common population. Therefore, the process of industrialization cannot be ignored or considered inadequate or redundant at one instant or go, but must be understood in terms of its pros and cons only. Rather than letting the 'waste' products of industries go into waste, which are again some input of another kind of energy only, must be utilized farther. Besides, the process of Industrialization, which allows the atmosphere to be polluted by the waste, must let the modification of technology take upper hand, so that old and outdated scientific apparatus cannot effect the environment any more.

The process of industrialization in terms of its factors and 'energy intake' and 'energy utilized' is shown in the following manner:-

(1)

Energy Required -------------------- _> **Energy Utilised**_

(2)

Pic: The process of Industrialization

(a). Resources and Renewable and Non renewable Energies

The natural commodities from which mankind derives benefits, are usually called the 'resource'. From resource man can derive 'energy' with which one can continue constructive activities or construct permanent features that may be utility oriented for one. Right from the wood cut from forest to coal or crude oil extracted from underground can be called as 'natural resources' that man has been utilizing either as commodities of utility or sources to provide with 'energy'. However, the most important feature about the natural resources is that while some of them are renewable i.e. which can be reproduced again, some of them are bound to be exhausted or tapered off from earth within a stipulated time period. Along with it, mankind can hope some more sources of energy being lost forever from earth. Coal as 'fuel' energy or crude oil as resource for petroleum used for automobile can be called as 'non renewable' energy, which we can be believed to be exhausted sooner or later from the earth.

b. *The Non Bio-degardable and Bio-degradable Objective Product:*
The way energy comes to be considered as a productive resource for industrialization process in form of renewable i.e. naturally refilled and non renewable i.e. which cannot be replaced anymore at its initiation, like wise the finished products at the end of it, meant for human utility, can also be considered either as absorbable to nature i.e. biodegradable- which results as natural to nature's process and therefore good, or as non biodegradable, i.e. non absorbable to natural condition, resulting as redundant on earth, and sometimes or more than often as nuisance or even dangerous to organic matters-living or non living ones. The technological processes of human science has allowed many natural elements or the combinations of more than one of them often turn into such composite substances that they become un-absorbable to natural conditions.

3. *Technological Achievement*

Besides the processes of urbanization and industrialization, man has also applied his technological knowledge for the utility for the purpose of human welfare. With the help of industrial process but not for the direct utility by man but for the whole community, man has used his knowledge for such activities as for establishing power station, mining ore, pumping out crude oil for various usage of transportation and other industrial production and even prepare rockets to go to the moon. Beside in the field of technology, man has also succeeded considerably in the arenas of medicine, biology and chemical industry. According to the scientific doctrine, the purpose of such activities is to provide mankind with material comfort by utilizing natural assets, which was not possible in the preceding eras and also to signify the progress of man's knowledge.

3.5.2. The Concept Of Management and Management of Environment

Management is a concept used in the process of both urbanization and industrialization for better functioning and smooth regulation of production respectively. It is a pragmatic concept for objective gain for achieving utmost result in the process. In larger sense administrative and the government of countries can also be called as individual management processes only. The concept of management, when used for environment can help in regulating the proper utilization of natural resources. Environmental management, however, unlike the concept of corporate management does not emphasize on the achieving the goal of maximum production of commodities. The management of environment is best complying when there is parity between resources and its utility. It is like

NaturalResources= Utility

It does not mean less or non utilization of natural resources either but proper and optimum level of utilization of both natural resources and its ancillary factors, ensuring in the process the lesser of the ill impact of the urban or industrial processes. For example, big cities and other urban areas usually are with the waste collection system that helps keep them in proper stead and free of pollutions. Preservation and conservation of natural resources also form part of environmental management only. The process of assessment is also a part of management concept. Likewise assessment of environment helps in monitoring the impact of industrial processes on the environment only.

3.5.3. *Environmental Assessment:*

is one of the management forms of application only. While in management practice it helps in asserting a situation, in environmental management it helps in finding the position of a subject or an objective issue relating to environment. In its objective approach, assessment can help finding the true condition of the impact of a particular material or subject on a place and its environment and thereby help in taking rightful measure in future. One of the most modern practice for finding or detecting the impact, that is the effect of any industry on its surrounding environment and making assessment of it is called the process of EIA- environmental

Impact Assessment. It is a science oriented and studious process which results in finding solution or reducing unwanted effect of any particular industry on its surrounding. However, then process fails to completely eradicate the influence of the polluting factors on environment. Presently, with the development of assessment process, there are other kinds of practice to find the impact of pollution on nature. ***Geomorphology*** is one of the latest scientific and technological methodology which, through the help of artificial satellites' positioning in earth's orbit can detect time and on the status of natural resources on earth.

3.6. *Critical Assessment of Man's Objective Perspective of Nature. (i.e. Environment)*

With the development of civilization, from its puerile stage in its early days few thousands years ago to present days at the end of second millennium A.D., man's utility of nature and natural resources also have grown proportionately, i.e. manifold than what used to be at the initial stages of it. However, the objective utility of nature, in stark contrast to its subjective influence on human kind, has ultimately bore grievous impact on society in the last two centuries by widespread destruction of nature, thereby giving rise to the crisis of various predicaments, _the crisis of conservation, crisis of development theories to ultimately moral crisis. According to modern ethicist Nigel Dower,_ "unlike other species man has always been on the exhaustive mode of resources since time immemorial,_ he has been used to exhausting forest, land and often of water resources too. But never had it been so widespread to bring earth on the threshold of exhausting marine biology. ......Environmental problems have existed in one form or others since time immemorial. Resources were used up, land became degraded, responses took place........... This can usefully sum up be summed up in the idea of global finiteness. The stem from the recognition of the combined and cumulative effects of what is happening everywhere.... And the fact that human practices in the latter half of the twentieth century are coming up against the limits imposed by the finiteness. This finiteness has always been there, of course, but it is now real constraint on human action."[*18]

Many other objective concept-oriented methods- such as management and assessment to keep in control the utilization of natural resources can only be partly helpful in bringing in the equilibrium or balance in nature and society if looked at the overall perspectives of present day status of environment. According to R. K. Turner and J.C. Powell, _"The multi-criteria evaluation technique has a number of clear limitations."[*19]. Again they express, _"Although the notion of an integrated and comprehensive residuals-impact assessment and management system, is intuitively appealing, there are conceptual and practical limits to it. The constraints are both practicable (i.e. the data and institutional resource demands) and philosophical..."*[20]

However, regarding the impact of both the subjective and objective perspectives of relationship between man and nature, scholar Carolyn Egri has expressed in the following manner-"The restoration of harmony or balance with nature can only achieved through subjective and objective understandings, as well as self- transformation in, all aspects of human existence –spiritual, intellectual, social and material."*[21]

___While making an Assessment of Man Environment Relationship we have found out that Man's relationship with nature is intrinsic and human society is an integral part of nature. However, unlike any other species on earth, man both eulogizes and utilizes nature, again both for his spiritual and materialistic gains. But in the subjective-objective relation with nature, man, over the centuries has developed inclinations more towards his objective relation than the subjective approach towards nature.___

While subjective relation helps in strengthening the bond between man and nature, resulting in a more positivistic attitude in the society, the objective perspective may tend to imprint society with a negativistic attitude towards nature, as in such a relation, man tend to take upper hand and use nature, making it ineffective in absence of the mutual bonding.

However, the most important out come of his subjective and objective relation with environment is, man being a 'rational' being by nature has succeeded in analyzing and scrutinizing the fall back of his (mis) deed and since has been trying to reprove it, as soon as he has realized it. Man has since been trying to find out the rationale in his deeds that he has been carrying out since time immemorial, and to rediscover his bond with nature that withstood the test of time and always had been inherent in his activities and never been looked at separately in the past. But man, in his bid to redefine his bond with nature has tried to find out the 'logic' behind it, so that he can renew his vow of reverence towards nature and try to restore it into its position of past glory as far as is possible. Man is needing to establish a new trend of Ethics that will enhance his faith in himself to retrieve the nature's glory of the past, even at the expense of personal needs and gains if the need (of retrieval) arises.

Therefore, an attempt has been made here to find out and reestablish the relationship between man and his ethics and his environment to further the cause of safeguarding mother nature, so that not only he can restore the glory of nature immediately, but even in distant future when any human being may forget and ignore the possible consequences of any of his destructive actions and try to destroy nature for his own gain, other beings of society may remind him of the possible consequences of his deeds, pledging by the nature-revering values of ethics.

References:-

1.   U. Kumar and Mahendera Jeet Asija, -*Biodiversity: Principle and Conservation* p1.
2.   Mark Rowland-*The Environmental crisis*-p.30
3.   U. Kumar, M. Asija-*Biodiversity*-p.23
4.   W.R. Sorley-*Ethics of Naturalism*,-p.24
5.   Stephann Budiansky- *Nature's Keepers*,-p.7
6.   Maarten Hajer and Frank fischer,-*Living with Nature*, p.12
7.   *Ibid.,* p.12
8.   Carolyn Egri-*Living with Nature* p.69
9.   *Ibid.*-, p.69
10. V.R. Potter,- *BioEthics: A Bridge to the Future* –p. 25
11. G.E. Moore- *Lectures on Philosophy*-, pp1-6.
12. Peter Simpson-*BookGoodness and Nature*-p.168
13. *Ibid.*-P. 171.
14. H.P. Bhattacharya -*Principles of Philosophy*- p.366
15. V.R. Potter-*Bioethics*-p.57
16. Jadunath Sinha- *Introduction to philosophy* - p.161)
17. Holmes Rolston III-p.27
18. Nigel Dower- *World Ethics*-p.158
19. R.K. Turner J.C. Powell- *Environmental Dilemma*-p.200
20. *Ibid.*,-p.201
21. **Carolyn Egri-*Living with Nature*-p.66**

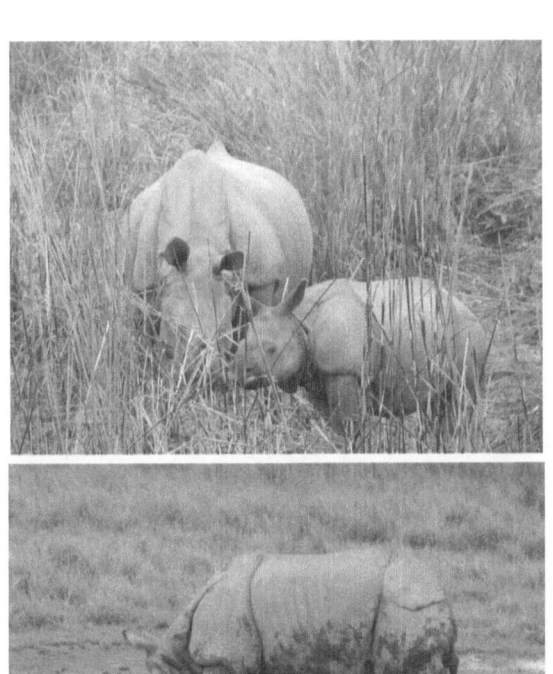

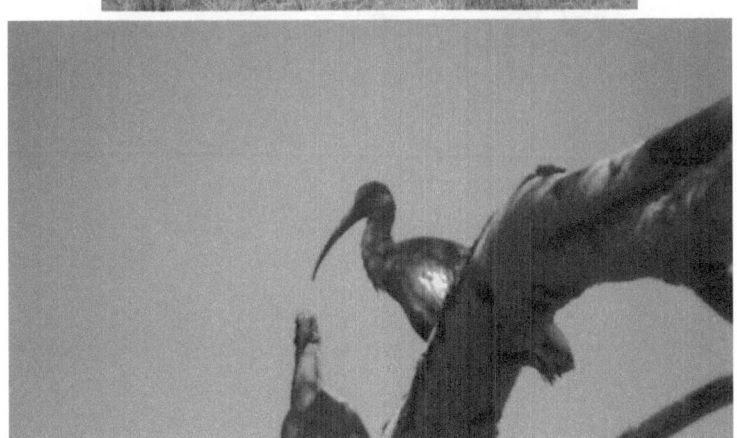

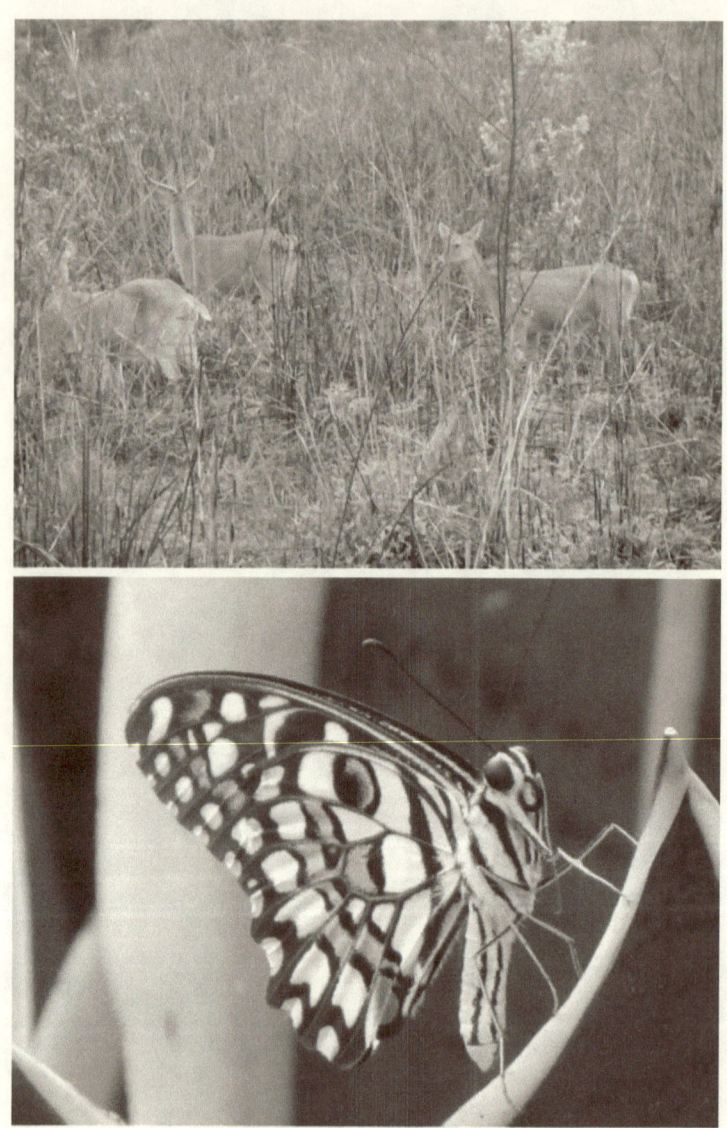

CHAPTER 4

ETHICS AND NATURE≈

4.1. Introductory

While trying to discover the finer characteristics of the relationship between nature and ethics, we must rely on the basic qualities of ethics to explain its relationship with nature. First we must make an assessment of qualities which have assured the basic establishment of its qualities. What are these qualities of Ethics that bring into the validity of their innermost congruity of views? The basic quality of ethics can be called as 'Value' which may be considered mother of all our basic qualities or even as the 'Index' of the qualities. All these qualities are based on 'emotion' which we can consider as the basis of all the qualities. Therefore when we can say that when we can call 'emotion' to be the plain on which qualities grow, then 'value' is the index of the growth of the qualities. However, we may go through the basic permutation and combination of the different facets of the ethics and nature and man to find out the answers to the ultimate order of relationship between ethics and nature, _ the basis of 'natural Ethics' for mankind that shows the perfect harmony between man's guide of moral value, i.e. Ethics and Nature, man's nurturer and provider of his surrounding.

≈**Environment and Nature**-Here the word Nature is being used instead of Environment. See Preface-I

4.2. *Ethical Naturalism'*:-

Naturalism as subjective approach to the philosophy related to nature has not been necessarily a propounding theme of ethical values. There are considerable numbers of believers of naturalism who propound that the primary consideration of nature's ideology, if there is any, _ must be based on certain ethical values that are complementary to nature's ways. On the other hand, there are quite a number of naturalists who believe that ethics derives its primary postulates from nature only. 'Goodness' in a person is believed to be representative of morality and there are number of both ethicists and naturalists who believe that it was basically borrowed from the conception of nature only. However, as we come to know that Naturalism, as a subject matter, does not necessarily represent ethics or ethical values of man and only basically means to be an alternative conception of materialism that espouses the idea of materialistic approach to nature, there is also the prevalence of the conception of ethical Naturalism that propagates the ethical values as it is believed to derive its basic natural conceptions based on morality or 'goodness' only. Environment and ethics, _ when simply put together, represent two different worlds of mankind_ while one represents the world outside, the other i.e. the later represents the world within or the world of mind. Therefore, we can say that they are positioned so diabolically that they do not reach out to each other and they are two genres in the world that are not connected to each other. In reality, it is found out not to be true_ for human beings, the representatives of the two worlds cannot exist without the guidance of each other. When the world of environment lies around us and perhaps could do without the existence of us the human kind, ethics is a product of human mind in form of a series of directives for proper conduct for mankind and as a subject directs the human mind for its restrains and commitments that seems practically has nothing to do with the world outside i.e. the environment. Again it seems the two worlds, each existing on its own and are separate identities which touch two separate dimensions of human world and its civilization. However, in spite of the seemingly obverse nature and contradictory implementation, both are not only the integral parts of the human life, they are supplementary to each other also. It seems the way ethics is inherent in nature, ethics derives its values from nature the same way only. The great Ethicist T. H. Green has also concentrated on the study of the contradiction nature and ethics bore on human mind,_ "The elimination of Ethics, then as a system of precepts, involves_no intrinsic difficulties other than_those involved in the admission of a natural science that can account for moralization of man"[*1]. Therefore, in the chapter for relation between ethics and nature, different aspects of nature and ethics will be discussed in prior in light of the comparative perspective of the other, besides bringing out the glaring differences between the two genres.

4.3. *Ethics in Ancient Time and Nature:*

Although ethics is believed to diabolically opposite to spontaneity and liberalism of Nature and its rules and regulations, many philosophers believe that Ethics as an applied practice uses the basic rules of nature only. Some scholars believe that the difference between the two is as much of inherent difference as two children of a mother can be. Ethics derives its inspiration for its postulates like duty, commitment responsibility etc. from nature only. Thus proper Ethics has inspired mankind to respect nature and give it due importance in social and intellectual world. However, we can call such a relationship between the two human concerns at such an early stage of mankind's civilization as very puerile and novice as the relationship was very rudimentary. However, both ethics and the perception of nature as two different conceptions had developed far more ahead on their individual account to be considered in the limelight of the other. Many of the ancient religions in the world separate their rules of ethics from their perception of nature or religious ideas. Even religions, like Christianity separate their perception of God from that of Nature, so much so that the latter is considered as the anti-thesis of the former. However, western philosophy cannot in overall manner be considered in that lime light, as the Greek Philosophy, which is the cynosure of western philosophy and part of its cultural heritage, preceded Christianity and it has been in general associated largely due to its philosophical ideas with perception of nature. Chinese philosophy β too, by and large, is also defined in terms of nature, _ such as natural forces, their cohesion etc. As in case of Hinduism, it has influenced the religious perceptions too, as we can experience the immense representations of symbolic presence of various animals in the religion. Perceptions of various natural elements metamorphosing in forms of various Gods and Goddesses indicate the amount of reverences expressed of it. Thus, natural perceptions have formed the basic ethico-religious perceptions of most of the ancient and old religions in the world.

βToaism of China, to certain extent Confuciousim also and Japan's Shintoism is also defined by Nature only.

4.4. *Man's Ethics versus "Nature's Law"*

While discovering the pattern or law in the happenings around us there has been efforts on some scholar's part to find such a system in nature's activities. Such a conception of nature has played a very important role among the practitioners of early ethics of Greek philosophy. They believed that under the casual appearance of things, the laws of nature act in unison to motivate things to occur. Therefore, the Greek scholars specially the Stoics, maintained that one should live one's life in accordance with nature (Virre conveniener naturoe). However, there was lack of concentration on the subject matter among the following generations till seventeenth century. In the twentieth century 'nature's law' has come into focus among the scholars again. One of the foremost propounders of nature and its law is Samuel Clarke, who in the seventeenth century expressed that there are certain relations and difference inherent in each and every thing in nature and careful observation makes such contradictory characteristics of it apparent in view of the observer, _ "… the reason for all men everywhere naturally and necessarily assents, as all men every agree in their judgment concerning the whiteness of the snow or the brightness of the sun.''*2 In a very simplified words Thomas Aquinas explains the natural law as, _ "To the natural law belong those things to which a man is inclined naturally: and among these it is special property of a man to be inclined to act according to reason." (from Summa Theologica, 11/I, Question 94, articles 2 and 4in 'The political Ideas of St. Thomas Aquinas).*3 However one of the foremost writers on natural law is John Locke who emphasized that we are not born with any innate ideas and we depend upon our sense experience for our knowledge. He believed nature is driven by certain laws "that allows (us) to call it a rule of morals" (Locke's 'Two Treatise of Government').*4 These rules of morals or conduct, according to him, are the laws of natural law which "can be described as being the decree of the divine will discernible by the light of nature and indicating what is and what is not in conformity with rational nature, and for the very nature, commanding and prohibiting." *5

Bishop Butler was a stout follower of John Locke and has been considered a 'devout' Natural Law-moralist by philosophical fraternity. He agreed with Locke on natural law in respect of conduct. However he emphasized on pleasure versus pain being related to natural law which he conjectured to be the dictum of God, i.e. man derives pleasure from virtuous acts, i.e. the moral ones. His effort to associate natural law with pleasure in terms of morality has ironically put him into the category of a utilitarian.

4.4.1 *The 'Conduct' or 'Character' of man versus 'Nature'*
The Ethics of human Philosophy comes down to the basics of 'Conduct' when its norms are brought into fore, as conduct is considered the forbearer of the morality postulate that Ethics professes. Conduct, as the basic rule of moral expression in relation to 'nature' may bring in many questions. The human conduct as 'standard of value' stands diabolically to the conformity of nature's ways. According to James Seth's view, human natureis related and defined by 'nature' only _ "(the) analysis of the process of volition prepares us to understand the distinction between nature, disposition or

temperament on the one hand and the character on the other.""[6] However, he has disagreed with Thomas Green and according to him man of nature differs from the man of knowledge. His belief of 'a natural man differs from the man of nature' he considered a by product of man's intelligence and virtue acting upon natural man to be his 'second nature'. However John Locke differs in holding such a view, although like Seth, he too believes that 'man is able to infer that God created man for a purpose.' He says, __ "When the will of God is known by the light of reason, it is called Natural Law, and when it is known by revelation, it is called positive law. Both are binding on men, and their difference is the manner in which they are disclosed by God and apprehended by man. ..... The law of nature is universally binding (essay VII), since it is so rooted in human nature that before the law can be annulled, human nature must be changed." *[7]

4.4.2. *Greek Ethics versus 'Nature'*

The Greek Ethics, as a branch of study is not only trend-setter as being 'way of life' for many Greek philosophers, it also emphasized on following the path of nature at its beginning, so that its followers remain within the bound of nature and practice restrain and austerity so as to learn to be 'happy' with whatever nature has to offer to individuals.

The Greek philosophers of earlier times, in spite of the great sophistication and intricacy of views, were great propounders of nature and its ways. Even before the Cynics and later their progenitors the Stoics were expressing their penchant for Nature's dictum, there were other philosophers who believed and deified Nature's ways by finding the Law on earth in it. 'Hylozoism' is the first such branch of philosophy that attempted in theorizing the law of Nature on earth. Hylozoism, which believed in life existing in some matter and life cannot be separated from it, suggests that here is a law which allows human kind to be aware of nature's beneficiary actions rather than being mystified by its 'voluntary' characteristics.

However, while trying to discover the finer characteristics of the relationship between nature and ethics, we must rely on the basic qualities of ethics to explain its relationship with nature. First we must make an assessment of qualities which have assured the basic establishment of its qualities. What are these qualities which bring in the validity of their innermost congruity of views? The basic quality of ethics can be called as 'Value' which we may consider mother of all our basic qualities or even as the 'Index' of the qualities. All these qualities are based on 'emotion' which we can consider as the basis of all the qualities. Therefore when we can say that when we can call 'emotion' to be the plain on which qualities grow, then 'value' is the index of the growth of the qualities.

With some instant scrutiny of the qualities, we may find love, care sincerity, dedication, devotion, perseverance etc. as the basic qualities of both ethics and nature. Even values of higher order that indicate thinking application i.e. ability to rationalize- such as morality, duty, commitment etc. are not only parts of higher human ethics, but to certain extent are parts of nature too. That man has achieved these ethical qualities from nature has been established by their very existence in nature. They are inherent in nature and natural beings embody the qualities to exercise them according to their necessity and capacity.

4.5. *Different perceptions of Ethical Naturalism*

We find considerable number of ethicists, with conflicting views on relationship of ethics versus Nature, as the modicum of their basic ethical perception lied with or related to their basic perception of the kind of ethics they relate themselves. For example, as we have already studied the perception of G.E. Moore, who was basically an 'Utilitarian i.e. one who believed in deriving best benefit from the surrounding i.e. Nature for the welfare of the 'human' kind, suggesting it is irrespective of the inconveniences that may be caused to the others of the living kingdom in the process. Therefore we may discover a tinge of non co-ordination between his view of ethics and his view towards Nature. We may discover such contention on his part from the following phrases:-

It remains obvious from the comment of G. E. Moore regarding his view towards nature in the following manner:-

"WHAT IS MEANT BY 'NATURE'?

What is meant by Nature; & what has philosophy to do with it - what kind of questions about Nature are philosophical, as opposed to scientific, questions.

This term "Nature", with a capital "N", is constantly used in philosophy, as elsewhere, as if we all understood what it meant; but I think it's important for philosophy to attempt to define it.

There are 2 senses, pretty sharply distinguished: a narrower & a wider.

(1) The narrower in wh. Phil of Nature is opposed to Phil. Of Mind - i.e. one in wh. Nature doesn't include our minds & mental process; the sense in wh. Whitehead uses it, when he talks about Nature being

closed to Mind ; the senses in wh. It is used when we talk of Natural as opp. To Moral science, & don't include psych. in the Natural Sciences.

(2) *A wider sense in wh. Our minds & mental phenomena, all those of living creatures on the earth or anywhere in the material universe, are included in Nature.*

<It might be thought that in the sense Nature is identical with the Universe; & so perhaps it is in extension; but certainly not in intension, since it is possible to hold without contradiction that that there are existents which neither are Nature nor fall within it. e.g. the Absolute. >

Both these conceptions are important conceptions & neither is at all easy to define.

We're obviously meant to confine ourselves to (1); &(1), with a certain proviso,= the material universe. The proviso is that if, as some Behaviourists & Materialists seem to have held, all our mental processes are, in fact, merely material processes, then we should define Nature = all that part of the material universe wh. is not mental. I think such views are certainly not true, & in that case Nature simply = the material universe.

(2) in any case needs, I think, to be defined by reference to material universe; it is the material universe & all mental entities that have a certain relation to it.

In any case, the def. of Nature, in our sense, depends on def. of "material universe": either it's identical, or we have to define it as material universe minus whatever is mental in it.

In any case, the def. of Nature, in our sense, depends on def. of "material universe": either it's identical, or we have to define it as material universe minus whatever is mental in it."[8]

He continues in the following way:

"Try to consider what actually happens when you think of Nature.

By "Nature", then, I think, we mean: All the entities which have a certain property.

But what property?

I feel great hesitation as to what I'm going to say; for it's certainly not easy to see for certain: but I can't help thinking that something like what I'm going to say is true, & that it contains very important points.

It seems to me that he connotation of the word Nature is almost certainly different nearly every time we use the word: though the denotation is always the same: that is to say we are referring to a class of things defined by an immense number of different properties. The only question is then of saying what sort of properties they are. [*9]

Again he talked about nature in the following way_

"What are we thinking of when we actually think of Nature?

I can't help thinking that we all of us are always thinking of some particular material thing or a number of them - a different one on different occasions, but always some particular one or group.

And here I mean by a material thing, a thing wh. is material in the sense in which my body most certainly is so: there is such a sense, what it is we shall be engaged in trying to define: but it certainly includes 2 things (a) having shape & size in 3 dimensions, in the sense in which my books has - a sense with wh. we are all familiar, though the analysis of it is difficult & (b) continuing to exist for a certain time, in the sense in which my body has done so.

Starting from this, part at least of what we mean by nature is, I think, this thing together with all those wh. have the property of being related to it in both the following ways:

(a) *are similar to it in the 2 respects mentioned*

(b) *are also positively related to it in this respect: that they either have been or will be, or both have been and will be, at every moment of their existence, in the same space in which it is or was.*

The first point I want to insist on is that both these things are necessary in order that a material thing may form part of the material Universe or of Nature."[*10]

From the above mentioned comments we can perceive his ambiguity towards the genuineness of the perception of nature as well as that of ethics. To Mr. Moore, the following conclusions on the factors are important:- (a) That value is un definable (b) Good is what is perceives as pleasure.

The universe of nature can produce materialistic outcome only and not any ethical or spiritualistic outcome. From his comments we can arrive at the following conclusions on his kind of 'Ethical naturalism'-(a) Although G.E. Moore is one of the forerunner in professing 'Ethical Naturalism', that his kind of Naturalism does not profess nature's concern. (b)That he believed nature is consisted of any materialistic assimilation and concoction rather than having spiritualistic content (c) That man's ego and concern stand larger than that of nature.

However, there are even more other philosophers whose views towards the Equilibrium of ethics and Nature is less ambiguous than that of G.E. Moore but still their goal remains Utilitarian. John Dewey, J.S. Mills etc fall into such a category.

They are followed by those of the ethical naturalists such as Thomas Green, W.R. Sorley who seem to profess moderate voices or even to some extent admitting Nature's influence on human kind, although they did not cease to be utilitarian by view. Followings are some of the opinions expressed by the renowned scholar Thomas Green, _"There are two elements, indeed, in the system of popular ethics inherited from the last century, which were long thought compatible with its complete reduction to the form of physical science. These were the doctrines of 'free will' and of a 'moral sense.'"*11

However, there are still some more philosophers whose views firmly fall into the belief of the 'Eternal Bond' of ethics and Nature, for which they make dedicated effort to establish the Ethical naturalism. Bishop Butler, Samuel Clarke etc. are such independent voices who established the tone of 'Natural Ethics'. Natural Ethics or Ethical Naturalism becomes an authenticated lineage of philosophy in twentieth century. We may discover the conduced view of Bishop Butler in his belief of the equi-balance of Ethics and Nature in the following words _ "It is highly probable that the first (morality) is formed and carried on merely in subserviency to the latter (nature), as the vegetable world is for the animals and organized bodies for mind."*12 Beside disagreeing with his interpretations, they seem not only to counter the dubious views of G.E. Moore and his followers, they also seem to set the trend of genuine views of 'Natural Ethics' only.

4.6. *Where does Ethics differ from Nature*

However, human ethics follows higher order of values in a gradual ascension of application in case of complicated social matters, as man gradually dithers and moves to greater consideration of ethical applications when his societal bonding becomes more complex, thinking and 'rational' oriented. Perhaps it is in this stage or level that the law of nature and human's ethics move away in their own individual course of formulation, and ultimately residing at their own plane of existence give the impression of having contradictory qualities. What is imminent and obvious at the same time is that when human ethics has continued to follow more and more stricter values, nature has allowed its wards to move independent ways and to establish their own identities with individualistic moral or value order.

4.6.1. *Why it is important to discover the qualities of the relationship of nature with Ethics:* The Environmental strategic Perspective

The reason to rediscover the finer relationship of ethics with nature has been an attempt since the time of development of philosophy in the height of human civilization. However, as we have already discussed that the necessity since in the twentieth century has been growing more and more as we find man's relationship with nature has been deteriorating more and more everyday. The reason is quite often than not ascribed to the growing utilitarian value of mankind that has corrupted the conventional ethical views man has been nurturing since ancient time and resulted into man being autocratic to cater to his own necessity, being oblivious of the existence of other living beings on the earth.

However, the necessity to re-establish the finer bond between the two man- related factors of mankind has been increasing day by day as many believe bringing into fore the relationship between the two factors and focusing into their commonalities and the ethos will make for the loss of faith between the two genres. It will allow mankind find a midway that would not only enhance nature's dignity in the view's of mankind of the newest generation, but also would allow to carry on the developmental activities for its progress without causing any harm to the former. After all, ethical values are the guiding light for mankind in dealing with its surrounding in rightful manner, and when such values become deviated from its age old role, it may lead mankind on a wrongful path as well.

Finding the finer qualities which complement for each other will not only enhance the bond between them, but would guide man to respect the individual domain of each of them.

4.6.2. *The Relationship of Man versus Ethics and Man versus Nature*

The common factor relating both to nature and ethics is but mankind and it is the same factor which brings into connection between the two related factors. Although ethics belong to the world 'within' and nature the world 'with out', and while the former is abstract in nature, the latter is materialistic in existence and it is only the 'perceived' law of the latter that is brought into consideration for speculation. However, what is important for man is the equilibrium of relation he is supposed to have between the abstract world of ethics and the presupposed law of the material world of Nature. Man has been maintaining with both the 'relations' of 'his' (i.e. mankind) in an individual manner and at individual or social level has barely associated one of the 'relations' with the other.

But we find that even at a very unconscious state of mind or a subservient level man associates himself or his world of 'within' with that of the 'without', i.e. nature. Because in spite of his intelligence or his 'knowledge' that sets him apart from the other beings of the natural world, man cannot separate himself from the legacy of nature and in spite of his great knowledge and ability to 'rationalize', he not only remains a seed of nature that has fructified in the evolutionary tree of nature, but remains a part of it too. While Nature has a 'a priori' existent in the world, man materializes a 'a posteriori' existence in nature's chronological order of creation and finds a place at a later period of it only.

Therefore, in spite of man, in his first impulse to separate himself from the other beings of nature for whatever the given reason-whether due to his 'egoism' as Dr. W.R. Sorley believes or due to his superior intelligence, man and his values in form of his ethics remain a part of nature only. According to him, _ "Both the conceptions (that of nature and Greater nature) are governed by the doctrine that Nature, whether in the larger or in the narrower sense, is a constitution or system." [*13]

4.7. FINDING ETHICAL ORDER OR MORAL SENTIMENT IN NATURE.
THE ULTIMATE PURSUENCE

Quite often we try to find any natural power that can be explained in terms of the mental or spiritual power of human kind, or to be precise, to know if such a power is only part of 'Nature'. On the other hand, Ethics, which is the moral directive for human mind, has certain root or even a kind of order with nature. A considerable number of authors have advocated and tried to establish the connection between ethics and nature, even by some found among those propounding 'Naturalism' to be ultimately resulting into 'Utilitarian Ethics'. However, the primary motive in trying to find a kind of order of ethical merit in nature is to find out in an indirect manner how much man's ethical value is originated and depended upon the Nature's basic ways and influence on human mind and psychology. Great scholars have attempted elaborately upon finding the 'conundrum' and establishing the inter-relationship between the two guiding factors of human life. T.H. Green has expressed in the following way,-

"The question, can the knowledge of nature be itself a part or product of nature? must not be confused with that commonly supposed to be at issue between spiritualists and materialists. It is one which equally remains to be put, in whatever way we understand the relation between body and mind. We may have admitted most unreservedly that all the so-called functions of the soul are materially conditioned. The question how there come to be for us those objects of consciousness, called matter and motion, on which we suppose the operations of sense and desire and thought to be dependent, will still remain to be answered. If it could be admitted that matter and motion had an existence in themselves, or otherwise than as related to a consciousness, it would still not be by such matter and motion, but by the matter and motion which we know, that the functions of the soul, or anything else, can for us be explained. Nothing can be known by the help of reference to the unknown. But matter and motion, consist in, or are determined by, relations between the objects of that connected consciousness which we call experience. If we take any definition of matter, any account of its 'necessary qualities', and abstract from it all that consists in a statement of relations between facts in the way of feeling, or between objects that we present to ourselves as sources of feeling, we shall find that there is nothing left. Motion, in like manner, has no meaning except such as is derived from a synthesis of the different positions successively held by one and the same body; and we shall try in vain to render an account to ourselves of position or succession, of a body or its identity, except as expressing relations of what is contained in experience, through which alone that content possesses a definite character and becomes a connected whole.

What then is the source of these relations, as relations of the experienced, in other words, of that which exists for consciousness? What is the principle of union which renders them possible? Clearly it cannot itself be conditioned by any of the relations which result from its combining and unifying action. Being that which so organizes experience that the relations expressed by our definitions of matter and motion arise therein, it cannot itself be determined by those relations. It cannot be a matter or motion."*14

The question here is, can we really find out a law of pattern, or even a system that will assert a certain kind of abstract rule, or even a very Godly way to explain the events and happenings on earth, including the human kind? Can we really find a kind of force or abstract power, or the creator or even can be considered as the basis of spirituality of human mind? What amount of influence nature can hold upon it even though it is considered as a material force only?

Or is it equal to the divine or 'Godly' power? The author Thomas Green believes in the same way. We can discover that when philosopher like John Locke believes it to be so, his counterpart Green does not believe it to be the same. When Locke, a naturalist believed that natural law is equal to the moral force, Green believed nature at most to be part of the almighty only.

Naturalism, on the other hand does not profess a supreme being or an Almighty at the helm of it. However, to imply a superior power at the helm of natural powers, Bishop Butler has mentioned of a 'Greater Nature' that is entrusted with the ultimate moral force. Joseph Butler, on the other hand was a follower of Locke and believed in the greater nature the same way Locke believed the moral force being at the helm. However, their explanation certainly differed from that of Thomas Green who explained the greater power as almighty, i.e., God only. However, his explanation of the Supreme being is in terms of nature only. According to him, _ "…. To deify nature…. It is to speak of nature without god in a manner only appropriate to nature as it is in God. Or _ to employ language less liable to misleading association, _ it is to involve ourselves in perpetual confusion by seeking for a completeness in the world of phenomena, the world existing under conditions of space and time, which, just because it exists under those conditions, is not to be found there. The result of the confusion will generally be that, being unable to discover any perfection or totality or independent agency among the matters of fact which we know, and having ignored the implication by those facts of a spiritual principle other than themselves, we come to assume that no perfect or self determined being exists at all. Or at any rate in any relation to us."*[15]

However, the question here is that while it is a metaphysical explanation, we have to find both a logical and pragmatic solution, as moral values, whether in spite of being abstract in nature has got any practical implications as well as applications too, and there must be also a force, perhaps abstract in nature existing on earth that imply the moral order in human society.

What is it that per forces the moral orders? To find a logical explanation to it and which is confounded on earth with its actual application in our lives, we have to again look for certain ground which is common to every aspect of human kind but also the per forcing or motivating force?

According to W. R. Sorley, he believes that,- "The standard of morality is thus found in human nature, as in human nature is so far as it is charged with a power of judging impulses and their ends: as we might say in so far as it is the vehicle of a spiritual principle... Conscience is supreme in man, and represents divine purpose."[16]

However, from Naturalism's point of view the various laws of nature that believed to cause the occurrences on earth are not random but are bound by certain pattern. It has certain purposes that perforce the applications of the laws; the same way a man carry out his activities with a purpose and to find the righteousness of them he depends upon his conscience, the purposefulness of them to assert his commitment. The same way we can say nature's objects fulfill certain purposes for which we can ascribe certain amount of consciousness to the objects. The same amount of consciousness also exists in mankind which allows him to exercise his conscience to judge or rationalize his doings. Therefore, it is our moral conscience that we can call as the ultimate moral order and which man derives from nature.

4.8. *Finding Ethical Order of Morality in Natural Selection*

Prior to learning about the Natural Selection in respect of ethical order, we need to scrutinize the views propounded by Natural selection theories from philosophical point of view. Basically, Natural Selection is a scientific explanation based on 'observation' and 'experience' on the existence and survival of Nature's living beings, including mankind. However, its testimony on development of animal kingdom including mankind brings in ethics into a dilemma of finding any or a kind of moral order in it. According to the primary theory of Natural Selection, the world is the ground for the survival of the fittest and in the competition to make some space for oneself, only the able ones survive to exist. Natural selection has been a theory basically established by Charles Darwin in nineteenth century, who also propounded the theory of evolution and natural selection was his ultimate conclusion on his conception of evolution and therefore any interpretation or apprehension regarding the moral order of any kind in it seems to be a far away conclusion.

Charles Darwin, discovered that unlike beliefs espoused by many religions including Christianity, the mankind was neither created by one particular 'personal god', as is professed in Christianity nor any particular human being was to start the genesis of mankind, but man originated from another species of Primate animals only. Darwin's theory, which upholds the origin of mankind as being part of a wholesome 'Cosmosis' process, believes that the various species are the resultants of long affliction of nature in which only those species which have in the face of the many trials of nature such as flood, earthquake, draught related famine etc. have succeeded in surviving, have ultimately succeeded in living on the earth only. The species yielding to the harshness of nature's decree, have also failed to survive and have ultimately become extinct from the surface of earth. The explanation to the omission of certain species from the tree of evolution has been justified in such manner and it has been called as 'Natural Selection.' In the long time period in which the process of evolution has taken place, the survived species have adapted with its surrounding by dint of physical morphemic process which helped them to currently live in what previously had been considerably an adverse situation for them.

However, the whole process of Natural selection and adaptation is basically a part of the perpetual development of animal kingdom, which is carried out in such a manner, so that the 'able' species can survive in the face of the constantly changing order of nature. About Darwin's Theory of Evolution, Alexander in his book speaks in the following way, _ "Natural Selection is a name for the process by which different species with characteristic structures contend for supremacy, and one prevails and becomes relatively permanent."[*17]

4.8.1. *Assessment of natural Selection Theory from Ethical point of View*

The Darwinian theory of evolution and its related 'Natural selection' is a naturalistic theory which is much based on scientific ideas and verifications, rather than being any subjective approach to the conception of evolution. It lacks any metaphysical explanation, nor morality, value or any other component of ethics being conjured in the whole theory. While ethics has no role to play in the process, as substantiated in it, it is rather a 'mechanical' process, as substantiated by Darwin, preconditioned to an unseen natural process. According to Dr. Potter,-"Darwin felt that the struggle was difficult to rationalize except as a means to progress, which he believed was the inevitable result from the natural selection."[*18] Therefore, in the process of the Theory of Evolution which is based on scientific verification methods only, it is of no point trying to derive any inkling of ethical value or metaphysical truth in it. However, even in its non esoteric conceptual ideas, some scholars have found certain pattern of events that seems to pertain to some invisible law. Dr. Potter believes it is due to the process of 'disorder' in nature that has caused to look for and find a 'perfect order' and such a quest make for progress of animal kingdom as well as mankind. According to him,-"A large proportion of human race is psychologically incapable of coping with large doses of disorganization and uncertainty. Mankind has an inborn desire to have some degree of organization in life and this desire leads many to gravitate in the direction of religion or science, both of which are identified as mechanisms for bringing order out of disorder."[*19]Again regarding the natural selection theory of Darwin, Teilhard de Chardin retorts,_ "What we find within the struggle to live is something deeper than a series of duels; it is a conflict of chances."[*20]

However, to find an ethical dimension to the theory of Natural Selection, i.e. the survival of the fittest, it rather shows to be a kind of inherent skill (in case of Darwin) and, or the influence of the 'outside', rather than the morality value of it. While we can find ethical justification in the motivation of Natural selection, rather than finding any moral or to be precise any non moral justification we can find its 'moral' applications elsewhere in our lives. However, John McKenzie had tried to explain the evolution of Ethics along with the development of species. According to him, _"In all development, there is a beginning, a process and an end. The development being starts from a certain level and moves onwards a higher level. .... The starting point and the goal are alike concealed from us; we only see the race. So it is also with moral life. The earliest beginnings of moral consciousness are hidden wit obscurity; and on other hand, we can scarcely form a clear conception of a perfectly developed moral life. We know it only in the course of its development.* [*21]

It has already been explained by many scholars that 'chaos' and 'order' are part of the natural selection process which is also believed in by Christian religion. According to it, disorder or chaos is a part of it so that it can cause to create newer order so that the progress of development or evolution can move towards perfection. The process use to have a 'purpose', as an explanation for its own 'reason de etre'.

However, the question that comes up in respect of it is that can present day environmental crisis to be categorized with the natural 'disorder' of the evolution process? Can it also be called a 'disorder' in the evolutionary process? Or whether the extinction of many species on earth for the same reason can be justified in the name of 'natural selection'?

Here we face an ethical dilemma which is the result of ethical folly of mankind who caused wanton destruction of nature. Therefore primarily man is responsible for such destructing acts and deterioration of environment. But can environmental crises and disasters be considered as part of such disorder too? Author like Dr. Von Potter believes that it is important that trying to establish order in societies may fail without accommodating or incorporating disorder.

The renown author of Bio Ethics speaks of 'disorder' of nature in the following manner:- "The survival of the fittest was a brutal process for using the raw material or disorder to achieve order, but it served a noble purpose in selecting new and better species, which were widely understood to arise on a continuing basis."[22]. However, 'disorder' according to him is-"knowledge led to power and the power to alter the environment led to new dimensions of order and disorder." [23]

4.9. THE NEW CONCEPTS OF ETHICS IN MODERN ARENA

1. Biocentrism: Anthropocentrism and Cosmocentrism:- Biocentrism is also a modern lineage of theories that philosophizes on the universe as centering around the organic world only. It is a kind of Naturalism which focuses not on the materialistic or metaphysical qualities of Nature but on the organism (i.e. living being) oriented that, according to it, is pivotal to the various factors of universe related to each other on such terms only. However, there is difference among the bio centric scholars, _ there are those who believe that man is the only superior intelligence in the universe and the universe is centering around mankind and everything belonging to universe is related to it. Philosophers with such views are called Anthropocentric and their idealism as Anthopocentrism. However, they have their opponent viewers, who believe man to be a part of the greater design of universe only and although considered superior in intelligence, he is a kind of being and is no different from other beings in universe. Only, like others he too fulfills certain purpose on earth only. Philosophers with such an idealism is called cosmo-centric and their idealism as 'Cosmo-centrism'. However, they basically follow the principle of Deep Ecology, a new conception born out of synthesis of various nature oriented ideologies and religions.

2. Deep Ecology: Its interpretation of Ethics has been in practice since early days of twentieth century in North America and has been used as a favorite tool for protection and conservation of Nature, primarily of flora and fauna of wildlife. It was established by a forest official by name Aldo Leopold, but it is a kind of philosophical thinking which is yet to develop or established any particular line of thinking of its own.

Regarding his views on nature scholar Strachan Donnelley expresses,-"First of all, we should note that Leopold accepted philosophically, morally, and spiritually a fundamental Darwinian tenet."[24] Regarding Leopold's ethical views he reiterates, _"The key to understanding, if not resolving, these paradoxes and Leopold's aesthetics and ethics is again, Leopold's particular philosophical appropriation of Darwinian evolutionary, biology, ecology, and ethnology: the admixture and intermingling of science and particular brand of human spirituality". [25] However, it has tried to established with all kind of 'Natural ethics of all major religions, specially the ancient ones including Hinduism, Confusianism etc. It has tried to highlight how most of the religions have been emphasizing on maintaining a kind of balance or rather an 'Equilibrium' between man and nature, whether it has been done in form of worshipping and devotion, or whether by making its ordain to make it a practice of respecting one's natural surrounding or even by making it a way of life by practicing 'natural' ways or living in its surrounding.

Deep Ecology, however, has its own small principles. But it also tries to scientifically establish that mankind is a part of a huge system of the 'Cosmos' i.e. universe and therefore like to call itself as 'Cosmocentrism'. They believe, thus they establish themselves as the ones not believing in 'Anthropomorphism', a kind of anti thesis of their own thinking-concern for the animal world and thereby which intend to establish itself as propounder of the belief that the world is 'man centric' only and does not consider other beings are as important as human beings are only.

Regarding the tenets it espouses, author Mark Rowland expresses,-"The deep ecology camp (i.e. followers) encompasses a spectrum of writings, from authors of very intellectual traditions and very different intellectual credentials"[26]. Again on its views on man nature relationship he expresses,- "According to deep ecology, our relationship with nature has been a 'bad' or 'unhealthy' one characterized by domination, disrespect, disharmony. Therefore, we need to rethink this relationship; to remove the offending elements from it".[27] Again its interpretation of the present day environmental problems, the author reiterates in the following way, -"The environmental problems we face today are according to deep ecology, the result of artificial separation of humans from nature."[28]

3. BioEthics_ Bio Ethics is the newest ideology introduced to the field of Environmental philosophy, as we find both philosophers and scientists are trying to bring into fold the rationalized authenticity to the reasonable application of newest inventions in the field of biology. With man's ability to create newer things, even to replicate organic substances believed to be most difficult ones and as the prerogatives in the domain of the supernatural being i.e. God only, man is facing the dilemma to proceed further, as the newer activities bring in the question of the moral authority to do so. It basically brings into the possibility of moral misuse of the privilege (i.e. immoral act) of creating by wanton usage of it, even immorally. The necessity, therefore arises out of the concern for vigil into the moral periphery and to put them into the bound of moral order so as not to allow any misappropriate actions to be carried out. However, there are quite a few 'bio ethicists' who believe there should be intermingling of biology which signifies man's progress in the field of medical science with the human values that would keep man harnessing his knowledge not only within bounds but also put to proper utility for mankind. According to V.R. Potter,_ "A science of survival must be more than science alone, and I therefore propose the term Bio Ethics in order to emphasize the two most important ingredients in achieving the new wisdom that is so desperately needed: biological knowledge and human values". [*29]

4.10. ETHICS' RELATION WITH NATURE IN INDIAN PHILOSOPHY

It is already to our knowledge about the immense influence ethics has exerted upon the thinking of Indian Philosophy. We are also aware of the ubiquitous presence of nature in the words in Indian philosophy as well. However, it is necessary to consider the amalgam of both in it and how both the genres have supplemented for each other to uphold the importance of each of them.

In the Rig Veda we find that humanity is born out of the great sacrifice of a great 'primary person (i.e. Adi Purusa) and therefore various natural objects considered sacred are offered to him. However, it is from religious point of view only which may differ from philosophical point of view. But we can safely say that Indian ethics has highly evaluated nature unlike many other philosophies and thereby has put a special place of reverence in the podium of ethico-religious feelings of common masses. Nature has become so much an integral part to Indian ethics that it is often difficult to find it without the mention of the former. For example, the 'Karma' beliefs of Indian philosophy, it is bound for any creature to be reborn, specially human beings, as different creatures of different categories, each category being the reincarnated forms entrusted to the amount of Karma _the deeds with moral righteousness that asserts the level of nirvana. The more 'good' deeds a soul commits to, the better living creature it is born into in its after life, that are bound by certain standard that stratifies the different animals into the different levels of attainment in accordance with their 'good deeds'. Ultimately a soul succeeds to purify itself through several of its human lives out to fulfill any deeds defined by Karma for achievement of Nirvana, the ultimate freedom from the bondage of livelihood and livinghood.

Karma can occur out of many reasons,_ such as committing the acts not morally endorsable or failure of duties towards elders etc., thus personifying it as punishment and the outcome of such offences. Ultimately the 'good' and 'moral' deeds of a person would allow him or her to achieve the ultimate goal of life, the zenith being Moksha or Nirvana i.e. the soul being free of any Karma and being part of the eternal and the almighty divine. Therefore, Mokhsa or Nirvana can be called as the moral zenith of Hindu ethics. However, the best way to achieve it has been more lucid and assertive manner mentioned in the MadBhagawat Gita where it has advised how an individual can achieve it by being a 'Sthitapragya' i.e. being resolute on one's principles and also a 'Karmayogi' i.e. one who fulfils duties without looking for benefit out of it. Author R.N. Sarmah expresses in the following manner, _ "The nature of human being does not change with time. The MadBhagawat Gita is based upon the fundamental principles of human nature hence it will always be a source of inspiration to human being."[*30]

4.10.1. *Ethical Relation to Nature in Buddhism*

We have already found nature being relegated to a relative role in some of the lineages in Indian philosophy. We can witness similar relation to nature in Buddhism as in Advaita Vedanta, where nature has only a relative importance in comparison to ethico-religious sentiments of Hinduism. Although in Buddhism nature is highly respected, it is also believed to be the expression of Maya the mundane illusion that makes human beings attached to the elusions on earth. In the book of Nirvana for Buddha, the protagonist, 'Mare" the Goddess of natural forces has been shown as trying to entice and distract Buddha in his effort of achieving penance. Such an explanation to nature is parallel to Advaita Vedantism, although many believe the latter was influenced by Buddhism only. In spite of such an interpretation of nature is an exception because of an observation from spiritualistic point of view, natural objects are intrinsically connected with rites and symbolic representation in Buddhism and thereby play an important role in carrying forward its messages to common masses. According to scholar Carolyn Egri, _"Buddhist relational ethics teach that moral actions are those which are informed, sensitive to and respectful of all beings (sentient or not) within interdependent relationship."[31]

4.10.2. *Ethics in Jainism*

Jainism is another religion which made significant mark with its doctrine of Moksha or emancipation and stringent ethical values. Barely preceding Buddhism in its birth, Jainism strictly follows the Karmavada theory in relation to rebirth and merit/ demerit of performance of duties. According to it, man relives again and again in form of karma particles called Astrava in 'Jiva', that is life of any being till he is free of karma by purification of soul through his acts enacting duties-enhancing progress and assurance in achieving moksha. Through the processes called Parinamika, Audayika, Aupashamika, Kshayika and Kshaaiauposhika. Again, it advises seven ways to refrain karma to work upon a being.

With help of Nirjara and Sanvar, one can destroy Karma and attain Moksha. Regarding the ethical values espoused by Jainism, author R.N. Sarmah expresses in the following way, _ "Jaina philosophers have made deep inroad into this field of human experience."[*32]

4.10.3. *Ethics' versus 'Nature' in 'Gandhism'*

It has been more than fifty years since Mahatma (M.K.) Gandhi's demise, leaving behind him the legacy of his actions, services and thoughts in form of Gandhism. Although Gandhiji himself never made any conscious effort to establish any particular lineage of his thinking and ideology, his admirers and followers have iconized it after his name which is synonymous with pragmatic approach to remedy the woes of the poor. Paragon of supreme sacrifices and tolerance he has left behind a legacy which if properly implemented might have, to great extent, improvise the social condition and remove the sorrows of the common people living under duress in the society. In present day context of environmental crises, Gandhi's tenets of non-violence, tolerance and sacrifice may hold significant importance in redressing the malaises of the society in particular and our natural surrounding in general. It is a well-mown fact that he advised his followers on going back to nature and he believed a person should live within the bounds of nature only. His insistence on weaving only hand made cotton cloth i.e. Khadi, strictly eating vegetarian food and living in natural conditions only reflects forms such views only. Gandhi's love of nature is evident from many of his views as he expressed joy and wonder at the manifold expressions of nature he witnessed during the tours and travels, which were part of his itinerary, that were carried out for his non-violent movement for achieving, or rather retrieving the independence of India. The people of Assam are aware of his care for the land, when he published in the Hindu paper and where he has addressed it as 'Daughter of Nature' (Kudrat ki Beti). He also wrote in details many nuances of his experience during his stay in Assam. Penchant for nature, it seems, also influenced the ethical perspective of Gandhi's ideology too. Apart from belonging to conservative Hindu family with stringent values, true to the tradition of vegetarianism and non-violence, he was nonetheless exposed to the liberal living culture of the West during his stay in London for academic reason and later in Darban to earn his livelihood. Therefore, his insistence on following the non violence path for attaining Independence for the country can also be attributed to his love of nature, for he wrote in Young India (26th November1929), _"God manifests Himself in innumerable forms in this universe and every such manifestation commands my spontaneous reverence". Back in 1920, he wrote in the same paper regarding non-killing of animals as part of 'Ahimsa' or 'non-violence policy',_ "A votary of Ahimsa(non-violence) therefore remains true to his faith if the spring of all his actions is compassion, if he shuns to the best of his ability the destruction of tiniest creature, tries to save it and thus incessantly strives to be free from the deadly coil of Himsa (violence)." He also emphasized on using natural ways for finding solution to problems of day to day life. He set example of his family people by putting into practice of 'naturopathy' for curing various illnesses with help of natural elements such as water, air, earth etc. He was inspired to do so by following Just's "Return to nature". Such an emphasis confirmed his belief in Meliorism -a form of philosophy, which prophesies that man can improve his destiny if he will follow the path of nature.

However, his love of nature and insistence on living within the bound of nature and to be less dependent on technological activities did not necessarily indicated his distrust of science and technology. In fact Gandhi was for using science in a manner that would have little adverse effect on man and his surroundings. He was opposed to setting up big industrial establishments, as it caused artificial immigration to urban areas from villages and such run off of locals created shortage of labour forces in villages as well as infrastructural problems of catastrophic proportions related to over population in locals of such urban establishments. Such concern on part of Gandhi shows how he was ahead of his time and while few of his cotemporaries worried about surrounding, he cared for the environment in terms of its distant future, albeit without any premonition of the impending disaster of catastrophic proportion for it beginning late in the twentieth century. He believed in opting for ways that would always be compatible with nature.

His views regarding the imparting of knowledge to children were much pragmatic in approach, as he believed teaching them how to work while earning knowledge would be the most appropriate way in reducing illiteracy in the country as well be self sufficient in economy in the most cost effective and convenient manner. It also allows economic viability while education would be distributed evenly at grass-root level. Many academicians see similarity between his method and that of John Dewey, who believed in utilitarian method of earning knowledge. Had Gandhi's educational policy been implemented in independent India, it might have shown great progress at educational level of common people and also would have subsequently ensured population control and economic prosperity, besides allowing its vast resources of forests and energy to be safeguarded and protected from destruction which is being carried out in the name of technological development.

Therefore, from further analysis and study of Gandhism i.e. the ideology of Gandhi, expressed and executed through many of his acts and deeds to retrieve the independence of India, and which is inherent with 'love for nature', we may be inspired to arrive at that conclusion that Gandhi believed not only in living within the bound of nature with a 'non-violent' policy, but also one to live happily while let live others. On Gandhi's ethical values author R.N. Sarmah expresses in the following manner, _ "Gandhi was a non violent revolutionary. His technique of social revolution, therefore is based on nonviolence. Since the practice of non- violence requires love, goodwill, co-operation, and fellow-feeling, Gandhian techniques include all these virtues."[*33]

4.11. Assessment of Relationship of Ethics versus Nature In Indian Philosophy
A Comparative Study of the Same in Western philosophy

As it is found that Nature is defined to be an integral part of not only the ethico-religious thinking, it is also of the same importance in the Indian philosophies as well,_ Nature comes to be revered as epitome of life in Hinduism. Although it has only relative importance while studied from metaphysical point of view, unlike in many other philosophies nature has been given its due importance in Indian philosophies. Apart from relative perspective and empirical existence in the view of metaphysical conceptions, it has been made to feel its magnanimous presence in the day to day life of an individual in Indian Philosophies and ethics. However, what is important here is that nature is being considered a means rather than an 'entity' vis. a vis. the ethical values and therefore a part of the greater entity, the Supreme Being only.

In the theory of Karmavada in Hindu scriptures, we find that nature becomes a 'tool' of experimentation in the crime and punishment perspectives of man's morality. We find layers of natural objects, particularly the living beings are attributed with different stratas of ethical connections_ with good deeds a good soul would move up through the different stratas in its life after life and ultimately would reach the highest strata, so as to reach Moksa which means that one has to relinquish one's natural body to immerse with the ultimate reality or the Supreme being, who does not have any physical existence. However, the important fact about its views is that the individual soul has to transcend various strata that are more and more ethically endorsable as the outcome of Karma would reduce proportionately because of the 'good' deeds and ultimately achieve the highest good in life. Here we find with increasingly attaining moral grounds one ultimately achieves the highest 'good', which is equivalent to 'Summum bonum' or 'Achievement of the Highest good' in western philosophy. Again, we can say that Nature, which has been involved in the process of achieving Moksa or Nirvana i.e. the ultimate freedom is a means or way for the ultimate good for the soul only. Here we can surmise that while nature is being considered here as means and as sacred, elsewhere in other areas of Indian ethico-religious feeling, it is not being attributed with any supreme authority or metaphysical force in its overall entity. Elsewhere in some other ethics related theories of Hinduism, we find nature being portrayed either as 'qualitative' or as 'illusory' as an entity. We can assume, in such respect, nature being considered as a materialistic force only, as it is often regarded in western philosophy. However, it is an explanation in terms of metaphysical reality only, and therefore 'relative' in importance, although we find nature or natural objects to be attributed with supernatural qualities in early scriptures of Hindu philosophy. Therefore we can conclude that the 'relativity' of nature's importance in Indian philosophy is in light of ethics only, and not from any other religious point of view.

References:-

1. T.H. Green - *Prologmena to ethics* –p.2
2. John Mc.Kenzie-*Manuel of Ethics.* -p.141
3. Thomas Aquinas -*'Ethics-p.*248*'*,
4. John Locke -*Butler's_Ethics*- p.43
5. John Locke- *Ibid.*-p. 11
6. James Seth – *A Study of Ethical Principles* p.49
7. John Locke -*'Butler's Ethics'* _pp.44-45)
8. -by G.E. Moore -*Lectures on Philosophy*- pp1-3
9. *Ibid.*-p 4
10. *Ibid-*5
11. T.H. Green-*Prologmena to Ethics.*' By -p.5,
12. Analogy by Bishop Butler, parti, ch.vii, worksi-p.126, *Ethics of naturalism*,
13. W. R. Sorley-*'Ethics of naturalism*"p.121
14. T.H.Green- *Prologmena to Ethics*- -pp13-14)
15. *Ibid.* 62
16. W.R.Sorley -*Ethics of Naturalism*- -pp122-123.
17. Mr. Alexander -*Manuel of ethics* Moral Order and progress
18. Dr. Van Rensselaer Potter -*'Bioethics'*- p.57
19. *Ibid.*-pp.55-56
20. *Ibid.*87
21. Dr. John McKenzie'- '*Manuel of Ethics'*. P.196
22. Dr. Van Rensselaer Potter -*Bioethics'* - p.57
23. *Ibid.*-p.56
24. *The Good in Nature and Humanity, ch.Leopold's Darwin*, p.168).
25. *Ibid.*-p169)
26. '*The Environmental Crisis*" pp.167-.168
27. *Ibid.*-p.168
28. *Ibid.*-, p.169
29. Van Potter- *Bio Ethics: Bridge to the Future*-, ch.1 p. 2
30. *Ibid.* -p. 2
31. Carolyn Egri-*Living with Nature, ch. The Environment*, p.64
32. **R.N. Sarmah-**.*Indian Ethics*-p.196
33. *Ibid.*,-p.245

CHAPTER 5

ENVIRONMENTAL CRISIS AND ETHICAL IMPLICATIONS

5.1. MAN CREATED (ANTHOPOGENIC)♦ crisis OF ENVIRONMENT AND ITS REPURCUSSIONS ON SOCIETY

As we have learnt before, the process of man created system of urbanization and industrialization have utilized the optimum amount of natural resources, i.e. the natural commodities that provide man with various utility purposes. As result of it, these processes are also causing enormous amount of waste which are the left out and unwanted part of them for being no more utility worth or being considered unproductive. These wastes, thrown aside either on the ground or in water or even in gaseous form to the atmosphere and thereby making these components of environment not anymore in their purer form, besides making them dirty and therefore contaminated. The process of contamination is called pollution which cause widespread degradation and even destruction of the elements on earth, thereby rendering them unworthy or dangerous for further utility. For example, in a colour- dyeing factory, after colouring the clothes, the left out chemicals are thrown in nearby water body causing pollution to the water and rendering it either as unworthy or dangerous to drink or use further. The more the natural resources are used the more waste and pollution are created thereafter as result of their utilization. The polluting conditions are not only

---

♦'**Anthropogenic**' is a scientific term used to mean man- created or generated by man. Likewise the 'term' anthropocentric means around man, i.e. everything concerning man in the pivotal role.

hazardous for human health, they are dangerous or even fatal for the species existing in the areas of the waste dumping. The water body used for throwing dyeing colour may result into the dissolve of the eco-system in it and thereby affecting other animals dependable on it for their survival. The heron or the cormorant living on the riverine species for their survival will not be anymore able to provide themselves with food and therefore go away or die due to the toxic effect of the water; thus putting the whole area dwindled of its natural condition or resources. Therefore it can be surmised that pollution does not merely affect one aspect of nature but set off whole chain of food dependents of nature and thereby triggering the degradation or destruction of the natural resources, both animate and inanimate. Thus human greed for more resources for his own welfare results into destruction of nature, making it more of an ethical issue rather than a materialistic problem. Therefore modern ethicist C.J. Barrow has expressed in the following way, _ "At the root of many environmental problems are unsound ethics and development and modernization. There is a need to promote new development ethics and to identify critical threshold so that action can be taken in time to avoid, mitigate or response to threat. It is also important to review opportunities to maintain or improve the well being of people other organisms and environment."*1

The degrading process taking root in society has left deep impact on human both environmentally and socially, root of which has already been traced out to the deviated ethical values, which were espoused and encouraged to propagate, at the end of medieval era in Europe in form of utilitarian ethics, for the utilization of nature for the benefit of mankind. He again has said, _"Humanity is at the 'crossroads', about to face or already facing a crisis or crises. Some of these problems are due to natural process, but many are wholly or in large part the result of human activity, which now has supra national (trans-boundary), in some cases global impacts. Problems are often caused by more than one group of people or more than one nation and those causing difficulties have so far tended to escape the consequence."*2

5.2. *Ecological Degradation and its Repercussion:-*
Physiological and Mental effects on Human Society.

At the zenith of civilization, mankind has proselytized the processes of Urbanization and industrialization and thereby has allowed the process of degradation occur at maximum possible way. In its rapid progression, it has gradually started to affect almost every area of human occupations i.e. whether materialistic, psycho –social or even purely psychological.

The Degradation of Environment has been two folds: - (i) Due to destruction and depletion of Environment in direct manner, i.e., by cutting down forest areas, causing desertification and desalination.

(ii) Degradation of Environment in an indirect manner, i.e., by causing pollution due to industrialization and urbanization. However, we must add another angle to these two processes-that is of 'The Population Problem' as the earth is experiencing unabated number of population added everyday to the existing number, which is creating a bigger and bigger problem everyday as resources on earth for supplying the population on earth is not only limited but also proving to be 'inadequate', specially in developing countries where the ratio of amount of food supply to an individual is always narrower.

5.2.1. *The Direct Process of Ecological degradation and Destruction*

The degradation of the environment has not only destructed many a phenomenal qualities of nature in certain areas, but also has put to threat the balance it has been maintaining among its components which help them retain their inherent qualities for their own existence. Regarding the destruction of the environment, the 'direct' ways by which man has been carrying on his act of annihilation, can be described in the following manner:-

In the act of destruction in direct ways, man has annihilated the forest in 'direct' manner i.e. there has been no secondary factor in between man and 'nature' that can be held responsible for its final degradation. Therefore we may hold man as the primary 'progenitor' of such heinous acts, which can be a very much 'conscious' acts on his effort and which means man did it with his 'knowing' self. They can be mentioned as follows:-

1.*Deforestation:-* From time immemorial and since the time of inception of human civilization, man has been using forest areas for development activities. They have not only used wood for the purpose of constructing houses but also as fuel for cooking and other necessities. In the early days of civilisation, people of some ancient cultures such as Maya and others used the planks of wood for constructing 'dam's in the river too. The primitive people used the leaves and barks of it to wear as cloth. At later stages of civilization, not only 'cotton' clothes were produced from the fibre of its flower, but they also learnt how to produce 'paper' from the bark of some particular trees, specially in the Nile valley civilization of Egypt and the Chinese civilization. The 'sap' of some trees were used for various purposes_ such as for making gum or in some case preparing essence or sometime even for drinking. The forest areas too were not only useful for human, but also were the breeding ground of the most other creatures on earth. The most important feature of the forest areas in their entirety is their contribution to the gaseous balance on earth as the tree kingdom i.e. the flora community in its abundance allows the carbon growth in atmosphere in check and that of oxygen aplenty, as it inhales the former and exhales the latter, and which is most beneficial for the growth of animal kingdom. However, the utility of the forest itself spells 'doom' for it as any 'utility conscious' people have been trying to cut it down often extensively for their own benefit. It is often said that the 'utility' conscious people of Roman civilization imported so many trees from the other side of Mediterranean sea i.e. areas belonging to the north of Africa that the enormously devastated forest areas have resulted into the creation of the Sahara desert. If such a 'fable' ever happens to be verified to be true, then it is the first historical instance of 'deforestation' in the world.

   2.*Desertification:-* It is another process of uprooting trees which results into destruction of local 'eco system' of an area. In the process however, trees are not directly felled, but often the excavating of the land areas results into no further growth of trees in it and thereby letting the living organism of the area get imbalanced over a period of time. Usually when in search of mineral ore or some other fuel sources, certain areas are extensively dug out and as a result trees are uprooted and the 'eco system' gets upstaged. The random digging out with excessive mineral on the ground render the soil un-useful and the whole area becomes not only un- aesthetics but also blockade the process of continuity of the neighbourhood ecology. According to authors U.Kumar and Mahendara Asija-"In most cases of desertification, there is a reduction in total species richness, an increase in the proportion of an exotic (nonnative) plants and a decline in overall biodiversity _the variety of life forms and the ecological roles they fill. Once desertification starts, it often causes changes that accelerate the process."[*3]

   3. *Desalination* is another process which occurs due to either the excessive usage of fertilizer for abundance of crop or as result of the desertification process. In the process of desalination caused due to over usage of fertilizer, the excess chemicals in it do not allow the oxidization process of micro-organism occur and as a result the earth on the ground fails to remain 'mucus' resulting into its dryness and becomes loose. Further, the dry soil runs away with rain and therefore the germination process is hampered. The 'run away' soil also causes **_'siltation'_** at the bottom of the receiving water body i.e. either a pond or a lake or a river making it shallow over a period of time and thereby rendering its water unsuitable for drinking or letting excess growth of unwanted weeds happen due to the incoming fertilizers. The silting process, compounded with additional growth of weeds due to excess amount of fertilizer brought down by rain water to the pond or any stagnant water-body results into the **_Eutrophication_** of it, which means depletion of the ecosystem and shallowness caused to it resulting into slow extinction of it.

However, from close quarters, we may discover that the processes of 'deforestation', 'desertification' and 'desalination' are in many cases supplementary and connected to one another. For example, the process of deforestation happening at a place may cause desertification subsequently in there. Again due to cutting down of trees leading to desertification and ultimately result into desalination of the area and has left a very debilitating effect on our environment. Thus, the direct ways of annihilation of nature has resulted into dwindling and often extinction of Nature's even species much faster than the natural processes. Author Michael Renner expresses,- "Changing precipitation patterns, shifting vegetation zones, and rising sea levels are caused by global warming threaten to disrupt wide range of human and natural systems….Many eco system cannot adapt to a rapid change in climatic zones; entire forest type could disappear."[4]

4. _The Increasing Population_
One of the brightest achievements of technology in the twentieth century is that it has succeeded considerably in overcoming the maladies effecting human health and help in reducing mortality. With scientific development in the medical front, man had succeeded considerably in finding remedies for such various maladies that had been affecting most of population in physical terms and thereby help in increase of the population or bring in more stability in health front over in the world. Although there are still places world over where such facilities are yet to make way, in overall it has improved considerably to make them self sufficient in health front and thereby increase the input and expertise of man power, both individually and collectively. However, the trend of health in modern world has shown that being healthy in physiological term is not enough as number of perameters for welfare of an individual needs implementations

before scrutinizing it, fulfilling various criteria of the socio-anthopological economy to substantiate the ground his well being. For example, a person needs to be well supplied with not only the basic necessities, but also the logistical right over the surroundings he or she lives in. When there is failure of such supply of basic amenities or rather the inadequacy of them, then his existence or rather the survival becomes conditional to the required supply or a liability in absence of it. The excessive population in a place or a country substantiates such a diabolical condition only in which the increasing population with increasing longetivity fails to be catered with even the basic amenities. Worst still is the fact that such over burdening population creates havoc on the already dwindling natural resources only. While providing good medical facilities that help in longetivity of an individual, the nation also should see that the growth of population is under control so the ratio of individual versus the resources, natural or otherwise infra structural remains constant and no individual is deprived of his or her basic rights, whereas the nation does not lose further resources to the growing demand of the growing population.

while in developed countries it has helped in prosperity and accumulation of wealth with help of thought out and well planned technology oriented facilities of infra structure and controlled population, it has not been so in impoverished countries where the concerned authorities fail to provide the inhabitants with rightful provisions of basic facilities. Besides, the concerned authorities have also failed to control wanton increase of population in keeping with their resources, whether natural or man oriented. Again, the developed countries too procure considerable amount of natural resources from such countries for additional production of commodities that makes them more wealth-oriented. Therefore, the utilization of natural resources becomes manifold than the natural replenishment of them. Man also has failed to produce the natural resources of crops and other agricultural products at the pace of the necessities of the growing population. Therefore there has been an increasing difference between the demand of such utilities and supply for them. As a result there have been considerable amount of destruction and misuse of natural resources which otherwise has created a dilemma of environmental justice and which should have been preserved for future generation for the prosperity of their posterity.

The predicament, experienced by present day society was much foreseen by some scientists ahead of their time. In the middle of nineteenth century, scientist Malthus has expressed how the growing population will increase exponentially in ratio to the food supply available to the mass. According to him, the earth has got limited capacity to feed its population beyond certain limit of its input and it is called 'carrying capacity'. Over a period of time when population will multiply food input will increase additionally only, leaving large section of society, mostly poor remaining impoverished. The ratio, if of population and food supply, was one to one at the beginning of modern era, it increased in difference of two to one, then four to two and then eight to three over the proceeding time. Therefore, not only the natural resources are having to be supplemental for the deficit of supply, they are also bearing the brunt of providing additional needs in form of fuel and other succors of life for the surplus population. Although technology is making up considerably in increasing the food supply, it is not seemingly enough if the population remains increasing at the exponential rate. Regarding the evidence of growing pressure of over population, C.J. Barrow expresses, _ "The malthusian thesis is that human reproduction capacity puts pressure on means of subsistence. A population may be said to have reached a crisis point if either its rate of growth or its size generates demand out of balance with prevailing environmental, economic or social conditions."[5]

5.2.2. The Indirect Processes of Ecological Degradation:
The Processes of Urbanization and Industrialization

The development processes of Urbanization and Industrialization can be called as 'responsible' for growing pollution of the atmosphere i.e. contamination of the components of the environment _ i.e. the air, the water and the ground (soil). The components of the environment, which, in the past, were never used to be contaminated and polluted beyond certain limitation and whatever amount occurred, it occurred naturally 0nly, till human civilization reached the age of modernization. In late nineteenth and early twentieth century, when new-found scientific achievement had made mankind enjoy the fruit of scientific inventions, they were unaware of the possible fallout of the newly acquired knowledge of the applied sciences. The two most devastating processes that man had established in the early nineteenth century in the name of development of humanity were the processes of Urbanization and Industrialization which in later days had vastly affected the congregated habitats of mankind with the adverse effects, the fall-out of which mankind was not aware of. Slowly, it occurred in a redeeming way the possible repercussion of all the 'development activities that man carried in God's own way, i.e. by recreating things that came as additional benefits besides nature's bounty that God has given him. The process of urbanization, and even that of industrialization in their puerile stages existed before, with the former being synonymous with the progress of some of the earliest civilizations in the world. However, neither any urban enclaves in ancient time were as devastating to the environment, nor they were so extensive in their propensity as it has been now. The congregation of human population in the urban areas, especially those in metropolitan cities has been consuming enormous amount of energy for the ongoing activities, along with the amount of energy going out as the waste product of it. It is the amount of waste in the conclaves of modern generation which has created the problems of pollution as it has invaded the world of environment's components with all the alien matters that do not go along with it i.e. destruct its elementary properties. The same can be said of the process of Industrialization, in which not only immense amount of land areas has been occupied by the industries, the waste materials contaminating the air with its emission, and that of soil and the water bodies by throwing the waste and effluents on them and has rendered the environmental components useless for further utility, but also has put the common people into jeopardy by letting them get exposed to such dangerous pollutants. When these processes are being considered as boon for the well-being of mankind, it has been achieved, as mentioned earlier, at the grievous harm committed to nature, which may not always be retrievable to mankind. However, the harm done to nature should not be the stumbling block for welfare activities achieved by technological achievement, as they are part of human progress only. What is most required here is that the nature, which has contributed so immensely for human progress should not be made to pay price for it and industries should be modified technologically not to harm nature in the process.

5.2.3. *Physical ElementsCausing Degradation and Destruction to Environment*

The various Physiological Implications of Ecological Degradation

We have found out that due to the various types of human activities causing destruction of our environment both in direct and indirect manner, the contaminations of the environmental components have occurred and as an outcome of it pollution of the components have resulted in affecting mankind in manifold manners, both at individual and global level. We may categorize the polluting agents in accordance with their types and sources from where they originated to how ultimately they are affecting us, both at individual and global level. *The list of polluting agents,* sources and also the types of pollution are given below:-

Air Pollution
The Polluting Agents
1. CO(Carbon Monoxide)

2. CO2 (Carbon-di-oxide)

3. S2O4-
4. Hno4 and other nitric combinations
Particules

Ground or Soil Pollution
PollutingAgents
1. InorganicEffluents
Phosphates, nitrates etc.

2. Cadmium molecules
3. Sulphates, carbon molecules etc.
4. of coal, crude oil, lmestones
from mining of mineral ores
5. Organic Effluents
Pulp, pulp water
6. Residues
7. Solid residues of food,
disposable materials

8. Animal bones and other substances
9. Mineral residues of coal,

Water Pollution
1. Nitrates, phosphates, carbon molecules
2. Chemical colours
3. Minerals, crude oil
4. Pulp, animal substances, 'black' water

5. Municipal organic substances
Noise or Sound Pollution

Sources of Pollution
Transportation:Primarily
Due to motor vehicles' emission
Also due to factory emission
primarily due to industrial emission
Also due to vehicles' emission such
as diesel and outdated railway mode

from factories,
railway emission also because of dredging
mining, carried outside, from

Sources of Pollution

Fertilizer factories

Paper factories
Chemical Factories mineral residues
cement and lime factories

paper factories
fruit & canning industries
municipal corporation's
Garbage dump, breweries, textile
Industries
leather factories
from mining of mineral ores
Cement and lime factories

Fertilizers, pharmaceuticals
Dyeing factories
from nearby mine or refinery
paper, food
Canning and leather factories,
Breweries, Refineries
municipal sewerage
Noise from machineries, vehicles,
Microphone

5.3. The Various Implications of Ecological Degradation

It has already become apparent mass population world over that the effect of environmental degradation and destruction is ubiquitous in manner and universal in nature. Degradation and destruction imply effect to both an individual and mass population and again in physiological and psychological manners.

5.3.1. *Effect on Individual*

Besides the degradation of the environment, including the atmosphere, pollution is not only putting into jeopardy the finer qualities of nature for its future survival, but also effecting human beings, both physical and often mental repercussions showing psychological effects in single or collective manners, besides causing socio-economic problems. The outcome can be not only individually, but also occur locally or even Globally effecting right from one single individual to mass population as well. One finest example of such effect at physiological level is that of 'sound' pollution, which mainly may occur due to the usage of loud speaker, heavy machination or even the constant movement of noisy vehicles on road. Due to such noises which are usually accompanied by high level of decimal, an individual exposed to it may be rendered lacking in or being less in hearing ability, besides an assorted number of ailing factors. An individual, exposed to such high level of sound, may fail in concentration in work place, leading to perhaps less compatibility, ultimately resulting in low self esteem. The lateral effects can be called as mental repercussion only.

Due to the pollution caused by both the processes of urbanization and industrialization, people can be affected both physiologically and often psychologically too. For example, in places where noise level is very high due to noise pollution caused by transportation or some kinds of machineries, hearing impairing or less of hearing abilities may occur occasionally to people exposed to higher decibels (the standard measurement of sound) may also produce less input in workplaces as it may affect his/her work-concentration. People working in mines suffer from assorted variety of heart and skin problems, those in congested urban areas from assorted stomach illnesses for drinking contaminated water and also from lack of concentration due to congested living conditions. Besides, in big cities, people suffer from such secondary pollutants as photo synthesis, in which the smoke mixed with fog in winter days creates smog causing severe breathing illnesses. There are many others in the list of such grievances of polluting agents in the environment.

5.3.2 The Effect of Pollution onNatural Resources and
Masses(Indirect Way) in the World in Collective manner

We, as a part of human mass on earth, and however small may it be in importance, have already come to realize the possible impact on not only an individual, but also being of such apocalyptic dimension that its effect is bound to be witnessed by the mass population as a whole. The destructions of environmental components has been so gigantic in proportion that it is not only some of the individuals that are effected but substantial proportion or the whole lot of human population is bound to be effected by such impact. The way the fine balance of beneficial elements- such as oxygen and nitrogen are being on treat due to the widespread destruction of the Rain Forest areas in the world, the same way the 'Greenhouse' effect, caused due to automobile emission is also dangerous for human kind. Besides, natural anti-phenomena like the 'Ozone layer hole' or 'Global Warming' in overall perspective may have as well spell peril for human kind. Therefore it is of utmost necessity to highlight the problems that may soon put into difficulty the day to day life of total population of human kind on earth.

(A)Depletion of Rain Forest: _ The incessant cutting down of woods in Rain Forests has been carried out without any foresight on its repercussion on the future generations. The Rain Forest Areas on earth, being mostly concentrated in some of the tropical regions met with the precondition of moistness and heavy rainfall, are so thick with areas of trees that sunrays can barely intrude through them. The thick top of trees called 'canopy' not only helps in retaining the moist underneath it, it also allows the highest number of species to breed in, letting them to be the richest areas of Flora and Fauna i.e. bio-diversity existing on the earth. However, it is not the single reason for its importance in the world. The huge areas in the world, covered by the canopies, help the world in retaining the required amount of oxygen which occurs as a result of oxygen cycle in the atmosphere. The atmosphere requires to balance among the various gases that prevail in it, so that gases required for living organism need not be overstepped by the gases neither friendly for living organisms nor for the atmosphere. Besides, the water vapour emitted by the huge wood regions in the process of exhalation helps in accumulation of the same in large amount so that rainfall occurs in regulated manner. It also helps in absorbing the carbon in the atmosphere in the process of inhalation which helps the harmful carbon molecules in becoming less in amount and therefore from dominating the stratosphere. However, the reduction of the tropical rain forest all over the world, specially the Amazon Rain Forest in Brazil as result of man's quest for materialistic persuasion, has put all

the 'natural' benefits into jeopardy and in fact the whole of living world will be in stake if such degradation is not sacked in time. Author C.J. Barrow expresses in following way about destruction of rain forest, _"Rain forest clearance is likely to upset a complex web of interdependence."[*6]

With the destruction of Rain Forest areas occurring in a rapid manner, not only the oxygen cycle of Earth's atmosphere is at jeopardy, but also the abundance of bio-diversity found in the tropical forest areas, as they are getting reduced everyday due to their depletion occurred at man's hand. The extinction of species at a rapid manner may jeopardize the manifold characteristics of bio- diversity in the world and thereby may weaken the genetic mutating process in the process.

(B)Acid rain

The emitted gases and particles of various harmful substances from factories and motor vehicles often mix with the water vapour or moist in the atmosphere and are carried away to far off places by wind. After certain time period, the harmful gases come down to earth along with the rain drops formed from the carrying moist and they cause harm or even injuries to the reigning harvest or even animals and other living beings residing in the vicinity of given area of raining. Usually such rain carries as harmful gas particles as that of sulphuric acid or nitrates usually emitted from chemical and other factories. They can cause blister on the leaves of the trees and may affect skin of animals and other living beings.

However, the most important fact related to acid rain is that the rain may occur not only in much nearer places from where the original sources of pollution reside, but also in places that are in no way might be related or connected to such places of origin of the acid and therefore the inhabitants of it may not be aware of possible repercussion of it occurring at unwarranted moments. Unless some technological devices are invented to predict and prevent such occurrences at such unforeseen places, acid rain will always cause peril for the 'eco systems' of places that are not connected to producing pollutants of atmosphere.

(C)The Green house Effect

The carbon molecules which are generally found as combination with other natural elements such as oxygen or nitrogen, often get emitted from factories or also as single combination with oxygen as carbon monoxide exhausted from motor cars and vehicles in the atmosphere. The accumulated carbon molecules which had gathered up in the atmosphere in larger quantity due to such emission from factories and motor vehicles and due to their comparative heaviness to other gaseous elements, they start accumulating in the atmosphere, then becoming like a blanket and covering areas over the earth. However, the carbon molecules which absorb heat do the same as the heat is radiated from the earth and it fails to go out of earth's atmosphere, making it warmer by a few more centigrade. Such change in temperature causes erratic ocean movement as usually the warm waters of it flow to the cooler parts of the world in osmosis process, and as a result the weather near and other parts of the land areas starts erratic patterns of it. It also helps in Global Warming.

(D)The Ozone Layer Depletion:- Above the layer of Stratosphere, lies another layer of Ozone, which is an element with three molecules of Oxygen and unlike the latter which has two molecules only and it makes as an balancing factor for oxygen counts in the atmosphere besides some other functions. Odorous and slightly pugnacious in taste and considered equally dangerous for living beings like the carbon dioxide or the carbon monoxide are, the gaseous substance has been protecting the biosphere from being harmed by the dangerous rays coming from the Sun and thereby affecting living organism.

However, it has not remained same over last one and about half decades, as it has been put to threat due to certain elements used for human luxury,_____ CFC i.e. Chlorofluro Carbon, a molecule used in some spray materials or foam beds or in making of the fridge get strayed to the atmosphere where the ozone layer lies and displaces one of the three molecules to reduce it to oxygen gas, thus letting the gas to be depleted in the effected area. Recently the depletion has be come so ominous that it has created a big hole in the layer the size of a small continent each in areas such as over South America and Antarctica, thereby letting the dangerous kind of rays to infiltrate into earth's atmosphere. Recently scientists in western countries invented technology to prevent the furtherance of the ozone hole occurring in the earth's atmosphere or even to close up the hole itself with the help of technology. However, to stop the problem from occurring at all, a kind of consensus required to prevail upon the mentality of people, so that they in collective manner refuse to utilize the unfriendly substance that harms the atmosphere in general and Ozone layer in particular.

(E)The Effect of Over- Population: _ Increasing population is over burdening the earth with additional input on its resources and stressing it limitation mark. The surplus population has tried to overtake land areas meant for reservation of wild species or forest areas. The outcome of it resulted into, according to M.S. Rathore, _ "They (Ownership, degradation of land,

commercialization of agriculture) directly or indirectly relate to the population, their property rights, and their changing socio-economic conditions."*7

(F)The Threatened Species : The Possible extinction of species

The WWF (an abbreviation for World Wide Fund)∀ which has been making efforts to safeguard the animals and fighting for the cause of the wildlife animals has been bringing out a book regularly and which has been called as 'Red Data Book'. It is listing the name of the particular categories of animals that are in danger of extinction or dwindling in number. They have been categorized as 'Threatened'- animals whose numbers are reducing and therefore the possibility remains to be extinct in near future; 'Endangered'_ which are already fewer in number and in very much danger of being extinct in near future, unless proper measures are taken to save them and retrieve with help of technology the extinct ones which have been either eliminated from the world by human greed or due to their own inability to survive in face of dwindling forest areas or necessary kind of food. Invariably, the numbers of extinct animal are growing day by day and the list of endangered animals being even longer than earlier, although many governments are taking steps to protect such endangered or threatened animals inhabiting in their individual countries. Therefore, it is becoming an utmost necessity for human being to protect these animals with rightful and proper ways. In India tiger rhinoceros snow leopards white-necked duck etc are Considered as endangered animals whereas elephants, sambhars etc are threatened animals. Likewise in a country like China the panda, a species of bear family is considered as endangered. In India, the government has established the 'Tiger Project' in areas where they still exist in numbers. Some other animals and birds figuring in the book of 'Red- Data' are as follows :-

Threatened	endangered	Normal	Extinct
Elephant	Tiger	Zebra	Dodo bird
Leopard	Panda bear	Ziraffe	
Himalayan Bear	Rhionoceros		
Polar bear	Koala Bear		

∀ **World Wild life Fund** is an organization that has been, since the middle of twentieth century which has been relentlessly attempting to protect and preserve various animals and other species at different locations over the world. They have been publishing a book at regular interval to inform the the present status of the condition of different species in the wilderness and their existing number.

(G)*The Global Warming*:_*The Climatic Change*

The Global Warming is another phenomenon occurring as aftermath of increased polluting factors in the atmosphere. It is the result of growing amount or number of warming up elements, _ especially carbon which is considered heavier than other elements and therefore absorbent of some of rays or sunlight and which are later reflected at dark time, causing radiation or heat in the atmosphere. The accumulating heat factor in large amount creates more temperature in the atmosphere, i.e. it causes the regular temperature to increase by a few more centigrade, as a result of which the usual temperature for the particular time period in the particular place will be more in intensity and more warmer than usually happen. However, such unusual warming, which may happen in an overall manner in the world, may cause the regular temperature of the world to increase by few centigrade which in return will cause the snow in the caps of high mountains melt because of the unusual warmth in the atmosphere. Such unusual melting again in return will cause heavy rain and the water in sea level increase and may cause inundation in many places in the world where it has never occurred before. Regarding the climatic change on earth, author Lester R. Brown and his associate Christopher Flavin have expressed in the following manner-"The global climate issue is an essential foundation of natural eco systems and ….. If we are entering a new period of climatic instability, the consequences can be serious indeed, affecting virtually all of Earth's eco systems, accelerating pace of extinction, and leaving few areas of economic life untouched. [*8]

The causes of Global warming can be attributed to be in two fold manner :- natural way and the artificial way. While due to the flares of the Sun increasing every few years (usually every eleven years) the temperature of the Earth's atmosphere subsequently may increase naturally, the repercussion is also temporary and its impact on atmosphere remains minimal and rebounding. However, when it comes to the artificial global warming caused by man's excessiveness of causing pollution and the subsequent 'greenhouse effects' caused to the earth's atmosphere, the probability remains that the impact of such action may become permanently damaging to the earth's atmosphere. The increasing warmth of the earth's atmosphere may permanently melt the 'capping' ice moulds of the two arctic regions on the two opposing poles of the earth as a result of which it would not only increase the water level of the seas and oceans, it would also cause severe flood situations subsequently and may permanently inundate many human habitats in low lying areas of the world and cause havoc to the living hood conditions of the the local inhabitants. Such a situation can be named as the secondary repercussion or co lateral harm of global warming.

According to C.J. Burrow,_ "Global cooling or warming may progress via transient steps, rather than steady change, and there may be different effects from region to region, for a time, as say, air mass movement or ocean current change."[9] Again he expresses, _ "Climatic trends are inadequately established and it is not certain whether human activity will counter or reinforce natural changes."[10] However, regarding the enormity of the problem of climatic change as a result of global warming, he reiterates, _"Many consider that enhanced global warming (accelerated greenhouse effect or anthropogenic warming) is the most serious challenge to be faced in the twenty first century."[11]

5.4. Assessment of Environmental Impact

Apart fro finding the root cause of the environmental problems, the need arises to assess the enormous impact on the present day society as a whole, all physically, psychologically or even futuristically on both mankind in particular and the earth in general. Even more important is the fact that different environmental problems affect a population differently, letting the assessment of the impact get mired and complicated.

The anthropogenic degradation of the environment, caused to different aspects of it has been resulting into different kind of impact on earth. For example, if deforestation caused to a locality may result into shortfall of rain in the area, likewise global warming can cause melting of snow in places which can be called as storehouses of water resource on earth, beside helping in balance of temperature; the repercussion of which is flooding or storm in unwarranted manner. Regarding the deforestation caused in many important and sensitive areas, author C.J. Barrow has expressed,- "… certainly when forests are cleared there may be alterations of water tables, soil changes, altered micro climate, etc."[12]. Again, on need of rain forests on earth he expresses,-"Rain forests behave like large water bodies: they moderate surrounding climate, reducing diurnal temperature fluctuation, maintaining humidity .."[13] Some of the most important environmental problems growing proportionately in relation to impact of transnational characteristics are _Global Warming due to Greenhouse effect resulting in Climatic Change and Ozone Layer Depletion due to pollution content in the atmosphere. Regarding the role of industry in society, author Satish Shastri expresses in the following way, _"Industry is central to economics of modern societies and an indispensable motor of growth. But today, industry is on the edge of the interface between people and the environment."[14] In The similar way regarding their impact on earth as outcome of human economical aspiration, environmentalists Lester R. Brown and Christopher Flavin express that,-"With the Acceleration of history has come escalating pressures on natural world, _on which we remain utterly dependent, even in the information age. New forms of environmental disruption _ Stratospheric ozone Depletion and greenhouse warming _ have began altering natural ecosystems in the past two decades, doing particular damage to coral reefs and suspected damage to species ranging from frogs to trees. In addition, the continuously growing global economy has collided with many of the Earth's natural limits. These collisions can be seen in such trends as the shrinkage of forests, the depletion of aquifers, and the collapse of fisheries."[15] Another environmentalist, B.B. Garg reiterates his views regarding the role of industry in human society in the following manner, _"During the early stages of industrialization, the environmental impact of industrial effluents did not pose major threat to the existence of living beings. However, with rapid industrial growth and population exploitation, environment has been exposed to hazards and the extent of damage to our environment has become a matter of serious concern to people in general and environmentalists in particular. Release of wide array of pollutants viz., toxic substances, gases and heavy metals has affected human health as well as the whole ecosystem. Man alone is the cause of this damage and alone can rectify it. No longer can warning signals be ignored under the pretext of modernization."[16] Again, on the ill effect caused by the unwanted residues of the by product on society, Satish Shastri speaks in the following manner,-"On one hand, rapid growth of production in all the fields helped to satisfy the needs of the people, but on the other it has forced man to live in unhygienic and degraded environment.""[17]

5.5. THE ETHICAL IMPLICATIONS OF ENVIRONMENTAL CRISES ON MODERN SOCIETY

The Introductory

In the study, however, the emphasis has been laid upon not only the physiological Impact the degradation of nature has caused and will do so in future on mankind, it is time for not only to analyze the impact and implication of Ethics has caused in our life in relation to such degradation, but also its possible repercussion on our ethical views and values in future, as it suggests a mercurial impact on 'ethical degradation' only. However, besides studying the ethical impact and implication on human mind and society in relation to nature, the emphasis is also on nature's impact on human mind beside the ethical values and how it has been personified in other spheres life of human kind. We can call them 'A Priori' and 'A Posteriori' implications of Ethical degradation. The whole episode of environmental degradation needs scrutiny to find out the proper classification for each kind of ecological, therefore environmental degradation, besides the assessment carried out on what are the factors and sections of our society that are associated with the activities causing the irreprehensible degradation to our environment. However, apart from dwelling on our perceptions of ethical values and otherwise the philosophical and spiritualistic conceptions, we also should scrutinize Nature's influence on our day to day life since time immemorial.

5.5.1. 'A Priori' Implications of Environmental Crisis

When regarding the various ethical implications we witness as fallout of environmental degradation, we can call it 'a priori' implications, as it results out in a series of effects that are ominous by their conspicuous presence in society. In fact many of us are almost always assured of the fact that it is only the 'Ethical' degradation of our age old values that were leading to the ultimate and almost irrevocable repercussions of environmental degradation. In certain ways they are also supplementary of each other's enormity. The 'a priori' implications, are being evident through the following assessments:-

(a) *The Tribals are Losing Their Age Old Value System of Revering and Safeguarding Nature due to the factors leading to Environmental Degradation, thereby letting them commit Further Destruction of Nature and falling trapped into the Vicious circle of Destruction. It has amounted to both Ethical Degradation of their Value System and Witnessing its Implications on their Society.*

The 'a priori' degradation of ethical values and the consecutive result in evidential implication on society get expressed in manifold ways. First of all we find the 'Tribal' people losing their age old value system, as they discover their operating areas shrinking rapidly due to cutting down of the trees or also non availability of game product on which they are depended upon as their staple food, as their areas are encroached upon by other communities. The tribal who had been revering nature as their primary idol of worshipping as well as their source of living hood and therefore never letting the equilibrium of their local ecosystem to become imbalanced either by cutting too many trees or killing too many games, have discovered themselves in a losing proposition as the outside factors have encroached upon areas that has put their own value system out of proportion or balance. The tribal communities are therefore finding themselves in the contradictory position of degrading their own value system by cutting down trees that their ancestors and they had been revering from time immemorial or killing the fewer number of animals existing in their areas leading to their scarcity or extinction and thus letting the imbalance of the eco system in their operating areas become ruined or degraded and thereby imbalanced. In a way the corrosion occurring in the value system of a tribal society is the first indication of the effects of repercussion of environmental degradation on human psychology in an overall manner.

(b) *The Cause of Over Population in many underdeveloped or developing countries leading to Economic Depression among Common masses, ultimately resulting into its Ethical degradation leading to its Implication of Environmental Degradation.*

People in general, mostly in countryside driven to economic depression due to initial overpopulation, then leading to scarcity food or less amount of it due to greater number of per capita division, and ultimately driving them to collect food from inside forest areas, leading again to the vicious circle of killing animals and often leading to their extinction in that particular area and thereby causing imbalance of the local eco system. On the other hand, quite often for the same reason of overpopulation which itself is a cause of pollution hazard in an underdeveloped or developing nation, lead the encroachment of nearby forest areas, thereby not only do they reduce the forest areas and number of animals living in it, they also forage it for pieces of wood and twigs for fuel leading to disturbance of the equanimity of wildlife, driving them away either out of it or to deeper forest and thereby upsetting the eco system. In more intent cases such bunch of people would prefer to cut down the trees of the forest areas for fuel or even sell or other games of animals and birds of it so as to make hard money for their livelihood. Often some of them even start poaching in restricted areas for much bigger amount of gain out of it. However, in this case it becomes apparent that the reason of overpopulation as the ultimate cause of 'Ethical degradation' leading to its implication on various actions of common people is the ultimate reason and result of economical degradation or poverty. Therefore we may rightfully call 'economical paucity' as the ultimate fall out of 'Ethical Degradation'.

(C) The Twentieth Century value of questing for comfort and Entertainment being also one primary reason that has lead to the Degradation and the ultimate Destruction of 'Nature' and Natural assets for us. It is one 'A Priori' implication that is leading to the Ultimate Destruction of Nature.

However, not always we can call the reason of 'economical degradation' as the ultimate result of 'Ecological Degradation' too. Quite often it is case of 'Pursuit' for comfort provided by modern technology at the cost of property gained from Nature's bounty and resulting from quest and thirst for material benefits. It merely shows greed and thirst for comfort on mankind's part.

5.5.2. The 'A Posteriori' Implications of Environmental crisis

Like the many a reasons leading to the ultimate destruction of our surrounding ecology and therefore the Environment, we may presume to apprehend also many a reasons over there that would lead to further ethical degradation amidst human kind that would result as the fall out of the absence of nature caused by such actions to both the physiological and the mental world, specially of human kind. The world is perhaps yet to scrutinize on the possible repercussion on human psyche that would grow up and develop in absence of the nuances of nature and be able to survive the trial and triumph of human's technological achievements. Such repercussions being considered as "A Posteriori', that is, the 'After Effect or Implications' of environmental degradation, on both human psyche and also the physiological world have been discussed below:-

(a)*After the process of destruction of Nature would become near complete, It is important to note how human psyche would react to Ethical values*:-While we have already talked about the 'A Priori' implication reflecting ethical degradation of human mind which has resulted into the ultimate environmental degradation, it is also time to think the possible repercussion of ethical propensity in respect of a spectacular diminishment of 'Nature' from human's day to day life. The absence of ethical guidance to human mind in respect of nature can be devastating to human psyche, some futuristic genres feel. However, what would be the 'de facto' implications of ethical propensity in a situation when actually such a devastating catastrophe occurs and mankind would be left to fend for itself? In such a situation how man's ethical values would be prioritized and dictated to cater to man's necessities?

However, the reason here to believe that with the increasing diminishment of Nature's importance in man's life would also affect the importance of ethical value in proportionate manner is that philosophers believe there to exist a very deep bond between the two. In fact an inseparable one between them, as a result of which not only they become integral to each other, but also complementary as well. While Nature provides the basis of ethical values by its exemplary tenets followed by its inhabitants, such as love, care responsibility, duty, obligation, proper judgmental attitude etc., Ethics in the process teaches human kind how to respect and to make itself realize as part of nature only, rather than as devoid of it.

From one point of view, we may assume that mankind may start undermining the importance of nature, their predilection for 'natural utility' had been thrust upon them vis a vis ethical values and may start further believing it to be 'redundant ', as they may find it a nominative science and not an experimental or materialistic science, that dictates the physiological good or bad to mankind. As the 'ethical dictation' or 'decree of ordain' would perhaps be disappearing from man's life, it is per chance that his life would become too wild to be ordained to any 'good' or 'bad' value or too mechanized, driven by certain dictions that would be concerned for 'great' human kind but not anymore for individual's 'good' or 'bad' or to cater for his emotion or emotional values. It seems, perhaps like all the 'inconsistency' of nature's ways, it suits a man's predilection to constitute a part in nature's inconsistent system! However, what appears to be 'method in madness' in nature's system, it has also dictated the basic human or ethical values _ like love, care, responsibility to mankind also based upon which all human development and progress whether in his mental world or in the world outside, has occurred. Therefore the sole mental power or 'will', the sheer ethical value had inducted in human mind the necessity to retain his 'humane' value to survive on earth, whether as part of the system or as the 'freak' or 'odd man (read here as 'species') out in the world and it seems to be the only or solely a kind of antithesis to the possible 'wildness' that may lead mankind's inroad into either the complete annihilation of the natural feeling or coax it to be part of the process of mechanization. As a result of it, he will never be able to perhaps enjoy such feeling like love and care in the world.

(b) ***From practical point of view, Ethical Degradation leads to Nature's Degradation and possible destruction of it in future, if the mishandling of the situation is allowed to continue.*** However, the most important feature of the issue is that in such an incomprehensible situation, common people will face unimaginable shortage of basic supplies that are acquired from Nature. As a result, ***the society may encounter further ethical devaluation as we may find common folks trying to destruct whatever little of Nature being left for their own survival's sake. In such a situation, we may call it a truly 'a posteriori' Repercussion of ecological Degeneration.***

It is being to everyone's knowledge by now that the world is getting shorter of its resources day by day, _whether they produce renewable or non-renewable energy, while non renewable ones are dwindling, renewable are yet to be harnessed properly. It is no wonder that sooner or later the world may become exhausted of the non renewable resources, as a result of which the poorer nations will be highly affected as they are dependent on the 'product' supply of resources from 'developed' countries, even though the 'raw material' resources are supplied by them only. In case of dwindling 'raw material' resources, the repercussion seems to become evident already by now as we find that outnumbering population of poorer and developing countries are starting to readily occupy forest areas that are providing them with natural resources. Lack of supply with basic amenities such as fuel and place to live-in has driven them to opt for measures that may further destruct the nature's equity. Besides there are whole genres of communities coming up mostly in economically weak countries, who in a bid to earn money in a quick and fast way have been targeting wild assets to fulfill their aspiration, resulting in rapid extinction of the many species of natural resources. Such acts of heinous proposition have only reflected the degraded values of present day society. In a way, it completes the cycle of recurrence of ethical degeneration resulting into not only destruction of nature, but of ethical values as well too.

However, they are all the implications, i.e. the repercussion of the ethical degeneration, the society is experiencing in recent era. The practical impact of man generated pollution, i.e. of ecological degradation has already been much evident and discussed in day to day life. Therefore, it is high time to bring into the perspective of finding the rightful solution to problems that has been being considered the most important and discussed about issue since the later period of the late twentieth century. There has been a desperate quest to find a solution both of pragmatic and specially of ethical kind, although the process of destruction is continuing almost everywhere in the world undaunted. The suggestions for finding the most rational one has been in plenty, although no one is being able to find the most useful and effective one to both stem the destructive degradation of the environment and regenerate the lost equities of nature.

In the context we have also to keep in mind that there has always been the problem of pollution in form of waste since the days of urbanization coming into practice as a mode of living hood. Therefore there has always been certain effort to keep in check the ill effect of the waste and managing it, although the problem seems to outgrow any effort in the last century as both urbanization related and technological achievement increased manifold and as well as has become wide spread. But both the progress and development of both urbanization process and that of technology being 'ubiquitous' in an ominous way and complementary to each other, a number of agencies in form of authorities has been trying to take care and handle it. Man has been establishing such authorities to take care of them with a central authority to sanction (for example, the kings in ancient time to the government offices in modern time) for the implementation. The role of such agencies needs to be assessed in the context of present day crisis of the environment in the world.

5.6. **Assessment of the Environmental Ethical implications**

The repercussion of environmental degradation has been of late too telling and evident in the day to day life of even common mass population, specially those residing in developing countries in the world, the root of which has been believed to be the deviated utilitarian values as in accordance with the views of most scholars and philosophers in the present day world.

With growing level of environmental awareness amidst almost all of its strata, the modern society is keeping abreast in finding suitable solution as remedy for the malaise of environmental crises being evident in form of various kind of socio cultural impacts, besides the environmental ones. However, there has been assorted kind of effort either to solve or find a solution which has proven to be either half measured or too inadequate to solve all the problems caused due to exhaustion of natural resources or degradation of it. The efforts made from different perspectives, either pragmatic or hypothetic have not been able to bring in satisfactory result, as the root of the problems remain to be addressed or the interpretation of them has been too vague or not sufficient to cover the parameters of solution. According to scholar Wolfgang Haber, _"Many ecologists have convincingly demonstrated that the present use of natural resources, with all the carelessness and harmful side- and after-effects, will inevitably result in disaster. This message, is however, meant as a general warning against resource depletion and environmental pollution and as a strong call to change the general attitude towards environment. The arguments are based on extrapolations of current trends of usage and pollution, the aim of the arguments is to challenge these trends and prevent them from coming true. It is to call for awareness." [18] Again regarding usage of technology he says,- "The time has now come to accept the lessons of ecosystem research, i.e. to recognize the exploitative nature, and to invest in intellectual and technical skills into supporting the protective and regulatory processes of ecosystems which alone will grant us sustainabilility and durability. Only in this way, can the doomsday syndrome be overcome."[19]

Of late, some of the environmental problems, however, have reached enormous propensity to be considered together with other environmental problems. For example, the global warming problem due to climatic change as a result of atmospheric pollution has become so gigantic that no individual country can hope to find a solution to it. Therefore environmentalist Elizabeth Edmondson has expressed in the following way, _ "Climatic change management strategies raise ethical questions concerning relative industrial capacities and distribution of consequences, responsibilities and burdens within the international political system[20]" Regarding the importance of ethics in finding the solution she says,_ "In climatic change management, ethical issues cannot be sidestepped or given diminished status.[21]

Taking into account on her emphasis on finding ethical solution, however partially, we can say that it certainly takes a very important role in finding our future solutions. In fact, philosophers of the modern society believe the root cause of all the problems has been rooted in the society itself and therefore has insinuated from it. It is none other but ethical value related, as ethics itself has been the moral, therefore the consciential guide of the society. *__Since ethical values basically dictates the dynamics of the society, that is, all the rationalistic activities of it, therefore it has been concluded by them that it is the degenerated values of modern society which in form of utilitarian outlook has ultimately driven it to the destruction of natural resources of the environment and therefore the degradation of it making it primarily responsible for the present day environmental crisis. But, the most important conclusion we can take regarding the remedial measures is that, if and while the problem is ethical value related, then finding solution by methods elsewhere such as techniological or even academic (such as ecological research) ones, may proof to be only relative in nature, and therefore temporal and partial only. For an ethical problem, the solution will have to be an ethical only.__*

The assorted problems born out of the environmental crisis are starting to affect human thinking and society in adverse way giving way to the arise of conflict of interest. Author Michael Renner expresses in the following way- "The degradation of land, freshwater and marine resources will become more pronounced with the onset of global climatic change and environmentally induced conflicts are likely to intensify."[*22] The piquant situation demands rightful scrutiny and moral judgment of the environmental crisis.

However, whenever, ethical judgment comes in relation to it, then also comes along the consideration of obligation and responsibility, because man cannot escape the burden of them, as he has been using nature as a kind of right. According to author Nigel Dower, our society has three kind of responsibilities in relation to environment, _ "In fact we can identify three dimensions to the moral responsibility,.... first to people living in future, second to kinds of being other than humans and third globally towards anyone anywhere."[*23] Besides, the necessity of safeguarding nature, i.e. environment as an act of moral responsibility has been creating dissension among those who are interested in using nature to optimum level or for the only benefit of human kind. Regarding our responsibility towards our future generations, Author John Stenmark expresses in the following way,_ "To summarize, two types of problem arise in dealing with the question of our responsibility to future generations: the population problem and the problem of obligation..."[*24]. The mutual paths of concerns has resulted into two opposite kind of actions, thereby causing conflict of interest. Moreover, man has to own the responsibility over the change he has caused to the surrounding nature. According to Authors John Kesperson and Jeanne Kesperson, _ "Even, where basic path of causality may be evident, the relationship among human causes, environmental perturbations and effects may be non linear and chaotic."[*25] Even the degradation of nature also has affected the finer qualities of human faculty and therefore according to C.J. Barrow, _"The loss of forest and woodlands is an aesthetic loss: they have been and continue to be a source of inspiration for scientists, writers, artists,...In some situations such qualities may provide enough incentive for conservation."[*26] The modern society has arrived at a cross point where both the related groups are bidding for take over of issues. The environmentalists are making effort for conservation, whereas utilitarian are for utilization of nature in optimum level. An ethics bringing in solution to the conflicts comes into the necessity for the present day society.

References:-

1. C.J. Barrow- *Developing the environment –ch. Preface*-p.3
2. *Ibid.,- ch. preface*,-p. i-ii).
3. *- U. Kumar & M.J. Asija Biodiversity, p.12*
4. Satish Sastri-. *Impact of Environment, p.10*
5. *Michael Renner. 5. Fighting for Survival, p.48*
6. *State of the world, p.7*
7. *M.S. Rathore-Environment and Development-p.23*
8. *Brown and Flavin-State of the World-p.3*
9. *C.J. Barrow-. Developing Environment-p.75*
10. *Ibid., p.74*
11. *Ibid.,-p.75*
12. *Ibid.-p.150*
13. *Ibid.,-pp.150-151*
14. *Satish Sastri-Impact of Environment-p8*
15. *Lester E. Brown and Christopher Flavin -State of the World -p.7*
16. *B.B. Garg-Impact of Environment-p.150*
17. *Satish Sastri-Impact of Environment-p.8*
18. *Wolfgang Haber-Environmental Dilemma:-p.36*
19. *Ibid.,-p.37*
20. *Elizabeth Edmonton,-Governing the Environment,-p.44*
21. *Ibid.-p.45*
22. *Michael Renner-Fighting For Survival-p.74*
23. *Nigel Dower-World Ethics,.-p.160*
24. *John Stenmark-Environmental Policy Making,-p.51*
25. *John and Jeanne Kesperson,-Global Environmental Risk-p.9*
26. *C.J. Barrow-Developing Environment,-p.150*

CHAPTER 6

CONCLUSION

After focussing on various aspects of society I have made attempts to various activities of human kind in relation to nature and their ultimate repercussion on the well being of society. They are as follows,-

In the first chapter, attempt has been made to discuss about the three primary aspects of society, _ first, it is the human being, who is the basic unit of the society, who together with other fellow human beings consists of the society. Then comes ethics, an abstract form of thinking, existing in the mind of world within, which dictates and directs man as moral guide in relating to norms and actions in the society. Then comes nature, where human society is based. It is the balance of these three aspects that assures the harmony and flawless functioning of the society.

In the second chapter, a discussion is made on the relation between man and its moral guide ethics, development of ethics in western philosophy along with the development of society in ancient, medieval and modern era along with the ethical views of the great Greek philosophers Socrates, Plato and Aristotle and then Indian philosophy from ethical perspective, also with the focus on Buddhism and Gandhism ending with the critical study of Indian and western philosophy.

The third chapter is engaged in bringing into fore the relation of man and environment in society along with the physiological description of environment, then its impact on human mind and therefore on society and its inspiration for creation of art, literature and culture, also its role and importance in religion and also nature's perspective in Indian philosophy. From the objective perspective of man's relation with environment, we find its growing utilization along with the civilization of society and critical analysis of it.

In the fourth chapter, Ethics has been brought into discussion in light of environment, its intrinsic relationship with the latter in spite of being two diabolically opposite genres and the modern and scientific theories by Darwin such as Origin of species and the Natural Selection, the moral standing in them from social point of view, the new ethical concepts revived and arriving in modern arena of society, the relation of ethics and nature in Indian philosophy and last of all the focus being laid on Buddhism and Gandhism, the ideology of Mahatma Gandhi, who is believed to be inspired by nature and took up the cudgel of bringing in independence to India with non-violent method.

In the fifth chapter, an attempt has been made to discuss the various methods of destruction of environment by man, the impact of it on human as well as the surrounding at local and global level, its ultimate repercussion on society in form of ethical implication and possible far off ramification in near and distant future.

In the last and concluding chapter, an attempt has been made to establish the connection among the various factors, both from positive and negative perspectives, functioning and affecting the society, both in active and passive manners. Here a discussion is made on the resurrection of nature revering values in society in recent time in form of Environmentalism, the conflicts caused by them, the possible new method of preserving nature, the reasons behind the degradation of environment, its ethical perspective, the views and values of different scholars and philosophers, the possible need of methods of resurrection of an environmental society of its values, and last of all, arriving at a conclusion after taking into consideration all the associated factors of the crisis for the well being of society and the posterity of the future generation.

It has now been established that at the threshold of twenty first century, *the environmental problems is a global crisis and finding a true remedy for it is a challenge to future humanity* which has spread over to all the corners of the earth. While some problems are localized, others are universal in their dimensions. But anyhow people from all corners in the world are suffering or at least facing with the repercussions of such global or localized problems. More important is the fact that certain regions suffer from such ecological degradation (such as acid rain, ozone depletion or at greater extent-global warming) which may be due to the industries existing in the neighbouring regions or country. The environmental problem has become too ubiquitous anywhere in the world to ignore its implications and it is found that not only of economical policies of individual government, but also of psychological and ethical set of mind of the concurrent generations. Therefore it is necessary to make introspection of our doings, both for ourselves and for the environment around us. It is time not only to find out the reasons behind such degradation and bring into fore the various analytical views, but also to discuss the necessity for usurping the neo-realization for retrieving and rehabilitating the environment. It is also necessary to find out the factors involved in it and to discuss the role they are playing, the alternative methods that would not only sustain developmental activities but also to differ from the concurrent methods harmful for nature and more so to find out an 'ethical' basis for such measures, so that it would bring about a permanent solution to the environmental crisis in the modern society and reinstate nature to its old foundation in human mind set. However it needs intent scrutiny to judge the good for our society as much as for nature and what stands correct for future humanity as well. Therefore critical judgment and assessment of the probable alter natives are in fore for discussion in the bid to find out the ultimate solution so that with reprieve and remedial methods the implications of environmental crises on our society can be put to null and void.

In the limelight of finding solution many other factors related to it, such as reasons behind the environmental and therefore 'ethical degradation', the usurpation of environmental ethical revolution, the puny measures already being taken up and practiced for the redemption of the environmental woes, the discussion of the tentative alternative methods as solution etc. are to be extensively scrutinized before arriving at the 'rightful' solution. They are discussed below :-

(A) **Discussion of Ethical Management and Assessment of Environment and Environmental Impact**
(B) **Global and Local Awareness**
(C) **Finding ethical reasons behind Environmental Degradation**
(D) **New Conceptions in the Horizon**
(E) **Conflict of Interest :Man versus Nature**
(F) **Finding Ethical Solutions**

(A)ETHICAL MANAGEMENT
AND ASSESSMENT OF ENVIRONMENT

Management of produced commodities out of human skill is a socio-psychological process, with which a person can derive maximum benefit out of the implementation of one's effort. The same process is utilized in relation to natural resources, the common perception is to get the maximum benefit out of the limited amount of resources. However, while the resources are diminishing rapidly from earth and since human being cannot survive completely without utilizing any of them, the necessity has arisen to use the resources as less as possible and get the maximum benefit from less of them. It also becomes a necessity to look at the crisis from ethical perspective, looking at the precarious condition the natural resources have reached. According to Lynton Keith Caldwell, _ "The management of man's relationships with his environment is a practical expression of a system of ethics; it is an application of values, beliefs and moralities to relationship not only between man and nature but man and man." [*1]

Management of environment is, as has been mentioned before, basically managing the natural resources and also the effluent or prevention of pollution from harming the ecology of the surrounding with optimum possibility as well as an implementation criterion. While prevention of pollution or destruction of natural resources is a prolong process, proper management can reduce not only pollution, but also protect natural resources from being misused, and being utilized proper way, so that there is minimal wastage of them. Certain policies which are ethically redeeming, should be followed in management of environment, so that they help in deriving maximum benefit for not only the 'management', but also the environment. Besides, it is a rudimentary need that *Ethical policies be a part of its Criteria.*

Such follow up would not only help in stemming the indiscriminate destruction of nature but also will put restrain and control in managing the environment in future as well. They are as follows:-

1. Technical or technological Remedy :- With rapid development of technology, gaseous emission from factory or vehicles can be reduced considerably, which ironically are technological products only, by the process of replacing old machineries or by using complete new technology altogether. The same can be said for noise pollution, in case of prevention of deforestation or poaching management staff can be equipped with advanced technical equipment or weapon for prevention of such acts.

2. *Administrative effort:*-- To make various environment related policies successful, barely formulating them would remain paperwork or unfulfilled vows as long as they would not be implemented. However, it can happen through the proper and sincere co-operation of the governmental administration only. In fact so much difference may be conspicuous with the policies being implemented or not with developmental activities in developed countries carried on in full fledged manner and getting half done in developing countries like India, indicating the performance of the administrations of each individual category of countries to their optimums. It can be said to be same when it comes to implementing policies related to environment also. However, the actions of the administration are reflective of general awareness of the environmental crisis by common population also, as the administration is comprised of them only. Therefore it is very important that common population is made aware of the extent and propensity of environmental crises on society, which only would ascertain the increased knowledge of the ongoing problem at administrative level.

3. *Ethical Approach made Towards Environmental Management*:-
Besides committing restrain and control in utilizing natural resources, certain policies that are ethically viable may help considerably in reducing the degradation process.

The fact remaining that since the world is consisted of limited natural resources, which may get exhausted soon if not used in rightful manner and no resources will be left out for our future generations, therefore it is of optimum necessity to safeguard the natural resources from being misused or exploited. Ways and means of skillful utilization of both the natural resources and the waste, besides following certain ethical policies there from will help safeguarding it for the future. They are as follows:-

*(a) **No Wastage of Natural Resources***: - while using various resources, often a considerable amount of them are allowed to go waste in the process of production of commodities from raw materials. Saving on such excess materials will allow not only lengthen the duration of production, it will also help save the natural resources for future.

*(b)**No part of waste of natural resources is beyond utilization*** :- It is usually customary that waste materials left after production being carried out from natural resources are thrown out either to the ground or water body and even to atmosphere. But no substances on earth are useless or less

useful, and they are inherent with latent energy, even the waste produce are. Therefore minute scrutiny should be carried out to utilize them further in useful manner. For example, after producing sugar and molasses or liquor from sugarcane the 'extracted' husk substances of it considered waste and usually thrown out, that which may cause ground pollution, can be pressed and used as alternative to wooden commodities. Again, the predatory plants that grow on an 'eutrophized' (silted) pond or lake fertilized by the soil and the water of it rich in nutrient can be collected to be mashed and pulped and used as fertilizer for crops.

Recycling of used products is also another method of getting the maximum utilitarian benefit from the product materials besides delaying the process of 'waste' disposal, and therefore less effluent. Also it means regenerating energy from the waste too.

(3)Skillful and Creative Alternatives to natural Objects

One of the primary measures for managing the natural resource is to utilize it at minimum level, even when it may be for our utmost necessity for safeguarding it for the future. For example, petroleum, which is energy for fuel of automobile or other vehicles is extracted from the natural resource of crude oil. However, by using the gasoline form of the resource indiscriminately not only we are exhausting the resources rapidly from the face of earth, it's wanton usage has also increased the pollution level of the atmosphere.

Similarly, rather than using wooden materials for utility commodities such as furniture or construction purposes, artificial materials produced from waste materials can substitute them. Therefore, certain policies taken up both by individual as well as by society may measure up to the saving of our natural resources.

a. **Ethical Assessment of the Role of Various Factors Responsible to the Environment and Its Well Being:** Finding Moral Criteria in It

The way proper management of environment is way to consistent and integrated process for the well being of nature and proper utilization of natural resources, rightful assessment of the related agencies of environment definitely will encourage to improvise upon their conventional views regarding it. Assessment, therefore can be called as part of the management process only. However, what is more important is that whether the assessment can be carried out from ethical point of view remains in question. It seems it remains a higher order of quest on the way for the solution of environmental problems, when even the basic requirements for amending the situations even from civic or political point of view remain undone or unfulfilled. Proper assessment of the role of the related factors may definitely focus on the required steps for betterment of the environment. Therefore, assessment can be a primary requirement for finding a basis for environment, even an ethical one.

The Ideal Role and Responsibility of an Individual

In the battle for the environmental causes, we may find an individual and his awareness towards the problem of environment to be the most important factor in fighting out for the given causes. Because, even when we are talking about the society or the local government or even the much empowered central government regarding the solution of environmental problems, each unit is basically comprised of individuals only and much depend upon individual awareness of each individual of the each unit only. Regarding the role of individuals in modern society, author Van Renssaeler Potter says, _ "Only man has the capacity to think a bout the future, and only man has the power to take step to prevent his own extinction."[*2] The level of awareness of an individual greatly help in finding solution of problems, specially of environmental kinds; for example, individual awareness against usage of plastic materials and its ill effect on environment, or the necessity of utilizing some recycled materials etc. Using alternative and harmless and perennial resources such as solar power for individual benefit suggests awareness on the part of such individuals only. Even more aware ones would try to find out substances or even discover materials that is less or not harmful to the surroundings. An aware individual may with or without the help of society use only herbicide that is not harmful for his agriculture in long term rather than use chemical substances such as urea or other materials that are harmful not only to his owned soil, but also its neighbouring ones in long terms, as the chemical substances would harm the humus or sticky characteristic of the land, letting the top soil erode over a period of time and expose it ultimately to easy erosion resulting into unnecessary silting of nearby waterbody.

However, apart from the physiological knowledge of the environment, it is most important on the part of an individual in being aware of the ethical implications of the whole issue of environment too. Because, only ethical solution to the problem may bring in a permanent solution to the problem of environment, because finding pragmatic solution to the problem may be never ending as the technological problems related to the environment may recur again and again, as there may not be any effort to find a permanent solutions to the causes that allow degradation of nature to occur. An ethical approach on an individual's part to find solution to the environmental problems by going back to the old value system of revering the Nature i.e. the environment around us, will only allow to restore the glory of Nature in the society in particular and the nation in general will find a permanent solution to the recurring problem of the environment. Regarding the need for individual picking up the cudgel of changing the outlook in the context of present day crises, the author Rensselaer had said again, _ "In the case of cultural revolution, an idea is judged in terms of present and not in terms of future. Only combined intellects from many disciplines will be able to assess the ideas that will best chart the course of mankind through an environment that is undergoing unparellel cultural and physical changes. "[3]

The Ideal Role and Responsibility of a Society

The idealism of environment of an individual society depends upon how much an individual society is aware of the problems of environment and its possible repercussion on society. Regarding the role of society beyond the periphery of an individual, author Rensselaer Potter speaks in the following way,_ "A basic problem requiring further study is this: the individual appears ill equipped by instinct to select an optimum environment for himself. Each of us has to be indoctrinated by society to get more exercise than we choose voluntarily, to eat less than an appetite demands, to learn new skills, to carry extra loads, and to develop interest outside ourselves."[4] Undoubtedly, an uneducated or a deprived society is certainly not aware of the repercussions of environmental fallout or completely ignores the question of environmental repercussion due to its own financial or other constraints. Again regarding the proper utilization of resources by society he says, _ "For society the problem is one of recognizing and utilizing the resources represented by interdisciplinary group and of encouraging individual participation in interdisciplinary groups at all levels of action."[5]. We may take into account the views of Lynton Caldwell in respect of it, regarding the kind of approach the society should make towards environment management, he says, _ "Understanding of man's behaviour would doubtless be strengthened by more adequate knowledge of actual perceptions of natural world, and his concepts of his relation to it. Information on environmental perception has been rapidly growing, but we are still largely dependent upon conjecture and deduction in discerning how man really understands their environmental condition. The knowledge is important to the process of environmental management chiefly as 'feedback'.[6] For example we may find the people depending on forest fuel ignoring the question of 'not collecting forest wood as it is damaging to the forest resource', because they are people left without any alternative for fuel required for their own existence. Therefore we need to create and ideal society who can show the deprived class to find an alternative__ for example creating an N.G.O. i.e. a non governmental organization, which will help the deprived section of the society to find alternative fuel either through perennial source of energy such as Solar energy or by collecting disposed or raw materials that would be an alternative source of energy. Gobar energy i.e. energy found from animal extract or from treated sewage can also be a source of energy for them. However, to keep update for solution, an aware society would keep an 'Feedback' and 'Feed Forward' system with local authorities, such as the local forest dept or environmental body such as Pollution control board, so that they can prevent anti societal factors such as poachers or one allowing his/hers individual automobile to emit particles beyond the given limits etc.

Ideal Role and Responsibility of the concerned Authority

The selected governing body of a society, whether in form of local administration or the government of a nation is the most important forbearer of responsibility when it comes to implementation of authority in rectifying the wrong doing relating to environment. Because it is entrusted with the ability to perforce the rules and regulations in form of law and order in the society by its people, it is also the most visible and trustworthy body to help the process of protection and conservation of the natural resources in a locality or a country. A rightful authority determined to perform its duty is bound to implement laws related to such purposes to ensure better protection to the resources whether the forest area or prevention of pollution of various natural factors. Usually the government forms a separate body at various levels of the country – state and central one to coordinate the duties of prevention, protection and conservation of the resources and implementation of law for the same at local and central levels. Besides, the concerned authority can provide its population with better facilities and infrastructure with proper planning for further prevention of diseases and pollution for the inhabitants. With proper assessment of impact of polluting agents they can control any unforeseen degradation of the surrounding environment also. In respect of the role of the administration Lynton Caldwell says in the following way, _ "Environmental administration is largely the management of men in relation to their environments, and therefore the behavioral tendencies of men and beliefs that motivate them are of practical relevance to the administrative process.[*7]

Assessment of World Bodies in Finding Solution To Environmental Problems in World Arena and The Latest Resolution
Organisational effort

Besides the occasional political effort, there are already certain organizational efforts on the environmental issues, which have even succeeded in making the causes of environment being pursued in more diligent and continuous manner, besides trying to safeguard many environmentally sensitive bastions, besides concerning with few other nature related issues. While they have carried out their issues globally by now, with the political concerns, it has been generally only the mutual environmental problems of two or more than two nations of some global issues only. One such most commendable organization is WWF, i.e. World Wide Fund for Nature which has made genuine effort to safeguard many of the endangered species and also those on the verge of oblivion from the surface of the earth. In fact it is their sincere effort which they have scrolled in the 'Red Data' book about the endangered species that the world has come to know about the precarious condition of such species. Another organization which commands respect and mention in respect of environmental causes is the Greenpeace organization which is focusing more on fallout of pollution and degradation of nature. However, unlike the WWF, it has focused more on the pollution, specially on hazardous substances on health related issues and the fall out of war on human as well as on nature. They have also succeeded in making their voice heard in political circles of different countries. Another organization, which has come up recently to focus is PETA, standing for People for ethical Treatment of Animal', which is making efforts to create awareness about the right of animals, not only of those living in wilderness but also the domesticated ones, which are quite often than not are objects of ill treatment. Besides, there are genuine and dedicated efforts of many other individuals for environmental issues, apart from the forerunners like Mr. Bahuguna to Dr. Karl Sagan, who were and had been trying their best to the restoration of ecology. Such overall efforts, after all, is focusing only as the necessity of time that can be called as 'need of the hour', as said in the language of Robert Elliot, _ "There are two reasons for this, one obviously practical and the other a little more than theoretical. The practical reason is that the more people there are who share the value response to wild nature, the more political clout environmentalism is likely to have and the more people there are likely to be willing to adjust their lifestyles and make the 'sacrifices' taking environmental values seriously requires. Obviously there is an instrumental basis for supporting environmentalist policies, having to do with such things as valuing present and future human recreational, aesthetic and scientific opportunities and more pressingly in consideration of future guaranteeing the continuation of conditions necessary for a tolerable life for humans. These concerns for human interests might spill over into a concern for interests of at least higher order nonhuman animals. Nevertheless, the appeal to the intrinsic value of nature gives an additional edge to environmentalism" [8]. Again he said,_ "And the pursuit of environmental policies by the liberal state does not violate the requirement of neutrality where citizens agree nature has intrinsic value and consequently desire that it be protected and preserved."[9]

b. Effort for Unifying World views at political as well as social and ethical fronts

The ever growing concern for environment against the resistance by authorities with vested interest, for the voice for environmental causes to be heard, there are efforts to make all the sporadic events for the same cause to be united, so that it becomes more of a stronger force to be recognized everywhere. There are efforts made in various levels; for example, individuals taking up measures on their own or social organizations such as some NGOs or institutes trying to develop environmental friendly commodities etc. However, being equipped with financial power, any effort made at political level had been more successful in unifying certain activities, if not all. As mentioned before, conferences and conventions held by United Nations Organization had been considerably successful in bringing in accords on common causes of environment among many small or big nations besides trying to acquire endorsement for implementation of certain international policies in the associated countries. However, some major countries with the power of financial nature as well as associating with the policy formulation had exempted themselves from participating or making commitment in many such efforts for the fear of either bearing much of the financial burden being financially a more powerful country or some of the issues going against some of the vested interests of the associated country. Still we can assume that because of such overall effort such environmental issues have generated more concern among usually ignorant or un concerted common population and had even drawn attention to individual environmental issues that may either concern their country or their locality.

However, since the middle of twentieth century, there is considerable amount of consciousness aroused among political and social circle with growing concern for rapid degradation of nature and natural objects. However, till recently, the voices still remained mostly confined to small groups of people some of whom made organizational effort to make their voices heard. There were quite a few concerned individuals who made efforts for their lonely voices to be heard and carried the burden of making other people be aware of the growing environmental problems. T. H. Bahuguna of India was such a concerned individual who motivated people to save trees against the growing machinery of deforestation. There were such concerned individuals in the west too, who took up various such environment related issues including possible nuclear war and its fall out. Dr. Karl Sagan of U.S.A. was such a scientist voicing his dissention to the degradation of nature late in twentieth century.

However, there were fewer rightful measures taken when it came to political effort. The measures, whatever, were taken up, mostly in the western countries were primarily 'preventive' of pollution in nature, as people started being effected by high amount of it prevalent mostly in the cities. Although there were few measures to protect certain species of flora and fauna, the destruction of forest resources as well as exploitation of natural resources remains continuous, even growing more at some places and countries.

Various groups or individual started facing opposition to their ideas, or even prevention as quite often than not it went against the interest of certain circle, often even with collaboration of government machinery. When some relented, some others carry on the fight. However, at the threshold of twentieth century, the measures taken for environmental retribution by political administrations of different countries cannot be said adequate, whereas those carried out under the entrepreneurship of individuals or by different organizations met with stiff resistance.

GLOBAL AND LOCAL AWARENESS

It must be taken into account that there has been a growing concern since the last quarter of the twentieth century for the protection of our environment in face of rapid degradation of it. Although most of the developed nations have succeeded in prevention of pollution and protection of natural resources in individual manner, they cannot rid of the overall responsibility of growing 'global' environmental problems. The developed countries have to bear the cudgel of being primarily responsible for such ubiquitous problems as ozone layer hole and global warming due to 'greenhouse effect', as they have initially set the precedence of unending chemical usage or uncontrolled gas emission before being concerned about the repercussions or taking up measures of preventing them subsequently. Besides, while the developing and under-developing countries are struggling to met out the developmental efforts in their own countries, it is not possible for them to make any financial contribution to the global causes of environment, the developed countries, besides being primarily responsible for pollution at 'global' level, are much more in financial capacity for redemption of the environmental problems than their less affluent counterparts in developing or under-developed regions.

However, 'United nations', the primary body to take into account the various activities of its member countries in particular and the world affairs in general, has taken up various measures for control and prevention of pollution and protection of environment through its various agencies. UNIDO and UNESCO, the subsidiary organizations to the former have taken up measures to redeem the 'crises' situation to certain extent. Besides conferences at global levels are being held both to dissipate misgivings between the 'richer' and the 'poorer' countries and bring into the fold of mutual understanding and also to make countries endorse measures for restitution of environmental protections at global level. Some of such conferences are being mentioned below:-

1. *The Convention on Environment held in Rio de Generio in 1992*
One of most strategically important conferences, held at Rio de Janerio at Brazil, in 1992, it succeeded not only in capturing the attention of political heads of most other countries, but also that of educational and religious institutions as well. Many important environment-related issues, such as 'Ozone layer depletion' and 'Global warming 'etc. were taken up so as to find out an universal solution. Certain 'protocols' were formulated and adopted to be implemented by the participating nations. No other earlier conferences such as one held at Stockholm in 1982 (i.e. as it is held at the gap of every ten year) or the one held at Montreal in the year 1989 could draw so much importance at world arena. However, the spirit of redemption over the 'environmental crisis issues' were dampened as many of the developed, therefore financially richer countries have refused to implement the protocol at a later time or refrained themselves from offering financial helps for the universal causes.

2. *The convention held in Johannesburg in 2002*:- The Convention held at Johannesburg ten years later to Rio De Generio Conference as per schedule could not generate much attention and therefore attending by many of the nations in it held early in the twentieth century. Many of the nations, _ developed, developing and underdeveloped as well retracted themselves from the earlier pledge to implement measures for environmental restitution, as they considered many of the measures as contravening to the financial interest of their own countries. However, it nonetheless reduced the importance of redemption of environmental issues as the necessity for it is always growing in rapid manner all over the world. Therefore we can say when the political agenda for such a cause has been in trouble water, the necessity remains for other agencies to carry on the issue of the causes of environment for its restitution.

3. *The Cancun Meet on Environment 2012 :-* The meet at Cancun in the year 2012 as the contiguous effort by U.N.O. every ten year to unify the world against the ever increasing crisis of the Environment, the most conspicuous one being Global warming/climate change again became futile as they did not agree upon a common ground to find a solution to it.

4. *The Kyoto Protocol:-* One of the most important resolutions taken in late twentieth century at political level keeping up with the growing awareness of destruction caused by man-made pollution of the climate world over is the one taken in the convention held in Japan under the auspices of United Nations in the year 1992. The convention highly emphasized on the role of western developed countries in attaining redemption of problems of climatic condition caused by pollution, for which it wanted to hold the western nations as primarily responsible. The resolutions asked the developed nation to pledge full co- operation with financial contribution in keeping with their affordability. The onus of bearing the cost of rectifying the climatic conditions has been entrusted mostly on developed nation as the world body representing most countries in the world believes they are more responsible than other nations for being forerunners in advocating for and utilizing maximum level of natural resources for human welfare and progress. The protocol was declared null and void after ten years (2006) as its time passed out for any agreement.

(C)FINDING ETHICAL REASONS BEHIND ENVIRONMENTAL DEGRADATION

'Ethics Behind the Environmental degradation':- The way the world has witnessed the evolution of culture occurring for mankind with the mode of living hood changing from stringent livelihood of common people to induction of luxurious or comfortable commodities in life by the end of twentieth century. However, with the advent of material gains in the lives of common masses, it is also evident that with the values of society which the common masses earlier espoused has changed with time to cater to the newer views towards life. Even common individuals started emphasizing more on gaining the material items laced with technological wizardry to express mettle or might in the society. While it was only confined to the privileged section of society till the medieval era, such materialistic views have taken over even the common individuals by the middle of twentieth century. Definitely man's view towards life has started centering around himself and not associated with his own surrounding anymore. Man's 'egoism' has taken over his altruistic feelings or as a matter of fact his sharing of feelings with nature. With such drastic change in ethical leanings among common masses, it has confirmed the influence of utilitarian values among them all. It is in a stark contrast from the conventional lineage among people in which belief in maintaining a fair equilibrium with nature and natural objects in spite of using her for man's own benefits prevailed.

The exploitation of nature caters to the need of mankind, which has resulted into rapid degradation of nature in form of deforestation and pollution of the natural components. From the analysis of events happening over the few hundreds of years, it can be confidently said that the change in ethical view is definitely responsible for degradation of nature,. i.e. our environment. In a way, change in ethical views at the beginning of modern era can be termed as ethical degradation as well, as it has lowered the esteem it had towards nature previously, which can be the reason for man's loss of aquiescence or parity needed between man and the animal kingdom.

The Reasons behind Ethical Degradation

As it has been surmised that ethics in general and ethical degeneration of values being responsible ultimately for the environmental degradation the world is experiencing currently and various scholars have given various reasons which according to them have lead to the degeneration of ethical values. However, the degradation itself manifested in different forms in human life that they can be called as the reasons behind such degeneration of values. Different scholars have emphasized on different reasons as primarily responsible for such degeneration. According to the rationalistic conclusion of the environmentalists only a balanced view of ethics would ensure a balanced environment on the earth, as the environment would not be susceptible to the wanton destruction by man for long. The different views held responsible for ethical degradation are being discussed below.

Different Views : Disorder, Knowledge, Conscience
Kaleidoscopic Views of causes of Environmental problems

1. **'Disoder in Evolutionary System as well as in society':_** It has been discussed upon the chaos or disorder in the evolutionary system in the light of origin of species. However, the necessity arises out to look at the implication of chaos or 'disorder' in society as well. The disorderly system is believed to be the reason, which occurs in the natural system so as to facilitate further newer creation to achieve or aim for greater perfection. The various other aspects of human life which also emulate similar pattern can also be said to aim for the same. However, when it occurs in a human society which generates the need to be 'orderly' so as to guide the mankind on the path of progress, result can be 'outrageous' to 'catastrophic', depending upon the extent of the outcome befalling it.

However, the question arising here is that the environmental degradation that has occurred on earth, and man's ethical values are being considered as befalling it, can it be considered as the 'disorder' of our society too, and for a reason, if it can lead to newer creation of a world with newer values for a perfect order of it. But what is causing concern here is that if the environmental damage caused as a result of its degradation and even if it can be considered as the 'disorder' in the system in the society, whether it can destabilize the society with its enormous impact and rather than be the cause for a newer order it can derail the society from the chosen path of it. Due to the ethical laxity the environmental aspects of nature, i.e. its components have not only degraded considerably but also have been destroyed irreparably in certain respect, for which it becomes questionable whether such a disorder, rather than being a way to a newer creation of world order will permanently become 'disordered or damaged, as there might not be enough scope for recreation with destruction of nature. However, with measures of redemption it is possible to turn the table of destruction and put the society on the path of restoration from further degradation of ethical values so that it would implemented on the society for the restitution of environmental qualities only.

2. 'Dangerous knowledge'
When utilitarian values have first set in the western society at the beginning of seventeenth century, it rather first came in more in the

unambiguous form of knowledge wrapped in number of scientific inventions. However, such inventions were harmless as it was conceived and as long as it added to the spreading extension of knowledge to its composite limits. However, sooner it comes to be implied for utilitarian reasons, precisely for the comfort of man in the name of welfare of his kind, it has taken a dangerous turn with unknown and unforeseen repercussions of it, both in society as well as on our surrounding. It indicates the necessity of scrutinizing the applications of our knowledge prior to utilize it for man's benefit without taking into account the possible effects on our surrounding. Such knowledge basically proves to be inadequate or not fully propounded, as it causes ill effect meaning its half done acclaimed knowledge. However, it must be admitted that it is only knowledge which has set man apart from other beings on earth and it is such a dimension of human intelligence which has allowed him to not only develop his civilization, but also to keep moving on the path of progress and posterity for times to come. Knowledge remains the cynosure of 'goodness' as long as it is not misused or misappropriated for the sole purpose of welfare of mankind, ignoring the existence of the other beings or about the fall out of its wanton usage of nature.

'**Knowledge, Nature and Man**':- However in light of the role of the 'indomitable' knowledge, which has believingly contributed to degradation of the both environment and ethical values in accordance with some scholars, knowledge needs to be scrutinized in the same vein as in case of ethics. In fact, ethics is part of man's greater knowledge, although both can be judged as independent genres.

There are also many philosophical scholars who have believed that Knowledge is part of human intelligence which has set him apart from other beings in nature. However, some scholars believe knowledge and intelligence are interchangeable, whereas others believe both of the two are two different dimensions of human mind although they complement each other. However, what is even more noteworthy is the belief that it is the entity which separates man from others in the organic world, for which man cannot be included in equivocal role of other beings in animal world or within the periphery of natural law. According to Thomas Green,_ "Now it is obvious that to a being who is simply a result of natural forces an injunction to conform to their laws is unmeaning. It implies that there is something in him independent of these forces, which may determine the relation in which he stands to them."[10] Again he says, _ "Can the knowledge of nature be itself is a part or product of nature, in that sense of nature in which it is said to be an object of knowledge?..... If it is answered in negative, we shall at least have satisfied ourselves that man, in respect of the function called knowledge, is not merely a child of nature. We shall have to ascertain in him of a principle not natural, and a specific function of this principle in rendering knowledge possible."[*11] However, we find that John Locke the first 'empiricist' philosopher, followed by Bishop Butler believed that man, including his knowledge is bound by the natural laws only. The idea of some of the modern time philosophers that man's knowledge is not bound by nature's laws has also given the dangerous edge to the perception that its values have to be separated from those of nature. More so, due to the acquired knowledge man is being considered as 'superior' than to any animals on earth and such a mental set up has encouraged him with the inclination to exploit nature, with which he neither want to identify with or consider himself as a part of it.

'Dangerous Knowledge: If man really is confounded by such Knowledge'

As soon as science and science-oriented studies have become part of human knowledge in the beginning modern era, man has learn to derive 'surprise' outcome from it, as a result of which patience to derive wisdom for it has become 'shorter' and shorter. Even more important is the fact that unlike in earlier time man no more prejudges the applied form of knowledge of its possible repercussion or negative effects in general. It remains a viable solution to all our maladies like the proverbial panache without taking into account its ill effects that may surface long time later. According to Van Rensellaer Potter, _"The feeling grows that scientists are finding it increasingly difficult to predict the consequences of their, that technology has become the sorcerer's apprentice of our age,"[*12] Again he says, _ "It is altogether likely that a documentation of the worldwide intellectual view of nature of man and his environment would confirm worst fears of those who are convinced that our stockpile of dangerous knowledge is already too large. As a matter of fact, the concept of dangerous knowledge has always been with us, and the public mind has always had an instinctive ambivalence toward science."[*13]

However, what is most important is that such knowledge has immensely contributed to the degradation of our environment, as mankind had not been capable of judging the impact of their applied knowledge. However, man's realization of it of late is making them willing to redeem the situation, which itself is nothing but the wisdom derived from his knowledge only.

3. *'De establishment of Conventional Values'*

As has been discussed earlier, it is our values which are lost, or in another word, distorted, displaced or are exchanged for the modern, i.e. utilitarian values, which has not only changed our views towards life but also our relation to our surroundings, we can safely call it the process of 'de-establishment of values. However, values are always susceptible to the influence of changing time, therefore change, although core values of ethics remain more or less unchanged as it emphasize on the moral accountability of an individual only. However, at the advent of modern time, when science has become associated with knowledge, therefore with ethics too, man's intrinsic values were changed drastically. Although the basic moral values were not changed yet, as science in its applied form did not initially interfere with ethical values, 'Hedonism', i.e. the ethics of pleasure, the degenerated form of moral values have gradually and serendipously insinuated into the old value system. As science had become applied for man's comfort in the garb of human welfare, gradually it has taken to producing commodities of pleasures that were produced in mass scale. However, the commodities of pleasure were always there since ancient times, although it was confined to limited number of people of privileged class, as common people by and large restrained from indiscriminate usage of them considering them to be unethical, besides usually the commodities being beyond their means. However, newer values have surfaced with the advent of science and mass production along with industrialization that had facilitated the easy availability of such commodities, which had further made them wish for more. A new kind of marketing value citing the example of human welfare by the help of industrialization process, was strategically emphasized originally by the colonial power so as both to utilize the raw materials gathered from their colonized nations, and also to churn wealth for themselves by selling the mass production made out of it.

The rapid growth of ways to earn money and the easy-some availability had made common people, specially those living in western countries in early nineteenth century completely obliterate their views towards life and the values. The conventional family system of nuclear with additional family members considered to be chief domain of cultivating fraternity began to be threatened under the duress of new social structure of single nucleus family encouraged by industrial set up. The 'state of a nation', the basic combination of political versus civic bodies had become stronger and stronger and started dealing directly with individuals, ignoring the status of society. As a result, society with collective moral values of team-man ship and cooperation has began to weaken, giving ways for individual personalities, with stronger 'egoistic' i.e. self obsession and benefiting, opinionated mental set up. It has become by and large the newer mental set up of the west, letting orient with its much starker values remained untouched till market-oriented industrialization took over their mental set up too in the twentieth century. Thus utilitarian values has received universal acceptance, making conventional ethical values sidelined to the obscurity of the edge of the society, and making ways to utilitarian ones to dominate the scene.

The process of change-over from conventional to utilitarian value with the string of events relating to the usurpation industrialization enhancing the process can be called as the de-establishment of the ethical values.

4. 'Obliterated Conscience'

When ethics has much to do with the sense of collective value, a human individual is equally dependant on his or her conscience to substantiate the rightfulness of a deed. However, there are certain levels of human mind before it reaches the level of conscience to make a decision. Again the collective conscience of individuals is called consensus. What is more important is the fact that conscience in a person has much to do with the origin of ethics in society and his power to rationalize his instinctive sense of judgmental behaviour manifest in an act of conscience. At the beginning of the formation of the society and civilization, man depended on his conscience to prior to proceeding for a deed or to judge its possible far reaching effect in future before opting for it. They would judge carefully any object or idea newly inducted to the society, before making decision for further usage or implementation of them. However, such attitude varies from society to society when it comes to the point of utility or application prior to committing an act. However, it does not necessarily do away all the evil of a society. It depends upon the standard of criteria an individual use in judgmentation, as the result an act produce may end up either being 'good' or evil. A society, therefore consisting of individuals making decisions based on their conscience is usually found to be as more conservative.

Therefore, we can presume till the late medieval era, societies were more conservatives because they were more consciensious, i.e. dependent on their conscience. But then in the west, gradually man has started studying science more and more as a part of acquiring knowledge which gradually had given ways to various scientific inventions at the beginning of the modern period in eighteenth century. The inventions had been proselyted by making mass production made easy access to common people to get rid of their common woes and lessen the burden of day to day life, which was called as 'welfare' of the masses by the producer of mass-production, who made immense wealth out of it. When people were given ways to their common impulse of desire and easily attained 'joy' out of the 'welfare' products, they had been blurted of their vision of rationality and judgment and yielded to the allure of the glistening gadgets. The development in the field of engineering and medicine also had immensely made life easier and comfort-prone besides conditioning it to longevity. All the feasibility of luxurious being carried out primarily at the cost of or exploitation of nature, the comfort of life that are being provided with the continuous improvisation of invention had made man obliterating his conscience. Even as the destruction had continued through the last two centuries, few had expressed their views against such acts, till it has reached with the last bastions of nature that conscience has 'pricked' for mankind, to create hue and cry over the destruction and with renewed vow for the redemption of the situation. It is the travesty of reality and tragedy of human history that it took so long for mankind to realize his own misdemeanour towards nature which has nurtured and grown him to arrive at such a state of progress and development. We however can say that man's conscience being conscience itself, had realized at the long hour the wrong being done and the felony committed to nature. As the author W. R. Sorley has said, _ ".. the authority of conscience thus seems to be derived from the divine purpose which it displays".[14] Again he said, _"The deliverance of conscience are immediate judgments as to the morality of action and affection. The approval of conscience is thus made the criterion of morality."[*15]

(D) NEW CONCEPTION IN THE HORIZON:
IN ENVIRONMENT ETHICAL FRONT

Along with the awareness of environmental degradation and the necessity arising out of it to preserve the natural aspects, newer concepts and methods have been thought out by different scholars and concerned citizens alike as instrument for their implementation. They are varied in nature and of different genres trying to solve different areas relating environmental problems. Besides, assorted notions of the crises have given way to thinking that are often more counter productive to the cause of the crises, both ethical and environmental creating hamper in the way of finding rightful solutions.

1. Advancement In Ethical Scenario in Latest Philosophical Agenda In Finding Solution to Environmental Problems

The view towards philosophy, specially the branch that is related to environment, more so with ethics has changed in the late twentieth century because of the various environmental problems coming to the fore due to its rapid degradation. While subjects like philosophy or ethics in particular bearing the inherent wisdom of mankind to contemplate over, it is quite often than not they are use to be sidelined in the bid for scientific, i.e. technological development. With ethics ultimately surrendering to changed moral values in late eighteenth century and endorsing utilitarian views, we have seen a completechange in the scenario with wanton destruction of nature and technological advancement in various fields of science. Those promoting development of science justified themselves ethically by saying that its primary purpose was for the development of mankind. However, the question arising here is if it is justified to degrade and destruct nature for the sole benefit of mankind; with rapid destruction of the environment and subsequent repercussion of it, of which man has become a victim himself has made him realize his own folly that it is all making of himself and the time has arrived to restitute the situation for saving our environment. In late twentieth century, man is realizing that like all other living being, he himself is an integral part of nature only, and it is impossible to survive for mankind without nature in spite of his knowledge and intelligence. More so, the attempt has been made to retrieve the old values to the fore so as to bring in the custom of revering nature. However, as the Utilitarian values took stronghold on society, there were quite a few numbers of philosopher who did the uphill task of retaining the age old values of ethics that was related to nature and was upheld by it in reverence.

At the foothold of twenty first century, we find that environmental has again become favourable among not only the philosophy related communities, but also among intellectuals related to other fields as well as among laymen. There are two parallel views being espoused regarding finding the solution for the created environmental problems. While some of the thinkers are trying to find pragmatic solution giving heed to ethics in applied form, others believe that there is need to make a complete change over the utilitarian views dictating man's outlook towards life and change in ethical values only would ascertain man's return to the age old view of revering nature and thereby ultimately retrieve and revive nature to its earlier glory. We find even the newer trends in current ethical views concentrating on efforts to dissipate the importance given on man's welfare by emphasizing on equitable distribution of importance to all the inmates of nature. A tussle has been going on between two parallel set of thinkers, and while one wants the concentration of values to be centered on and around human beings and in their necessities, the other wants it to be concentrated equally on all living and other beings in accordance with necessities, human beings being just one of them only. While the former is called Anthropocentric, i.e., human oriented, the latter is called Cosmocentric, i.e. man being a part of the huge cosmos only. Deep Ecology endorses the views of Cosmocentrism as it believes in upholding the views that all the objects and living beings are inter-related by an unseen law of nature and each one is necessary for the ecological system and therefore needs to be held in reverence.

There are however, attempts to synthesize the various nature related qualities of different philosophies into one and emphasis is given in bringing them into one fold so that the newly found ethical values comes even more stronger in views against the utilitarian ones. We can witness such synthesizing process taking place in Deep Ecology as it has brought in views of Hinduism (India), Confucianism and Taoism (China) etc. to give it a broader perspective of nature and to relate to its various phenomena and also to focus on the glorious characteristics of nature as various sections of human kind discover, each in its unique way, so that all the perceptions regarding the qualities of nature come under one umbrage and strengthen the environmental ethical views of those believing in retrieving the old ethical values.

2. Environmentalism and Activism

The latest movement of environmental awareness comprises assorted sections of society focusing on different environmental related issues and looking at them from different perspectives. Most other lineages of environment related thought founded in twentieth century, such as Meliorism or Deep Ecology are usually viewed from ethical or philosophical perspectives, whereas environmentalism, as the newest movement for environmental protection is known, is also looked at from political perspective and is with the political agenda for proper implementation of regulations for prevention of environmental degradation. However, the movement, because of its multicultural approach and the multitude of environmental issues affecting assorted kind of people, is unlike most other recent movements being confined to academics or intellectuals and comprised of various sections of people such as common people to intellectuals and even corporate bodies from variety of industries etc. Besides, according to R.C. Guha, environmentalists should be careful to the cause of their concern. He reiterates, _ "(The last quote) seems to point to an uncomfortable gap between the environmental debate and environmental movement. Scientists and ideologues were concerned with the resource shortages and the disappearances of species. They were critical of direction of economic growth and its impact on the local, national and global eco systems. Set against the prophets of doom was the growing popular interest in the wild and the beautiful, which not merely accepted the parameters of the affluent society but was wont to see nature itself merely one more good to be 'consumed.'"*16 Therefore it is a necessity for the environmentalists to be concerned merely on the restitution of the ecological world for the sake of the environment i.e. a biocetric' approach rather than view it from an anthropocentric perspective.

3. Some Measures Noteworthy at The Ethical front
Since the middle of the twentieth century, as many big metropolitan cities have started getting covered with pollution dust, it dawned not only to philosophers but also to any intelligent individuals that it was nothing but the overall outcome of the industrialization process. Compounded with the problem of deforestation, as man needed more and more land areas besides the natural resources on it to produce various commodities, the realization has occurred to safeguard whatever of nature have been left as species of flora and fauna has become extinct from earth and there were increasing level of pollution compounding to the global problem of ozone depletion, greenhouse effect and Global warming, acid rain etc, besides some other assorted local problems. The irony remains in the fact that man realized his folly not when nature got decimated almost to 'oblivion' point, but when various groups of population started getting effected by man's various acts of pollution and nature annihilation began effecting their life both physically and psychologically.

(a) 'The process of Disobedience'
The usurpation of new ideas about restoration and protection of the environment around us in the middle of twentieth century had been random, few and far between and started in pockets of environmental problems where usually the population of the adjacent areas was effected by them. The problems at the global level were yet to be their concern and

most even were not aware of the growing prevalence. But the disturbances caused to create awareness of whether local or global problems were largely in peaceful manner. Often when they could get attention from local population they were susceptible to opposition from connected agencies too. In connection with a 'Logging' protest held in Oregon state in U.S.A., scholar Allan Holland says that, _ "Notice that in many respects, the logging protests conform to these definitional conditions. ..... These acts are obviously public, non violence ones that involve law breaking and are aimed at changing the policies of the government. They are conscienciously motivated and addressed to a sense of justice in the public at large and perhaps in those who legislate, create and administer these policies in the national government."[*17]

John Rowls, an environmentalist, has pointed out the methods of the 'disobedience' for the environmental issues which technically stand apart from any other social or political issues. First, environmental cause, or to be precise the issues are not any moral issues in which right of any individuals are brought up to the fore. secondly, no other means other than a 'non violent' method would justify in performing of protest for such causes, as any other method would contravene its basic rules of preserving natural assets only.

Again author Peter Laslett has focused on the counter effects possible verbosity with which an environmentalist may put forward his concern, _ "The laxness in our attitude and action gives too much room for ecological fanatics to dwell upon its alarmist exaggerations."[*18] Therefore, according to the scholars the concerned environmentalists are in need to tread a careful path between extreme views and intellectualism, with radical views to put forward their concern in rather a non violent manner in their mission of disobedience to the conventional political and philosophical attitude to the cause of environment.

(b)Environmental justice

Environmental Justice is the iconic discipline which highlights the necessary justice to environmental causes and related grievances. It is a standard by which one can judge issues like human or animal right, right of environmental refugees or depleted forest land and its inhabitants etc. However, the primary theme of the conception of environmental justice is the equal distribution of the usable natural resources among the present and few of the next generations. Regarding the need environmental justice author Val Plumwood expresses in the following way, _ "Logic shows though that environmental concern can't just be a recognition of prudence which does not also involve recognition of injustice."*[19] Regarding the primary view of environmental justice, author Roger Kasperson said, _"whether at national or global levels, environmental problems increasingly are fraught with questions of equity and fairness"*[20] Again, according to Mikael Stenmark, the policies of environmental justice should be based on principle of Proportionality, principle of Minimal Wrong, principle of Equal Distribution and principle of Restitutive Justice.

(c) *Right and Equal right to Animals*

At the second part of twentieth century, man has become not only aware of his overall political and socio-ethical right, he had started to take into consideration the right of the animal world too. With the growing depletion of forest area on earth, it has definitely been not only obstructed of 'natural' development and growth but also interfered of its right and therefore tempered with its very existence. It has been necessity of the time to act quickly to retrieve the due 'right' to the animals both wild and domesticated to reinstate them in their earlier conditions, as they are part of the animal kingdom and like human being they also have right to exist on earth. Unable to compete with man's intelligence and wit, the animals are being relegated to fringe of their kingdom and their survival on earth. Man has highly interfered with existence which is part of their legacy on earth only. However, paradoxically to the rapid degradation of environment and its components, there are efforts on man's part to retrieve the qualities of both nature and its inhabitants by man himself. 'Right to Animal' is one of such efforts only.

If ethically assessed, the 'right to animal' falls into the global order of ethical rectification the twentieth century has witnessed, first it was the concept of democracy, the right to vote, which is followed by the right to vote by women. That consideration to animal right has come up at the end of twentieth century in the order of the ethical rectification has only been a natural act of the growing 'ethical process' only. According to Peter Singer,_" Many philosophers have proposed the principle of equal consideration of interests, in some form or other, as a basic moral principle: but, as we shall see in more detail shortly, not many of them recognize that this principle applies to members of other species as well as to our own."*[21]

However, in making such effort, man has put into dilemma some other issues related to man himself. Many believe when there are many other grievances for mankind itself, such as poverty and malnutrition, education and development etc. animal right should not claim any relevancy in such context.

However, assessing such outlook from ethical point of view, we can surmise such an explanation as emanating from 'egoistic' attitude of man, as he is asking for his own 'complete' welfare ahead of the animals and thereby disassociate himself from responsibility of reprieving the animals' right he has already tempered with and the fact that animals too form part of the universal system. The dilemma, therefore can be believed to have caused by the 'Anthropocentric' view of men who believe in man being the only benefactor on earth and nature exists and the universe moves with its concern for man's welfare only.

(d) Sustainable development in the Light of Rehabilitating Nature: Ethical Purview

Sustainable development is the newer concept in the arena of environmental issue, and it can be called an applied form of the ethically viable conception of 'let us not harm nature while man treads on the path of progress', i.e. both mankind and nature should strive to develop in their individual 'natural courses' and none of the factors should interfere with the development of the other. For example, The widespread usage of chemical fertilizer such as Urea, the booster of crop development is, as has been learnt later as the cause of soil erosion and that it makes the soil clogged with chemical and therefore lose the mucus quality of it. As a result of it, the top soil flows down with rain water again to silt a river or any other water body in the process. Organic fertilizer made with animal droppings such as cowdung or with vermicompost can easily substitute for such artificial materials, helping both in growing good crop and not doing any harm to the top soil, therefore to the environment. Again, chemical pesticide used in the field to deter pest, weeds or predators can highly hamper with the local eco system and disturb its balance. But by using herbicide for the same purpose and made of natural pest and predator deterrent, can be prepared to be used instead of the chemical one, which will not only do good for the crop, but also the eco system, therefore the environment. The marketing technique used for chemical can also be applied for the 'naturally' produced items for mass production that may thus help in replacing the chemical items ultimately and bring respite to both the farmers and the nature itself.

However, the concept of sustainable development as an ethical approach to the environmental problem has still been being at developing stage and confined to limited areas of agriculture and those affected by deforestation.

It is yet to define pollution effected domains of environment. But such an objective solution based on ethical tenets may certainly help mankind by helping remove the problem of environmental degradation. Regarding applying of ethical values in the concept of sustainable development, author Joachim Spangenburg says in the following way, _ "Thus, the limits to the material flows based on ethical concerns translate into limits to economic growth."[22] Again scholar F. Douglas Muschett expresses in the following way, _ "The ethical dimensions of sustainable development are two folds (1) our relationship to fellow inhabitants of our country and planet and (2) our relationship to the land and plant and animal inhabitants in the world."[23]

(E) CONFLICT OF INTEREST: *Man Versus Nature*

1. *Ethical Dilemmas of Man versus Nature*

As the concern for environmental protection is growing day by day, making considerable number of people being aware of it, it is also bringing up certain questions that have born out of the clashes of interest amidst various groups of people. For example, when certain sections of people bring up the issue of animal right and ethical treatment to them, there are others who feel mankind as a whole is yet to achieve full right, so the question of that of animals need to be in the backburner. Besides, certain other measures for environmental protection are thought to hamper the interest of living conditions of others. When there are moves to make further areas as reserved forest areas, some population living in those areas for generations, specially certain tribes have to evict such areas. Then again, the question of human right comes up ahead of the animals. Such situations earmark the ethical dilemmas human society in present day suffers from, which again push behind the agenda of environmental issues to the forum of utopian theories. Besides, in many other respects, whether in the agriculture or the industry sectors, such dilemmas come up whenever the issues of environment figure in the agenda. While in the agricultural sector it is a necessity to produce in bulk the necessary commodities for as demand of an ever-growing population is in need of huge amount of supply for which the artificial chemicals such as urea, phosphate, ammonia etc are required to improve the output of it. But then again, as mentioned earlier, fertilizer does immense and often irreparable damage to the ecology in the surrounding areas of its usage. Therefore, by taking into assessment of the producers of mass industrial product, G. Wayburd says, _ "Nowhere are environmental dilemmas more acutely felt than in the relationship of industry and business with rest of society; nowhere are generalizations and over simplifications about such dilemmas more likely to confuse the issues."*24 However, it is technology on the other hand which can produce in bulk the organic fertilizer that is good for the ecology also.

2. 'Man and Nature's Relation in peril'

The devastation of natural assets, both renewable and non renewable has highly degraded the environment on earth. It also shows the chasm that has occurred in the relation between man and nature. Martin Bueber, the renown European philosopher has explained the relation of man versus nature in the following way, _ man use to have his relation with another being either as 'I -You'or as 'I –It' manners. When it comes to addressing someone in the first term of relationship, it means familiarity or intimacy usually reserved for family people. That also suggests cordiality and mutual respect on part of each of the partakers. However, 'It' of the relationship suggests only a distance presence in a relationship which however, when the relation is based on 'I- It' equation, man reserved the feelings in a manner that the 'It' of the relation is considered an objective, inanimate existence. Therefore the relation become banal or 'feelingless, i.e. not palpable. According to Bueber, man's relation with nature originating from a sense of mutual respect and therefore of cordiality existed in earlier time which suggests the 'I You' relationship. However, with advent of materialism, the two icons in the relationship has become distant from each other, the chasm between the two ever growing more to become an 'I-It' relationship. The differentiation of the relationship between man and nature is but indicative of a cordial relationship turning into an impersonal, therefore banal relationship between the two factors.

3. Human Right and environment :- While the process of utilizing natural commodities in a very fast manner, making way for over-consumption of the by products by fewer number of communities on earth, whereas, considerable number of people in many countries, mostly in Asia and Africa has been suffering from poverty born out of assorted problems, including those related to environment because of inequitable distribution of natural resources or their by products. Many of such impoverished people are also the producers or providers of raw materials i.e. natural resources, forming the ground level manpower of the industrialization process governed by the handful of population. However, the very distribution of equity of natural resources, originally coming from the concept of utilitarian values

is not only causing inconsistency in economic conditions of people, but also has lead to poverty. However, in the cycle of over exhaust of natural resources and impoverishment of certain sections of society has again lead them to misuse the left out and preserved natural resources. Among such communities or groups of people, there has been growing discontent over preference for preservation of animals in wild, as their common perception is that human and their rights should be protected and get precedence over that of animals, and if necessary, even at the cost of their habitation and existence of some of them. Such notion has caused direct conflict of the interest of the species and that of man, creating further hamper in the process of the preservation of the wild animals.

4. *Population Growth and Land Use: An ethical review:-*
Demand and Supply of Food and Natural Resources
While fighting for the preservation of the dwindling numbers of many species of animals other than human is in the process, number of mankind has been growing rapidly and the growing numbers have been causing problems for land using and utilizing and also in the process of planning too. While human numbers are growing in exponential manner, that is, multiplying at a rapid pace, the supply for their consumption is not growing at the same ratio. In certain respect, such as land sharing, the resource itself is stagnant in growth with respect of no possibility of growing further. As a result of growing, that is, the surplus population is starting to occupy land areas that are reserved as forest areas for wild animals. Besides, they are deforesting the reserves of natural resources for the need of not only fuel and energy, but also for various other utility purposes and thereby putting the existence of wild species in jeopardy. There has been widespread discontent among population in some countries, specially the developing ones as their population is in ever growing trend leading to not only the conflict between man and animals but also between communities of people and the concerned authorities. Regarding the problem caused by growing number of human population, G. Wayburd says, _ "The biggest environmental problem of all is that there are so many of us on the earth; the greatest dilemma is that the best way of reducing population growth- short of war, famine and disease- is to raise the standard of the poor through economic growth."[25] Although the problem of 'Human Right' and population growth can be supplementary to the issue of land use, the problem of population itself can cause the basic economical problem that may bring in ethical issues. As has been mentioned earlier, the land areas meant for human utility

remain inadequate in terms of growing population, and in fact lead to lesser share of it resulting into lesser input for individual. It, on the other hand leads to demand for more land and often unethical occupation of reserved land meant for wild life and their preservation. Such an approach to put into jeopardy the process of conservation of species already dwindling in numbers, survival of which are very much in importance for maintaining the ecological balance on earth.

(F) FINDING SOLUTIONS TO THE ENVIRONMENTAL CRISIS
Different Perspectives
The concern for environment ever growing, there are sincere efforts for finding the rightful solution to the problems of environment, after the initial efforts of making the general population aware of it. The rapidly growing problem, finding a rightful solution for the vast extension of it has been as good as looking for the needle in the haystack. Even finding certain solution may touch upon the problem only single-dimensionally. Again there is the question of approaching the problem in 'subjective' or 'objective' manner. Many scholars and even some philosophers have offered ideas of objective kind, who had attempted to bring in a solution to the manifold problem. There are others who believe it needs a subjective approach as solution. Those who have been looking for the solution on ethical ground can be said to make a subjective approach. However, the question is, will such a solution bring to end the environmental crisis which ranges from deforestation to pollution to also repercussion of both and also their prevention, along with the global problems of ozone depletion, Greenhouse effect, climatic change, acid rain etc. Although many of the problems are interrelated, _ for example, Greenhouse effect causes global warming, or to be precise, climatic change, the total coverage of areas by the cataclysm's continuous presence is far more vast for any objective solution even to be implemented by any unified force of different nations. It is often even more difficult for a single country to solve a single problem, such as atmospheric pollution or water pollution, as it may incur huge expenditure for a country specially a developing or underdeveloped one. However, a subjective solution such as an ethical one, by which common population is made aware of his role in environmental problems and also in its solution, which in turn would opt for ethical ways, shun activities that are harmful to nature, can at best help in prevention of many problems. It can be a solution as an immediate effect, although much more positive outcome may become conspicuous in the long run made with such an approach. Therefore perhaps the best

possible approach to achieve the best result is by following certain ethical policies with dictum to solve and prevent in objective manner at primary level of the problem by each individual and that will help considerably to restore nature's equilibrium even to great extent. Policies that are ethically viable should be implemented in objective manner probably then bring in the solution which is the need of the hour.

However, there can be many other alternatives to such a solution, which should be brought out to the fore for the best possible result. Different scholars have forwarded different solution to solve the environmental crises in different way. They are as follows:-

Different Views
Rehabilitating Nature: If Sustainable development a Restitution measure Finding 'alternatives' to natural resources

The importance of sustainable development has already been discussed about from point of view of maintenance of equilibrium between nature and development of human welfare activities. While measures are growing day by day to make common population aware of the rapid environmental degradation there are, and also there are quite a few preventive measures to stem further degradation, as we have come to learn already, there are fewer or inadequate measures for recovering or restoring what has already been lost of the natural assets. From objective point of view, there are effort to introduce 'ex-situ' condition, which is an attempt at establishing in repetition of the species existing earlier in the particular locality. Such an attempt is in parity with the process of 'In-situ' which emphasizes on safeguarding the last bastion of nature on 'as is where is' basis, which means no human interference with the existing 'naturalness' condition of it. However, the subjective approach is made on basis of recovering the value of nature; i.e. to make an ethical re-examination of it. According to author Holmes Rolston III, in spite of man attempting to rehabilitate nature, for example by planting trees to make up for loss of lost forest areas may not exactly compensate for the value of it already lost. The value of nature cannot be replenished when it comes to the rehabilitated form, as it may lack not only the 'naturalness' of earlier condition, but also the value it evoked in the people of the locality and also that of man's interference. However, it also necessarily does not mean that the new condition should not be appreciated; especially when the earlier condition was completely lost and sincere attempt being made to recreate such a condition, however inadequate it might be. Although rejecting many of such 'rescuing' methods for nature, author Ernt Nesse the deep-ecologist believes that instead of no forest concept, the concept of value added man made 'natural condition' may be valuable in many other respects.

1. *'Global Ethics'*

Ethics as a moral standard has been existing in almost all the societies in the world in independent manner. However, there are varying degrees of standard in them, and when some are stringent of their values, other are lax in maintaining such a criteria for their standard ethical norms, although there are certain common codes of conduct in the ethical values perpetrated by the societies, each of the societies, like individual rivers taking their own turn and traverse and the course, use their own development policies and standard to relate to different social problems.

Generally, in spite of the mutual likeliness of standard, the world ethics can largely be considered into two different trends,_ one is oriental, whereas the other is western. The oriental ethical norms formulated long time back in history, is more 'static' in content, more or less over the enduring periods of history, whereas western ethics is volatile and susceptible to constant change in time because of its inherent qualities. While in the oriental ethics, also inclusive of Indian ethics, a considerable emphasis has been laid upon 'Crime and spiritual punishment' mentioned as 'Karmaphal', western philosophy has been revolving around the ideas of 'Good' and 'Pleasure'. Indian philosophy has included nature in its agenda as to be defined by ethics, it is only in the early Greek days and then later in early modern period that western philosophy has defined nature in ethical terms. However, each trend again has been factionalized into different individualistic ethico-religious groups, as each one has been influenced not only by individual religious and ethnic thinking, but also by the perception of value of individual locality.

However, because of the individualistic course of formulation, ethical value of different groups may relate to matter differently. Over the same issue while one society may response quickly, another may act in delayed manner. Usually, tribal communities are sensitive to environmental problems and are capable of ethically define any events related to nature. But, not all societies are willing to relate to such issues considering them to be unimportant, and therefore banal.

However, in the present day context of environmental problem, it is becoming a rudimentary necessity for all the societies to be aware of the ever growing problem and bring in an ethical solution to it, if not universally then at least at the level of individual locality. However, such an approach also points out to the necessity of congruous views among different societies. Only a unified front and uniform views on the problem will help in to create a common concern and therefore a common ground to fight against the ills of the continuous crisis. Only when there would be common criteria of ethical values uniformly endorsed by all societies equally aware of the perennial cause, we can hope to solve the universal problem of nature, already developing far and wide to make various societies to have common problems as well as repercussions. Environmentalists as well as philosophers believe as soon as there would come to be prevalent an universal code of conduct for all, called 'Global ethics', only then we can hope to arrive at a common consensus about environmental issues.

Regarding such an ethics, we can definitely say which definitely will unify not only the views relating environmental issues, but also the value system itself. It will help people express themselves in uniform livinghood based on environmental values. Such unified society will be able to face the assorted human problems of overpopulation, physical illness, poverty etc and possibly eradicate them more easily than they are being able to do so. Besides, there is the universal problem of the local ethics submerging into Global Ethics, as cultures of different communities may hamper in the process. According to authors Brandon Gleeson and Nicholus Low, _ "we live in a world of many cultures and if the communitarians are partly right, from these different cultures and different values loyalties grow. Today we regard such multiplicity as a virtue. Yet if there is a global Interest in humanity and its earthly environment, as intuition suggests, then we also have to find values which transcend national cultures .... What seems to be needed, then, is an Ethics which bridges between the global and the local."[*26] However, global ethics as a norm of directives of moral values must follow certain ethical principles and policies to endure in the science and technology dominated world. They can be as follows:-

2. *'Grand Narrative'* :- The 'Grand Narrative' is a definition considered as mode of discourse. However, in the environmental context, grand narrative brings into picture the contemporary thinking process which influences the mental set up of both intellectuals as well as common people. The 'grand narrative' of the first part of twentieth century was to highlight 'modernism' and its characteristics and advantages, along with ascribing 'goodness' or 'badness' of an act if one followed or did not do so respectively. By almost making it a kind of moral support to the 'primary' theme, the propagators of such a narrative succeeded in emphasizing the market criteria for 'saleability' of any modern item or idea. However, author Arran Garre believes it is "discourse about actions, usually a number of actions often coming into conflict with one another, with some prevailing over others." [27] According to him, _ "Life is first of all lived as inchoate narratives that prefigures the stories we tell _ we grow up into a world that is already structured and organized by narratives." [28]

3. _Planetary Citizenship_:-In the wake of the 'globalization' in the economical front and the necessity of the universalisation of the environmental issues have arisen the necessity of finding a common ground for bonding among the residents of the world to relate to the problems in a uniform and egalitarian manner. There is, therefore like the suggestion for ethical environmental Governance, there is also importance given for formulation of the idea of a 'Planetary Citizenship'. 'Planetary Citizenship' is the universal theme of binding the concerned population under one roof for solving the environmental issues. The advantage of citizenship is being taken under the consideration of attaining certain minimum right to certain civic facilities universally. However, when the environmental issues are taken into consideration into its perspective, such 'citizenship' may help considerably finding universal solution to the issues and also help in hastening the process. Besides, as 'right' entails 'responsibility', the planetary citizens enjoying such right are also bound by safeguarding the assets of the world, i.e. the environment.

The common standard of planetary citizenship is 'cosmopolitanism', that is, the emergent living standard of divergent religions, ethnicities, nationalities and all other cultural and political identities. Cosmopolitanism accepts and absorbs all kind of divergent thinking rather than discarding of ideas and follow unilateral thinking process: it rather prefers Unilateral thinking process. Environmentalism is a far reaching process which is possible to be appreciated by cosmopolitan outlook only. When some profess the need for distribution of responsibilities among the world citizens for protecting the environmental value, some others speak for decentralization of political powers for the same purpose. However, the necessity arises to transcend from localization to globalisation in both respects, for the Scholar Daniel Arcibugi says, _" Today new social and political subjects are appearing in international life. I do not wish to overestimate their importance, but associations such as movements for peace human right and environmental protection are playing a growing role in the political process.

For the political dimension to exist for the world citizens, it is necessary for appropriate institutional channels to open up. This is the objective that marks out the cosmopolitan project."[*29]

However, the way cosmopolitanism is a requirement for planetary citizenship, it itself can be the first step in environmental governance. Regarding the citizenship, Janna Thompson expresses in the following way, _"World citizenship is a traditional cosmopolitan notion that some think might be revived to deal with environmental crisis."[*30] While the 'value for nature' is its ethical dimension, and penchant for democracy is its political connection, then planetary citizenship will help mankind in establishing the first of 'universal governance' with earthbound dictates and cosmopolitan beliefs that may truly help the environmental causes in future. However, in view of Daniel Archibugi,_ "In short, something more than internal democracy is called for. That may be summed up as democratization of the international community seen as a process of joining together political with different traditions and states of development. This is what a group of scholars have defined as the cosmopolitical democracy project".[*31]

4. *'Global ethical Value or religion,'*

Finding solution to the environmental problems, the ethical way shows another alternative to bring in respite to those who concern for a better future and without any harm to the natural environment around us, _ a global religion based on ethical views. The reason of preferring a religious outlook over an ethical governance or mere environmental ethics can be attributed to the fact that religion exerts more influence on the views of some people than ethics and politics may do. According to some scholars, therefore, it can also be a stronger medium to convey the messages of environment and can be a fitful reply to the views of those espousing the exploitation of the environment. Speaking for the necessity of spiritual approach in life Stephen R.l. Clark expresses in the following way, _"that archaic unity was broken by the dichotomizing intellect, and our spiritual crisis is echoed in our ecology. "[*32]

Traditionally, in most cases of the different religions, nature and ethical values based on nature are highly revered and emphasized upon respectively. Even now those who follow a stringent dictum of religion, would also follow the view perpetuated by his or her own religion regarding environment. A religion with more strong ethical views is bound by the fact that the followers also would follow it word upon word. Religions whose followers are asked to revere the nature do so and usually without putting up any question. There are some scholars who believe such dogmatic belief in religion would help also when such conception as universalisation of environmental causes be introduced to religions that necessarily do not preach nature as an entity to their followers. When a uniform belief is universalized through the convention of religion, it may be followed with more fervour and its ethics being more deep in its impression among them. Such scholars believe that universalizing such a religion would help mankind in coping up with the problems of environment of which the basis will be environmental ethics only. According to Lester Mondale, _"That the various liberal religious groups, taken in their wholeness, constitute another family of the world's great religions is realized only when we pass beyond introductory characterizations to the larger perspective in which we see these groups in revolt against inadequate and outmoded concepts and practices of the traditional faiths."[33] Again he says, _"Prominent among the spiritual pioneers of our new age will be no sanctimonious monks or nuns of starveling preachers; ......Self denial in the interest of richer interrelationships there will be of course. And detachment from the overwhelming plenitude of things there will also have to be".[34] According to him, _ "The religious professional is driven more by psychological necessity than by anything purely spiritual. He has no choice but to find in the practices of traditional religion the occupation for the mind, the outlets for the emotions the activities for muscles crying for employment, the goals for striving, that will bring all the many elements of selfhood into a focus of integration.""[35]

One of the most important qualities of ethics is value and by dint of value ethics judges the importance and validity of an issue. On the other hand, value can be called as the index of any other value to be judged in ethics. Ethics values the qualities such as morality, duty, responsibility, judgment etc. The same way it ascribes the subjective value on any other objective assets depending upon the importance and necessity each of them have in our society. However, there are ways and standard of valuing an issue or an object. For, when man make a subjective approach to start valuing something, then it is automatically transfigured to objective value. However, here the difference lies between valuing objectively and valuing ethically, i.e. subjectively, as Holmes Rollston III expressed, _"But we may still want to say that value exists where a subject has an object of interest."[36] Regarding man's value system, again he opinion of 'valuing' is expressed in the following way, _"We human carry the lamp that lights up value, although we require the fuel that nature provides. Actual value is an event in our consciousness, though natural items while still in the dark of value have potential intrinsic value. Man is the measure of things, said Protagoras. Humans are the measures, the valuers of things, even when we measure what they are themselves."*37

5. *'Environmental Ethical Governance'*

Ethical Governance is another conception which is in reality neither governmental nor any implementation of legal procedure but a few ethical principle basically used to maintain fairness for man and nature alike. Although similar to the concept of global ethics, it is a conception bound by economical theories and to some extent with political motivation. However, both the conceptions of Global ethics and Ethical Environmental Governance have taken advantage of 'globalization' of economic condition in the world. However, in what manner the environmental issues are being conditioned to the 'globalization' theoretical concept depends upon individual interpretation of each of the conceptions.

In respect of governance, however, it is believed that there has to be certain political interpretation as well, if not any governmental interference. According to the theme of governance, 'democratic' reform, the establishment of an International Court of the environment and a world environment forum are to be made functional with political motivation only. According to authors Brendon Gleeson and Nicholas Low,-(they) are not only useful starting point for institutional reform but may also empower global power in civic society."*38 Again, regarding role of 'political ethics' they reiterate, _"Humanity has developed political ethics (variously framed) for political scales up to the nation state, different of course in different national cultures. But now the globalisation of certain aspects of human culture (economic globalisation) and an appreciation of global relationships within non-human nature and between humanity and nature (ecological globalisation) have over reached these scales, requiring a new political scale supernational) for which we must political ethical framework. The climate negotiations are a key example of the ethical complexity that global environmental governance reveals. These negotiations also reveal the limits of voluntaristic governance, pointing inexorably in the direction of government based on democratic authority and accountability.*39

However, when a super-national governance is talked about, there is the necessity for the 'national' states to transcend their limitations of local politics, ignorance about environment and issues related to it and bureaucracy etc. before it succeed in reaching such a level. Taking the best advantage of 'globalization' process, which is fortunately taking place in twentieth century as a form of expansion beneficial to many and considerably succeeding in replacing the theme of war, the conception of governance of ethical environment can best succeed as a form of economical tool promising development for all and without interference to individual governments.

However, the 'governance of Environmental ethics' is not without criticism, regarding its political and economical considerations, rather than the ethical ones. Given the opportunity, both its political and economical considerations at global level may ignore the necessity to take into consideration of the fragility of ecology of individual locality while taking into account the 'global' nature of an issue. But such considerations should not pose a problem, considering the 'priority' being laid on the needy issue, i.e. environment. After all, it must be taken into account the views of Gleeson and Low in their following sentences, _"In the new millennium a new challenge awaits us, to address another dimension of human folly that threatens the entire planet. Enacting 'government for environment' is a task we cannot delay."[*40]

6. *Finding Ethical establishment for society* : *Reestablishing social Value Or Ethical management*

At the onset of post modern era, with the degradation of nature, an established fact in our society, it has dawned on mankind that it has much of a degraded ethical system as well. Much of the values espoused in time earlier to modern era have been lost with the advent of the Utilitarian values, which taught mankind to respect nature and live within its bound. However, as the utilitarian 'ego centric' conception saves professed economy-oriented values, the exploitation of nature has followed its dictum, after which man could see the shortfall of such 'pleasure' oriented values. After reaching the full circle, there is a conscious effort to retrieve the lost values and re-induct into society. However, the process is bound to be complicated than what it was in earlier setting. While values relating to environment became a part of the social conceptions at the beginning of civilization, it was simplistic in interpretation and it remained an inherent quality of the human society. However, as utilitarian values have conceivably eroded the conventional values of the society in modern era and consequently there is an attempt at retrieving the values that prevailed in earlier time, complexity of the situation has arisen as society has become a complex structure already and there are many other parameters to be touched upon to successfully implement and prevail upon with such values in society. Therefore, ethical interpretations are in need to be generated in view of politics, economics and development, mental set up and living standard, and even with ethics and most of all management, the skill to consistent and integrated approach to any deeds.

However, the question here is, the management being talked about is only management for a proper environment or the ethical management of it. While the bare management of environment can be highly successful with the following of certain ethical policies, without basically changing any basic moral or ethical views of society, ethical management suggests changing the complete contemporary set up of the society and make an ethical set up, so that values relating to nature is inducted into the society along with other restrained and stringent values that profess higher level of mental set up of it. The mottos of such society should be:-

(a) Respect for Nature
(b) Environmental Ethics should be the Criterion of Economy policies.
(c) There is to be cohesive relations among inhabitants of the larger society, so that the ethical policies are implemented right and proper.

7. Finding 'Order' for the society

The state of Chaos, as endorsed by the views of Evolutionary theory is believed to have occurred in pursuance of perfection in the society. The disorder or chaos, which time and on are caused, or rather triggered by eventuality programmed to the necessity to cause it, so as to make the existing world of species can move on the path of creation. The crop being destructed by flood or sudden drought, there being a wide spread diseases etc, are some of the hampers caused by the process of disorder. However, at the height of civilization, when man has surpassed the test of natural obstructions with technological skill, the disorder caused to him has equally been of higher in order as well. Man has experienced disorders of different kind, especially at higher order of thinking, mostly at ethical level, which has allowed man to carry on with different experimentations of views towards life. However, the way he cannot rid of the disorder process, the same way he can hope to attain perfection as the subsequent fortuitous event as well. In which way he experienced ethical disorder, the same way he can hope to attain even a higher order of ethics to be integrated to his life. The higher order may also integrate the various parameters of the modern complex life with its manifold characteristics, to be folded into the new ethical order of his life. Perhaps it is the conventional ethics which was too static to be evolved into the evolutionary process of society and thereby left behind in the process to accommodate alternative thinking so as to carry on the order of it. However, such a disordered contention has allowed man to introspect the ethical values of his society and then integrate it into the system in a new formation, so as to achieve a perfect order for it.

8. *Setting up an International Court*:- Among the possible solution brought out for safeguarding natural acuities against the perpetrators who help in the process of degradation is setting up an international court so as to book the guilty for their misdeed. Many present day environmentalists believe that setting up an international court will considerably help in reducing the activities of those acting against the interest of environmental protection and conservation both at local and the global levels. However, such a consideration may help in solving the crises only partially but not in their entirety.

9. Spreading knowledge of Environment through Education

Making common citizens be aware of the environmental problems and spreading the messages of protection and conservation of it is another tool that helps considerably in finding solution to the environmental crises affecting our society in particular and nations in general in the long run of our future. However, such efforts are rather the means than the end in the process. Still in can cause tremendous effect on the psyche of common people on the path of creating concern for the nature which is the very basis of living hood of not only of the animal kingdom but also our very existence only.

However, it is a method which is not easy to be achieved within a short period of time, especially in a developing or underdeveloped country, as considerable amount of finance is involved in a big country like India. Besides there are other hampers in form of section of people in society, who are uprooted or living on the edge of society and making living hood with natural resources of the surrounding neighbour hood. Such messages are contradictory to the very nature of their existence. Therefore barely informing about the environment and the crises related to it may not be the only rightful criterion for such a mission. It is also a rudimentary necessity on the part of those who have been taking up the cudgel of spreading the messages to adopt different strategies for different location or groups of people for the reason that each of them may be related to the environment in a different manner. For the evicted ones or those living on the resources of forest areas in an illegal manner, the necessity is there to show 'alternative' to their mode of living patterns. While the former should be given an alternate shelter in reclaimed land of government occupied areas, the latter should be shown alternative and cheap resources such as solar power or energy from animal droppings etc. Besides, the practices of environmental education should be field work oriented, i.e. education in 'applied form' so that the learners can find it useful as applied knowledge, rather than as academic ones.

Therefore as strategies of environmental education, the followings can be pinpointed as the necessary steps for its development:-
   (a) Children should be imparted with the knowledge of environment from an early age with 'practical and curriculum' oriented methods with 'ethical' notions, so as to make them develop not only positive attitude towards it, but also with ethical motivation to protect and preserve the natural resources.
   (b) The environmental education should become flexible and 'bendable' according to the necessity of the learners, specially the ones belonging to the village areas. Such imparted knowledge can empower the learners with greater possibilities of utilizing their knowledge in more environment oriented manner.
   (c) The education of environment should be carried out in an applied form, keeping in mind the fact that even the people affected by the environmental grievances should be able to appreciate it, and be shown to the choice of finding alternative ways to their environment-harmful ways.

10. Finding a moral criteria: Creating a Think tank
While ethics has become the most important strategy for reinstating both environment and the values in society, there is a need to make it a permanent feature of the society. Because, if ethics remain a strategy for the society for reinstating the environment, the sooner the purpose will be fulfilled the possibility remains that ethics will be shorn of its necessity as quickly. The possibility remains that the society may go back to its original

views of utilitarian values and the problem of environment may reach the full circle only.

Therefore there should be a conscious effort to form a permanent basis of thinking based on values related to nature, i.e. environment. It should be in form of a 'Think Tank' which should dictate the mottos common people should adopt while formulating their own views and principles in relation to nature. The views should make comprehensive knowledge of the environment whereas the principles should dictate as their guide in relating to the activities of day to day life that would ensure as 'environment friendly' only. Thus by establishing the moral criteria for the strategic importance of the 'Think tank', the society can be ensured of a permanent way of finding ways with lost environmental values, if making ways for a permanent solution to the environmental crises.

A CHALLENGE TO FUTURE HUMANITY

With the study of various aspects of environment, their degradation, the reasons behind them and finding the possible ethical solution to the present day crises and the impending ones in future, we have to arrive at the possible conclusion finding remedy that would also bring in respite to the impact of the ever growing problems of environmental degradation.

However, while looking for solution, whether pragmatic or ethical one, emphasis should be laid on following certain principle at the grass root level of the society, that is an individual, because an individual person is the basic root or unit of a society. Therefore, only when an individual person would follow the ethical or technical policies, only then the society would be able to overcome the hamper in the process of implementations of the policies and the effort of prevention of degradation and restoration of environment would be complete. Likewise society as a whole too can follow certain ethical policies or principles. The fact that man is the root of the society it also is the part of nature and universe. An ethical approach in life of an individual towards nature will only ensure the survival and continuity for the coming generations in future.

References

1. L.K. Caldwell,-'*Environment: A challenge for Modern Society, ch. Environment Management as Ethical System*,-p.234
2. Van Rensselaer Potter- '*Bioethic-Ch. The role of an individual in modern society,* -p.109
3. *Ibid., Ch. Role of an individual in modern society*, - p.79
4. *Ibid*. pp.112-113
5. *Ibid*:-pp:110-111.
6. L.K. Cldwell-'*Environment'*, p.235
7. *Ibid.*, p.235
8. Robert Elliot-*Philosophy and The Natural environment*-Ch. *Ecology and Ethics of Environmental Restoration-p.36*
9. *Ibid*, pp.37-38
10. Thomas Green-*Prologmena to Ethics*-p.10
11. *Ibid.*-p.12
12. Van Rensselaer Potter-*Bio Ethics.*-p.76
13. *Ibid.*,-p.79
14. W.R. Sorley- *Ethical Naturalism*-p.113
15. *Ibid.*-p.113
16. R.C. Guha- *Environmentalism: a Global History'Ch.5-The Ecology of Affluence*-pp.82-83.
17. Allan Holland-*Philosophy and Natural Environment*-p.18
18. Peter Laslett-*Governing for the Environment*,-p.167
19. Val Plumwood- *Environmental Culture*-p.116
20. Roger Kasperson-*The Environmental Risk*-p.
21. Peter Singer-*Applied Ethics*-p.221
22. Joachim Spangenberg- *Governing of Environment* -p.32
23. F. Douglas Muschette-*Principle of Sustainable Development*-p.9
24. G. Wayburd-*Environmental Dilemmas- ch. Case Study*-p.204
25. Ibid.,-p.204
26. Nicolas Low-*Governing for the Environment*-p.11
27. Allan Garre-*Ibid.*,-p106
28. *Ibid.,* 107
29. Daniel Achibugi -*Ibid.*,-p.206
30. Jana Thompson,-*Governing the Environment'*-p.139
31. Daniel Achibugi-*Ibid.*,-p.203
32. Stephan R.I. Clark-*Philosophy and Natural Environment*,-p121
33. Lester Mondale- *Values in World Religion*-p.96
34. *Ibid.*,-p.32

35.   *Ibid.*,-p.9

36.   Holmes Rolston III-*Philosophy and Natural Environment*,-p.16

37.   *Ibid.*,-p.15

38.   *Brendon Gleeson and Nicholas Low*-p.22

39.   *Ibid.*,-p.22

40.   *Ibid.*,-p.25

BIBLIOGRAPHY

<u>Name of the Authors /Editors</u>   <u>Name of the Books</u>

Ackerman, C. book:- *'Theory of Knowledge'*_published by McGrow Hill Publishing Co. Ltd., 1965

Agarwal, S.K., book :-*'Environmental protection'*-published by Himangshu Publications 1ˢᵗ Ed., 1993

Arnold, David and Ramchandra Guha book:-*'Nature & Culture and Imperialism'* published by Oxford University Press, 1995

Arora, M.R., book:-*'Ecology'*- published by Himalaya Publishing House, 1997

Attfield, Robin and Besley, Andrew editors- book:-*'Philosophy and Natural Environment'*- published by Cambridge University Press, 1994

Barlingay, S.S.,_book:- *'A Modern Introduction to Indian Ethics'*_ Published by Penman Publishers Delhi, 1Ed., 1998

Barrow, C.J.-1. book:-*'Developing the Environment: Problems and Management'* published by Longman Group Ltd. 1995
2. book:-*'Environmental Management:Principles and Practice'*-published Rouledge, 1ˢᵗ ed., 1999

Bennet, R.J. and Chorley, R.J.-Book:-*'Environmental System'*-published by Princeton University press, 1978

Beitz, Charles R., Cohen, Marshall and others, editors--Book:-*'International Ethics'* published by Princeton University Press, 1997

Berry, R.J.-Editor-Book:-'*Environmental Dilemmas:Ethics and Decisions*'-published by Ist. Ed. Chapman 7 Hall, 1993

Bernard, Theos- Book:-'*Hindu Philosophy*'- published by Philosophical Library, New York, 1947

Bharadwaja, V.K.-Book:-'*Naturalistic Ethical Theory*'published by University of Delhi, 1978

Bhattacharya, Hari Mohan-Book:-'*Principles of Philosophy*'–published University of Calcutta, 1944

Bhattacharya, Dhirendra M.-Book:-'*The Chief currents of Contemporary Philosophy*' published by University of Calcutta, 3rd Ed., 1

Bhende, Asha A., and Kanitkar- Book:-'*Principles of Population Studies*' published by Himalaya Publishing House, sixth Ed., 1998

Brown, Lester and others, Editors-Book:- *State of the World*'published by Earthscan, 1999

Brown, Peter G., Book:-'*Ethics, Economics and International Relations*'-Published by Edinburg university Press, 2000

Burnhill, David Landis and Gottlieb, Roger editors-Book:'*Deep Ecology and World Religion*' published by State university of new York, 2001

Budiansky, Stephan-Book:-'*Nature's Keepers*'-published byWeidenfield and Nicolson 1stEd.1995

Caldwell, L.k-. Book:-'*Environment:Achallenge to modern society*'-Published by Natural History press, 1970

Calvert, Peter and Susan-Book:-'*The South, the North and the Environment*'Published by PinterPublishing House, 1999

Carlsson, P. Allen- Book:-'*Butler's Ethics*'-published by Monton & Co.

Cartledge, Bryan, Editor-Book*:-'Health and Environment'* published by Oxford University Press, 1994

Cartwright, John –Book:-*'Evolution and Human Behaviour: Darwinian perspectives of Human Nature'*published by McMillan Press Ltd., 1ˢᵗ Ed., 2000

Chandra, Pratap –Book:-*'The Hindu Mind'*-published by Indian Institute of Advanced Study, Simla-1977

Chatterjee, Satishchandra-Book*:-'Problems of Philosophy'* published by Dasgupta & Co., 1ˢᵗ. Ed., 1949

Corwin, Rothann and Others, editors –Book:- *'Environmental Impact assessment'* published Freeman, Cooper and Company1975

Das, D.L.-Book*:-'Fundamentals of Philosophy'-* published by M.V. Press, Calcutta, 1967

Das, Rasbihari- Book*:-'Kant's Critique of pure Reason'* published by Progressive Publishers, 2ⁿᵈ. Edition, 1977

Dasgupta, Partha and Goraeb Maeyer, Karl-1. Book*:-'Environmental Management in Developing Countries'*
2Book:-*The Environment and Emerging Developmental issues'* published by Oxford University Press, 1ˢᵗ Ed., 1997

Dasgupta, S.R.- Book*:-'Some Problems of The Philosophy of Religion'*Published by Sahityashree, 1ˢᵗt Ed., 1965

Dasgupta, Subhayu-Book:-*'Hindu Ethos and Challege of Change'*- Published by Arnold Heimann, 2ⁿᵈ Ed.

Devaraja, N.K.-Book:-_*'Philosophy of Culture'* published by Kitab Mahal Pvt. Ltd., 1963

Dewey, John-Book:- *'The Theory of Moral Life'*-published by Wiley Eastern Private Limited., 1ˢᵗ Ed., 1968

Dower, Nigel –Book*:-'World ethics'* published by Edinburg University Press, 1998

Dreyer, Oleg Bella Los and Vietor Los-Book:-*'Ecological Problems in Developing Countries'*-published by Janata, New Delhi, 1st Ed.1989

Edward, Mile- Book:-*The Philosophy of Religion*'published by Progressive publishers, Indian Ed., 1975

Ellen, Roy -Book*:-'Environment, Subsistence and System'*- published by Cambridge University, 1st. Ed., 1982

Falkenberg,-*History of Modern Philosophy'* –published by Progressive Publishers, Calcutta, 2nd Ed., 1960

Fisher, Mary Pat-*'Religions Today:An Introduction'* published by Rouledge, 1st Ed., 2002

Fisher, Frank and Hajer, Maarten-Book:-'Living with Nature'published by Oxford University Press, 1st. Ed.1999

Gandhi, M.K.-*'Essence Of Gandhism'*-published by Navjivan Publishing house, Ahmedabad, 1st Ed.

Gaudie, Andrew –Book*:-'The Human Impact on Natural environment'*-Published by Blackwell Publishers, 5th. Ed.2000

Gellner, David- Book*:-'An Anthropology of Hinduism &Buddhism:A WeberianTheme'* Published by Oxford University 2001

Ghosh, G.K.-1Book:-*'Environment and Woman Development'* published by Ashish, New Delhi, 1st Ed., 1995
2. Book-*'Environment and Development'*, published by Ashish Publisng House, New Delhi, 1st Ed., 1995

Ghosh, Subodh Kumar-Book:-'Important Philosophical essays' published by India Book Distributing Co., 1st. Ed., 1997

Gleeson, Brendon and Low, Nicholas-editors - Book:-*'Governing for the Environment'* Published by Palgrave Publishers, 2001

Goel, Aruna –Book:-*'Environment and Ancient Sanskrit Literature'* Published by Deep&Deep Publications pvt. Ltd. 2003

Goel, Dharmendra –Book:-*'Philosophy and Social Change'*-published by Ajanta, New Delhi, 1st Ed., 1989

Grambine, R. Edward,- Book:-*'Environmental policy and Bio Diversity'*-published by Island press, California, 1st Ed., 1994

Green, Thomas-Book:-*'Prologmena To Ethics'*-published by Oxford at Clarendon Press, 5th Ed., 1936

Grove, Richard H., Damodaran Vinita and Sangwan Satpal, editors-Book:-*'Nature and the Orient: The environmental History of South and South EastAsia'* Published by Oxford University Press, 1stEd., 1998

Guha, Ramachandra-1. Book:- 'Environmentalism:A Global History'published Oxford University Press, 1st ed., 2000

Guha, Ramachandra and Gadgil, Madhab-2. Book:-Use and Abuse of Nature, Ecology and Equity, published by Oxford University, 1stEd., 2000

Gupta, R.K., Malik, B.S.-Book:-'Animal Ecology, published by Pragati Prakashan, 1993

Hamlyn, J.N.-Book:-*'The Pelican History of Western philosophy'* published by Panguins Books, London

Heptullah, N.-Book:-*'Environmental Protection in Developing Countries'* Published by Oxford, IBH, New Delhi, 1st Ed.1993

Hertsgaard, Mark,-Book:-*'Earth Odyssy:Around the world in Search of our Environmental Future'*published by –Abacus 2000

Hick, John and Hempel, Lemont, Editors-Book:-'Gandhi's Significance for Today' published by McMillan Press Ltd., 1989

Holgate, Martin-1. Book:-'The Green Web'-Earthscan- Publication Ltd. 2. Book:-'From care to action:Making sustainable World'Published by Earthscan Publication Ltd., 2nd Ed., 1997

I., Mohan-Book:-'Environmental Awareness and Development Concept' Published by New Delhi, Anmol Publication, 1st. Ed.1996

Iyer, Raghawan-Book:-'The Moral and political Writings of Mahatma Gandhi" published by Oxford Cauldron Press, 1st Ed., 1987

Jatana, Renu and Trivedi, I.V.-Book:-'Impact of Environment'- published by Printwell, Jaipur, 1st Ed. 1995

Kapur, J.N.- Book:-'Ethical values for Excellence in Education and Science' published by Wishwa PrakashananNew Delhi, 1st Ed., 1996

Kellert, Stephan and Farnham, Editors-Book:-The Good in Nature and Humanity, Island Press, 2002

Kohli, V.K.-Book-'Environment Pollution and management'–published by Haryana Vivek, 1st Ed., 1995

Kumar, U andAsija, M.J.-Book:-Biodiversity: Principle and Coservation' published by Agrobios,(India), 2nd. Edition, 2004

Kasperson, Roger and Jeanne-Book:-'Global Environmental Risk'published by United Nation University PressEarthscan, 1st. Ed., 2001

Lotze, Herman –Book:-'Outline of Philosophy of Religion' published by McMillan Co., 1954

Maithani, B.P.-Book:-'Environmental Planning For sustainable Development of hilly areas' published by Mittal publications, New Delhi, 1st Ed., 1992

McCormick, John –Book:- *'The Global Environmental Movement'* Published by John Wiley and Sons., 1995

McKenzie, John- Book:-*'A Manuel To ethics'*-published byOxford University Press, 3rd Impression, 1977

Miller, Jr., G. Tyler-Book:-*'Replenish the Earth: A Primer in human Ecology'*published by Wordsworth Pub. Co.1972

Mondale, Lester- Book:-*'Values in World Religions'*-published by Starr King Press, Boston, 1958

Moore, G.E.-Book:-*'Lectures on Philosophy'* published by George Allen &Unwin Ltd., 1896,

Muschett, Douglas F., editor-Book:-*'Principles of sustainable Development'*, published St. Lucie Press, Florida, 1997

Pathak, Rajkumar,-Book:-*Environmetal planning, Resources and Development'*Chugh, Allahbad, 1st. Ed., 1990

Patil, V.T., Editor-Book:- *'Studies on Gandhi'*published by Sterling Publishing. Ltd., 1963

Plumwood, Val-Book:-*'Environmental culture:The Ecological Crisis of Reason'* Routledge, 2002

Potter, Van Rensselaer- Book:-*'Bio Ethics: Bridge to the Future'* published by Prentice –Hall, Inc., 1971

Radhakrishnan, Sarvapalli-book:-*'History of philosophy: Eastern & Western'*- published by George Allen & Unwin Ltd., 1st Ed., 1953

Raghuramaraju, A., Editor-book:- *'Existence, Experience and ethics'Essays for S.A. Shaida* published by D.K. Printworld (P) Ltd., 1st Ed., 2000

Raj, Hans –Book:-*'Population studies'* published by Surjeet Publications, 6th Ed., 1998

Rathore, M.S., Editor –Book:-*'Environment and Development'* published by Rawat Publications, 1996

Rao, K.N., Trivedi, P.R., Singh, U.K.-Book:-*'Introduction to Ecology and Environment'* published by Indian Institute of Ecology and Environment, 1992

Renner, Michael-Book:-*'Fighting for Survival'* published by Earthscan, 1997

Robert, Stephan R. and Farnham, T.J. editors-Book:-*'The Good in nature andHumanity'* published by Island press, 2002

Rogers, Arthur Cayon-Book:-*'A Student's History of Philosophy'*-pubished by The Mcmillan Company, new revised ed.1925

Rowe, Christopher -Book:-*'Introduction to Greek Ethics'*- published by Hutchinson of London, 1ˢᵗ Ed., 1976

Rowlands, Mark-Book:-*'The Environmental Crisis'*-published by 'Mc. Millan Press, Inc., 1ˢᵗ Ed. 2000

Sarat Chandran, K., Prof.-Book:-*'A Critical Study of Indian Philosophy'* published By Oriental Book Company', 1ˢᵗ Ed., 1967

Scarre, Geoffrey-Book:-*'Utilitarianism'*-published by Routledge, 1995

Semple, Allen Churchill-Book:-*'Influences of Geographic Environment'*Published by Henry Holt & Company 1911

Simpson, Peter -Book:-*'Goodness and nature'*-Published by Martinus Nijhoff Publishers.1987

Singer, Peter-1. Book:-*'Ethics'*-published by Oxford university press, 1994 -2. Book:-*'How Are We To Live'*-Published by Oxford University Press 1997 Editor-3. Book:-*'Applied Ethics'*-published by Oxford University Press-1986

Singh, Shekhar, editor-Book:-*'Environmental Policy India'*-published by IIPA, New Delhi, 1ˢᵗ. Ed., 1984

Sinha, Jadunath-Book:-*'Introduction to Philosophy'*, published by Sinha Publishing House, 1977

Sharma, R.N.-Book:-*'Indian Ethics'*- published by Surjeet Publications, 1993

Sinha, R.K.-*'Environment and Natural Resources'* published by Commonwealth, New Delhi, 1ˢᵗ ed. 1

Sharma, B.K., Kaur, H.-Book:-*'Soil and Noise Pollution'* published by Goel Publishing House, Meerat, Ist Ed., 1994

Shrivastava, O.S.-Book:-*'Demography and Population Studies'* published by Goel Publishing House, 2nd. Ed.1996

Sidgwick, Henry –Book:-*'Practical Ethics'* published by Oxford University Press, 1998

Sondhi, Madhuri and Walker, Mary M., Editors-Book:-*'Ecology, Culture andPhilosophy,* Published by Abhinav Publications, 1ˢᵗ. ed., 1988

Sorley, W.R.- Book:-*'Ethics Of Naturalism'*-published by-William Blackwood& Sons., 2ⁿᵈ Ed., revised, 1stEd., 1876

Stenmark, Mikael-Book:-*'Environmental Ethics and policy making'* Published by Ashgate, 2002

Teetan and Keeton, Morris-Book:-*'Ethics for Today/Ethic Tomorrow'*published by Van Nostrand Company, 5th. ed., 1973

Thilly, Frank- Book:-*'A History of Philosophy'* published by Central Book Depot, Allahabad, 1978

Tripathy, S.N., Sudhakar Panda- Book:-*'Fundamentals of Environmental Studies'* 1999

Trivedi, P.R., and Cherry Sudarsan, Editors- Book:-*'Global environmental issues'* published by Commomwealth publishers, New Delhi, 1ˢᵗ ed., 1995

Trivedi, R.N.-Book:-*'Environmental Pollution and Its Impact on the Organism'*published by Bharati Bhavan, P&D

Ward, James-Book:-*'Naturalism and Agnosticism'* published by Adam and Chales Black, 1899

Wehrmeyer, Walter and Mulugetta, Yacob, Editors-Book:- *'Growing Pains'* published by Greenleaf, 1999

Yutang, Lin-Book:-*'The wisdom of Confucious'*-published by The Modern Library Copyright, 1938

www.ingramcontent.com/pod-product-compliance
Lightning Source LLC
Chambersburg PA
CBHW031839170526
45157CB00001B/353